Race
Relations

OPPOSING VIEWPOINTS®

Other Books of Related Interest

Opposing Viewpoints Series

American Values
America's Cities
America's Prisons
Crime and Criminals
Criminal Justice
Culture Wars
The Death Penalty
Economics in America
Education in America
The Family in America
The Homeless
Immigration
Islam
Mass Media
Poverty
Social Justice
Violence

Current Controversies Series

Hate Crimes
Illegal Immigration
Nationalism and Ethnic Conflict
Police Brutality
Youth Violence

At Issue Series

Affirmative Action
Ethnic Conflict
Immigration Policy

Race
Relations

OPPOSING VIEWPOINTS®

David Bender & Bruno Leone, *Series Editors*

Paul A. Winters, *Book Editor*

OPPOSING
VIEWPOINTS®
SERIES

Greenhaven Press, Inc., San Diego, CA

Cover photo: Photodisc

Greenhaven Press, Inc.
PO Box 289009
San Diego, CA 92198-9009

Library of Congress Cataloging-in-Publication Data

Race relations: opposing viewpoints / Paul A. Winters, book editor.
    p.   cm. — (Opposing viewpoints series)
  Includes bibliographical references and index.
  ISBN 1-56510-356-4 (pbk. alk. paper) — ISBN 1-56510-357-2 (lib. ed. alk. paper)
    1. United States—Race relations. 2. Race discrimination—United States. 3. Racism—United States I. Winters, Paul A., 1965– . II. Series: Opposing viewpoints series (Unnumbered)
E184.A1R316   1996
305.8'00973—dc20   95-9016
                                   CIP

"Congress shall make no law . . .
abridging the freedom of speech,
or of the press."

First Amendment to the U.S. Constitution

The basic foundation of our democracy is the First Amendment
guarantee of freedom of expression. The Opposing Viewpoints
Series is dedicated to the concept of this basic freedom and the
idea that it is more important to practice it than to enshrine it.

Contents

Why Consider Opposing Viewpoints?

"The only way in which a human being can make some approach to knowing the whole of a subject is by hearing what can be said about it by persons of every variety of opinion and studying all modes in which it can be looked at by every character of mind. No wise man ever acquired his wisdom in any mode but this."

John Stuart Mill

In our media-intensive culture it is not difficult to find differing opinions. Thousands of newspapers and magazines and dozens of radio and television talk shows resound with differing points of view. The difficulty lies in deciding which opinion to agree with and which "experts" seem the most credible. The more inundated we become with differing opinions and claims, the more essential it is to hone critical reading and thinking skills to evaluate these ideas. Opposing Viewpoints books address this problem directly by presenting stimulating debates that can be used to enhance and teach these skills. The varied opinions contained in each book examine many different aspects of a single issue. While examining these conveniently edited opposing views, readers can develop critical thinking skills such as the ability to compare and contrast authors' credibility, facts, argumentation styles, use of persuasive techniques, and other stylistic tools. In short, the Opposing Viewpoints Series is an ideal way to attain the higher-level thinking and reading skills so essential in a culture of diverse and contradictory opinions.

In addition to providing a tool for critical thinking, Opposing Viewpoints books challenge readers to question their own strongly held opinions and assumptions. Most people form their opinions on the basis of upbringing, peer pressure, and personal, cultural, or professional bias. By reading carefully balanced opposing views, readers must directly confront new ideas as well as the opinions of those with whom they disagree. This is not to simplistically argue that everyone who reads opposing views will—or should—change his or her opinion. Instead, the series enhances readers' depth of understanding of their own views by encouraging confrontation with opposing ideas. Careful examination of others' views can lead to the readers' understanding of the logical inconsistencies in their own opinions, perspective on why they hold an opinion, and the consideration of the possibility that their opinion requires further evaluation.

Evaluating Other Opinions

To ensure that this type of examination occurs, Opposing Viewpoints books present all types of opinions. Prominent spokespeople on different sides of each issue as well as well-known professionals from many disciplines challenge the reader. An additional goal of the series is to provide a forum for other, less known, or even unpopular viewpoints. The opinion of an ordinary person who has had to make the decision to cut off life support from a terminally ill relative, for example, may be just as valuable and provide just as much insight as a medical ethicist's professional opinion. The editors have two additional purposes in including these less known views. One, the editors encourage readers to respect others' opinions—even when not enhanced by professional credibility. It is only by reading or listening to and objectively evaluating others' ideas that one can determine whether they are worthy of consideration. Two, the inclusion of such viewpoints encourages the important critical thinking skill of objectively evaluating an author's credentials and bias. This evaluation will illuminate an author's reasons for taking a particular stance on an issue and will aid in readers' evaluation of the author's ideas.

As series editors of the Opposing Viewpoints Series, it is our hope that these books will give readers a deeper understanding of the issues debated and an appreciation of the complexity of even seemingly simple issues when good and honest people disagree. This awareness is particularly important in a democratic society such as ours in which people enter into public debate to determine the common good. Those with whom one disagrees should not be regarded as enemies but rather as people whose views deserve careful examination and may shed light on one's own.

Thomas Jefferson once said that "difference of opinion leads to inquiry, and inquiry to truth." Jefferson, a broadly educated man, argued that "if a nation expects to be ignorant and free . . . it expects what never was and never will be." As individuals and as a nation, it is imperative that we consider the opinions of others and examine them with skill and discernment. The Opposing Viewpoints Series is intended to help readers achieve this goal.

David L. Bender & Bruno Leone,
Series Editors

Introduction

"What are we to make of this dismaying evidence that the relationships among us are getting worse?"

William Raspberry

Race relations in American society are becoming more complex as the nation's racial makeup becomes increasingly diverse. Interactions of growing populations of Asian and Hispanic Americans with blacks and whites bring new opportunities for cooperation, competition, and conflict. But relations between blacks and whites, the traditional topic of books on race relations, continue to be the focus of much attention. And three recent books on black-white relations present "dismaying evidence" that things perhaps "are getting worse." In his autobiographical account, *Makes Me Wanna Holler: A Young Black Man in America*, reporter Nathan McCall relates how the inchoate anger he felt as a young black man became focused by his prison experience into a clear-eyed look at discrimination against blacks in America. In *The Rage of a Privileged Class*, reporter and author Ellis Cose records the anger many middle-class black Americans, who have ostensibly achieved success, feel when confronted with persistent discrimination and racial insults. Journalist Jared Taylor, on the other hand, in his book *Paved with Good Intentions: The Failure of Race Relations in Contemporary America*, expresses the anger that a number of white males feel at being blamed for the problems of blacks and others. In looking at race relations in America in the 1990s it seems that much of the debate is dominated by angry voices.

Explaining why he believes middle-class blacks are angry, Cose argues that because discrimination persists in American society, it is most keenly felt by those blacks who have made the largest investment in the American dream. People assume, he says, that the post-civil-rights-era progress blacks have made into middle-class status is a sign that discrimination has been largely eliminated. He disputes this view as "utterly at odds with the reality many Americans confront daily." Among stories of racial discrimination experienced by middle-class blacks, Cose tells one of a black woman who finds her career in business limited by the color of her skin. As she watches whites with no more qualifications or experience than herself advance up the corporate ladder, while she and other blacks do not, she comes to feel that discrimination is placing an insurmountable obstacle in her path to success, Cose relates. "The bottom line is you're black," in her words. "And that's still a negative in this society." For Cose, her story illustrates that a promise of the American dream—that if you work hard, you will be allowed to advance to your full potential—has been broken. "Why," he asks, "a full generation after the most celebrated civil rights battles were fought and won, are Americans still struggling with basic issues of racial fairness?"

Discrimination against middle-class blacks is not the only problem that blacks write about, nor is it the only cause of anger. Through the story of his prison experience, Nathan McCall describes the anger felt by young inner-city black men at unfairness in the justice system, at the circle of violence, prison, and death these men are trapped in, and at the low value society places on their lives. Having always felt like "a black intruder in a world not created for me and my people," he says, his spiritual growth during three years in prison focused his anger on what he came to believe was its true cause—structural racism in American society. With this realization, McCall writes, "no longer were my angry feelings about the vast white world simply vague, invalid impulses dangling on the edge of my mind."

On the other hand, some whites say they are increasingly angry at the constant charges of racism, discrimination, and responsibility for causing the problems of others. Jared Taylor protests, "Most whites probably cannot find in themselves the desire to oppress or persecute blacks." He feels that with the successes of the civil rights movement since the 1960s, whites have largely eliminated their personal prejudices and blacks have made visible progress into the mainstream of American society. Further, he argues, discrimination or racism by whites cannot possibly explain the violence that results in blacks' being killed by other blacks or imprisoned for violent crimes. A backlash by whites has thus emerged against policies such as affirmative action that benefit blacks and that have been justified as remedies for racism and discrimination, according to Taylor. "Only for so long will whites watch blacks use race as a weapon," he says.

Cornel West, a Princeton University professor of philosophy and author of *Race Matters*, warns that in this climate of anger, before race relations in America can be improved, "we must acknowledge that as a people—*E Pluribus Unum*—we are on a slippery slope toward economic strife, social turmoil, and cultural chaos." The causes of such strife, turmoil, and chaos as well as ways to improve the situation are debated in *Race Relations: Opposing Viewpoints*, which contains the following chapters: What Is the State of Race Relations? Does Discrimination Persist in the American Economy? Is America's Justice System Biased? How Should America's Political System Respond to Minorities' Interests? What Should Society Do to Improve Race Relations?

What Is the State of Race Relations?

Chapter Preface

In early 1994, a controversy arose over a speech delivered at Kean College in New Jersey by Khallid Abdul Muhammad, a spokesman for the Nation of Islam (NOI), the black Muslim organization led by Louis Farrakhan that preaches black nationalism, separatism, and self-reliance. During his speech, which was based on the NOI's publication *The Secret Relationship Between Blacks and Jews*, Muhammad made derogatory remarks about Jewish people, calling them "the hook-nosed, bagel-eatin', lox-eatin'" Jews who in the past dominated the U.S. slave trade and who today are "sucking our blood in the black community."

In response to the speech, the Anti-Defamation League (ADL), a Jewish civil rights organization, sought to draw attention to Muhammad's anti-Semitic remarks and to what many Jews fear is a rising tide of anti-Semitism among blacks. Jacob Neusner, a professor of religious studies at the University of South Florida at Tampa, is among those who condemned Muhammad's speech. He fears that the growing popularity of Farrakhan and the growing acceptance of the NOI's separatist views among blacks—views he feels are laced with anti-Semitism—portend a worsening of relations between blacks and Jews. Black nationalism is "racism, no worse and no better than the white kind," in Neusner's opinion, and "will end up in the anonymity of sheets, like that of the Ku Klux Klan." The ADL called upon black community leaders to condemn Muhammad's speech and to repudiate the separatist views of the Nation of Islam.

Most black leaders did condemn the anti-Semitic remarks— Louis Farrakhan himself rebuked Muhammad for the mocking tone of his speech—but many stopped short of condemning the message of black nationalism that Farrakhan preaches. Thulani Davis, a teacher at Barnard College in New York City, contends that to focus on the problem of black anti-Semitism masks whites' fear of black people and distracts attention from the larger problems of poverty and lack of opportunity that plague blacks. Supporting the NOI's message of self-reliance as a positive force for blacks, Thulani challenges: "Anyone who really wants to deal with the impact of Minister Farrakhan had better start standing on the same street corners he stands on, going in the same doors."

The controversy over Muhammad's speech is one illustration of what many people think is a declining state of race relations in America, characterized by charges of racism from all sides. The viewpoints in the following chapter debate the sources and the accuracy of people's perceptions of this hostility.

"The racism that made slavery feasible is far from dead in the last decade of twentieth-century America."

Racism Is the Cause of Problems for Blacks

Derrick Bell

Economic statistics show that blacks as a group lag behind all other groups in income and other measures of wealth. In the following viewpoint, Derrick Bell argues that, although slavery has been dismantled and despite moderate gains for blacks from the civil rights movement of the 1960s, racism persists in America, reflected in the statistical economic disparities between blacks and whites. He concludes that blacks will "never gain full equality" with whites because of this institutionalized, structural racism in American society. Bell is a scholar in residence at New York University in New York City and author of *Faces at the Bottom of the Well: The Permanence of Racism*, from which this viewpoint is excerpted.

As you read, consider the following questions:

1. According to Bell, where was the onus of slavery laid prior to the 1960s?
2. Why are whites unwilling to support economic programs and reparations for blacks, in the author's opinion?
3. How are whites encouraged to believe that racism is a thing of the past, according to Bell?

When I was growing up in the years before the Second World War, our slave heritage was more a symbol of shame than a source of pride. It burdened black people with an indelible mark of difference as we struggled to be like whites. In those far-off days, survival and progress seemed to require moving beyond, even rejecting slavery. Childhood friends in a West Indian family who lived a few doors away often boasted—erroneously as I later learned—that their people had never been slaves. My own more accurate—but hardly more praiseworthy—response was that my forebears included many free Negroes, some of whom had Choctaw and Blackfoot Indian blood.

In those days, self-delusion was both easy and comforting. Slavery was barely mentioned in the schools and seldom discussed by the descendants of its survivors, particularly those who had somehow moved themselves to the North. Emigration, whether from the Caribbean islands or from the Deep South states, provided a geographical distance that encouraged and enhanced individual denial of our collective, slave past. We sang spirituals but detached the songs from their slave origins. As I look back, I see this reaction as no less sad, for being very understandable. We were a subordinate and mostly shunned portion of a society that managed to lay the onus of slavery neatly on those who were slaves while simultaneously exonerating those who were slaveholders. All things considered, it seemed a history best left alone.

Raised Awareness About Slavery

Then, after the Second World War and particularly in the 1960s, slavery became—for a few academics and some militant Negroes—a subject of fascination and a sure means of evoking racial rage as a prelude to righteously repeated demands for "Freedom Now!" In response to a resurrection of interest in our past, new books on slavery were written, long-out-of-print volumes republished. The new awareness reached its highest point in 1977 with the television version of Alex Haley's biographical novel, *Roots*. The highly successful miniseries informed millions of Americans—black as well as white—that slavery in fact existed and that it was awful. Not, of course, as awful as it would have been save for the good white folks the television writers had created to ease the slaves' anguish, and the evil ones on whose shoulders they placed all the guilt. Through the magic of literary license, white viewers could feel revulsion for slavery without necessarily recognizing American slavery as a burden on the nation's history, certainly not a burden requiring reparations in the present.

Even so, under pressure of civil rights protests, many white Americans were ready to accede to if not applaud Supreme

Court rulings that the Constitution should no longer recognize and validate laws that kept in place the odious badges of slavery.

As a result, two centuries after the Constitution's adoption, we did live in a far more enlightened world. Slavery was no more. Judicial precedent and a plethora of civil rights statutes formally prohibited racial discrimination. Compliance was far from perfect, but the slavery provisions in the Constitution did seem lamentable artifacts of a less enlightened era.

Racial Discrimination Persists

But the fact of slavery refuses to fade, along with the deeply embedded personal attitudes and public policy assumptions that supported it for so long. Indeed, the racism that made slavery feasible is far from dead in the last decade of twentieth-century America; and the civil rights gains, so hard won, are being steadily eroded. Despite undeniable progress for many, no African Americans are insulated from incidents of racial discrimination. Our careers, even our lives, are threatened because of our color. Even the most successful of us are haunted by the plight of our less fortunate brethren who struggle for existence in what some social scientists call the "underclass." Burdened with life-long poverty and soul-devastating despair, they live beyond the pale of the American Dream. What we designate as "racial progress" is not a solution to that problem. It is a regeneration of the problem in a particularly perverse form.

According to data compiled in 1990 for basic measures of poverty, unemployment, and income, the slow advances African Americans made during the 1960s and 1970s have definitely been reversed. The unemployment rate for blacks is two and a half times the rate for whites. Black per-capita income is not even two-thirds of the income for whites; and blacks, most of whom own little wealth or business property, are three times more likely to have income below the poverty level than whites. If trends of the 1970s and 1980s are allowed to continue, readers can safely—and sadly—assume that the current figures are worse than those cited here.

Statistics cannot, however, begin to express the havoc caused by joblessness and poverty: broken homes, anarchy in communities, futility in the public schools. All are the bitter harvest of race-determined unemployment in a society where work provides sustenance, status, and the all-important sense of self-worth. What we now call the "inner city" is, in fact, the American equivalent of the South African homelands [where black tribes were segregated under the system of apartheid]. Poverty is less the source than the status of men and women who, despised because of their race, seek refuge in self-rejection. Drug-related crime, teenaged parenthood, and disrupted and disrupting family life all are manifestations of a despair that feeds on self. That despair is bred anew each day by the images on ever-playing television sets, images confirming that theirs is the disgraceful form of living, not the only way people live.

Whites Fail to Understand Blacks

Few whites are able to identify with blacks as a group—the essential prerequisite for feeling empathy with, rather than aversion from, blacks' self-inflicted suffering. . . . Unable or unwilling to perceive that "there but for the grace of God, go I," few whites are ready to actively promote civil rights for blacks. Because of an irrational but easily roused fear that any social reform will unjustly benefit blacks, whites fail to support the programs this country desperately needs to address the ever-widening gap between the rich and the poor, both black and white.

Lulled by comforting racial stereotypes, fearful that blacks will unfairly get ahead of them, all too many whites respond to even the most dire reports of race-based disadvantage with either a sympathetic headshake or victim-blaming rationalizations. Both responses lead easily to the conclusion that contemporary complaints of racial discrimination are simply excuses put forward by people who are unable or unwilling to compete on an equal basis in a competitive society.

For white people who both deny racism and see a heavy dose of the Horatio Alger myth as the answer to blacks' problems, how sweet it must be when a black person stands in a public place and condemns as slothful and unambitious those blacks who are not making it. Whites eagerly embrace black conservatives' homilies to self-help, however grossly unrealistic such messages are in an economy where millions, white as well as black, are unemployed and, more important, in one where racial discrimination in the workplace is as vicious (if less obvious) than it was when employers posted signs "no negras need apply."

Whatever the relief from responsibility such thinking provides those who embrace it, more than a decade [since 1980] of civil rights setbacks in the White House, in the courts, and in the critical realm of media-nurtured public opinion has forced retrenchment in the tattered civil rights ranks. We must reassess our cause and our approach to it, but repetition of time-worn slogans simply will not do. As a popular colloquialism puts it, it is time to "get real" about race and the persistence of racism in America.

To make such an assessment—to plan for the future by reviewing the experiences of the past—we must ask whether the formidable hurdles we now face in the elusive quest for racial equality are simply a challenge to our commitment, whether they are the latest variation of the old hymn "One More River to Cross." Or, as we once again gear up to meet the challenges posed by these unexpected new setbacks, are we ignoring a current message with implications for the future which history has already taught us about the past?

The Power to Arrange Politics and Culture

In those innocent days, before desegregation had really been tried, before the New Frontier and the Great Society, many of us blacks had lovely, naïve hopes for integration. . . . We thought that prejudice was an individual thing and that relatively few whites were virulently afflicted. We thought that the leadership classes in this country were far better than the racist few and that they would make an effort to lead their fellow whites to richer understandings. We hadn't considered the nature of racism very much.

In our naïveté, we believed that the power to segregate was the greatest power that had been wielded against us. It turned out that our expectations were quite wrong. The greatest power turned out to be what it had always been: the power to define reality where blacks are concerned and to manage perceptions and therefore arrange politics and culture to reinforce those definitions. When we were segregated, we hadn't ground into our considerations the nation's long history of racial subordination. From the dark and cramped box of segregation, the rest of the country out there looked bright and shiny. We thought the only thing it lacked was us. We didn't understand then how normal a part of national life racism had become.

Roger Wilkins, *Mother Jones*, November/December 1992.

Such assessment is hard to make. On the one hand, contemporary color barriers are certainly less visible as a result of our successful effort to strip the law's endorsement from the hated Jim Crow signs. Today one can travel for thousands of miles across this country and never see a public facility designated as "Colored" or "White." Indeed, the very absence of visible signs of discrimination creates an atmosphere of racial neutrality and encourages whites to believe that racism is a thing of the past. On the other hand, the general use of so-called neutral standards to continue exclusionary practices reduces the effectiveness of traditional civil rights laws, while rendering discriminatory actions more oppressive than ever. Racial bias in the pre-*Brown v. Board of Education of Topeka, Kansas*, [1954] era was stark, open, unalloyed with hypocrisy and blank-faced lies. We blacks, when rejected, knew who our enemies were. They were not us! Today, because bias is masked in unofficial practices and "neutral" standards, we must wrestle with the question whether race or some individual failing has cost us the job, denied us the promotion, or prompted our being rejected as tenants for an apartment. Either conclusion breeds frustration and alienation—and a rage we dare not show to others or admit to ourselves. . . .

Gunnar Myrdal, author of *The American Dilemma*, and two generations of civil rights advocates accepted the idea of racism as merely an odious holdover from slavery, "a terrible and inexplicable anomaly stuck in the middle of our liberal democratic ethos." No one doubted that the standard American policy making was adequate to the task of abolishing racism. White America, it was assumed, *wanted* to abolish racism.

Forty years later, in *The New American Dilemma*, Professor Jennifer Hochschild examined what she called Myrdal's "anomaly thesis," and concluded that it simply cannot explain the persistence of racial discrimination. Rather, the continued viability of racism demonstrates "that racism is not simply an excrescence on a fundamentally healthy liberal democratic body, but is part of what shapes and energizes the body." Under this view, "liberal democracy and racism in the United States are historically, even inherently, reinforcing; American society as we know it exists only because of its foundation in racially based slavery, and it thrives only because racial discrimination continues. The apparent anomaly is an actual symbiosis," according to Hochschild.

The permanence of this "symbiosis" ensures that civil rights gains will be temporary and setbacks inevitable. Consider: In this last decade of the twentieth century, color determines the social and economic status of all African Americans, both those who have been highly successful and their poverty-bound brethren whose lives are grounded in misery and despair. We rise and fall less as a result of our efforts than in response to the needs of a white society that condemns all blacks to quasi citizenship as surely as it segregated our parents and enslaved their forebears. The fact is that, despite what we designate as progress wrought through struggle over many generations, we remain what we were in the beginning: a dark and foreign presence, always the designated "other." Tolerated in good times, despised when things go wrong, as a people we are scapegoated and sacrificed as distraction or catalyst for compromise to facilitate resolution of political differences or relieve economic adversity. . . .

I want to set forth this proposition, which will be easier to reject than refute: *Black people will never gain full equality in this country. Even those herculean efforts we hail as successful will produce no more than temporary "peaks of progress," short-lived victories that slide into irrelevance as racial patterns adapt in ways that maintain white dominance. This is a hard-to-accept fact that all history verifies. We must acknowledge it, not as a sign of submission, but as an act of ultimate defiance.*

"It is simply not reasonable to attribute all *black problems to the single cause of white racism."*

White Racism Is Not the Cause of All Problems for Blacks

Byron M. Roth

Many researchers on race relations attribute statistical disparities between the economic position of blacks and whites to the
endurance of white racism in the structure of American society.
In the following viewpoint, Byron M. Roth argues that the assumption that white racism is to blame for the problems of
blacks is not supported by any positive evidence, especially in
light of the fact that the number of successful blacks is growing.
The economic position of blacks will not be further enhanced
by attacking white racism, according to Roth. Roth is a professor of psychology at Dowling College in Oakdale, New York.

As you read, consider the following questions:

1. What is the prevailing view on prejudice, according to Roth?
2. According to the author, what groups of blacks have done
   well in terms of education and employment?
3. Even though white racism exists, according to Roth, why is it
   unwise to blame it for problems blacks experience?

Consider the following comments on prejudice presented in a popular textbook on social psychology by David O. Sears et al.:

> In the United States, racial prejudice against blacks by whites has been a tenacious social problem. It has resulted in an enormous catalog of social ills, ranging from the deterioration and near bankruptcy of large cities, to poverty, shorter life expectancy, high levels of crime and drug abuse, and human misery of all kinds among blacks themselves.

In a similar vein the distinguished black psychologist Kenneth Clark (a past president of the American Psychological Association)—whose research was cited by the Supreme Court in the 1954 school-desegregation decision [*Brown v. Board of Education of Topeka, Kansas*]—gave the following explanation for black-white differences in SAT scores in a 1982 op-ed piece in the *New York Times:*

> Black children are educationally retarded because the public schools they are required to attend are polluted with racism. Their low scores reflect the racial segregation and inferiority of these schools. These children are perceived and treated as if they were uneducable. From the earliest grades they are programmed for failure. Throughout their lives, they are classic examples of the validity of the concept of victimization by self-fulfilling prophecy.

The Prevailing View on White Racism

The above statements are fairly representative of the views of social scientists commonly heard in the popular media. Under the prevailing view, white America is endemically racist and racism is the primary cause of the problems that blacks confront. Racism is claimed as the primary, almost exclusive cause of poverty, crime, illegitimacy, drug abuse, and educational failure among blacks. In fact, it is the assumption of widespread racism which is the justification for most of the laws and policies associated with the civil rights movement—laws and policies that a large majority of social scientists support.

But even modest reflection must give one pause. It is simply not reasonable to attribute *all* black problems to the single cause of white racism. In fact, it is almost always the case that complex social phenomena are caused and influenced by a multitude of factors. It is of course true and indisputable that, in the ultimate sense, everything about blacks in America today can be traced to the racism of the white Europeans who enslaved their ancestors. In addition, it is probably true that historical black responses to centuries of abuse have played a prominent, perhaps determinative, role in many of the responses of blacks today. But to say that is by no means to outline in precisely what ways past racist practices shaped the behavior patterns common today. Nor is it clear what impact current white attitudes have upon blacks in the very different circumstances of the late twentieth century. These are questions of great importance for blacks and whites and the future of America, and it is unlikely that the answers to them will be simple. At the very least, we should examine the empirical evidence with great scrutiny before accepting this or that answer as if it were a foregone conclusion.

Is Historical White Racism Responsible?

For instance, it is a reasonable hypothesis to assert that the educational difficulties blacks face may be due to the fact that historically blacks were denied the fruits of educational success by racist practices. But that is a very different hypothesis from one that suggests that these educational problems are the result of current white racism. Indeed, these hypotheses are radically different and would lead to very different policy prescriptions for improving black educational performance. The historical-racism hypothesis would recommend an effort to change the attitudes of black children about the current opportunities that educational success can provide. The hypothesis that current racism is to blame would suggest attempts to eliminate racism among whites, especially those in the schools. There are, however, many reasons to question the impact of current racism on black children today. It is by no means clear how the racism of some white teachers—I doubt that even the supporters of the white-racism hypothesis would argue that all white teachers are racist—undermines the education of black children in Atlanta, Georgia, where, according to Abigail Thernstrom, "white teachers have almost disappeared from the school system." Even more unclear is how the attitudes of white teachers could have affected children in the earlier segregated schools of the South when virtually all teachers in segregated black schools were themselves black and were given considerable freedom in what and how they taught.

Certainly the segregationist practices in the South of the past may have demoralized black children and interfered with their motivation to learn, but that is very different from arguing that America today denies educated blacks fair opportunities. The latter is merely an assertion and one that runs counter to everyday experience. . . .

Illegitimacy in the black community, to take another example, is a very serious problem. Some 64 percent of all black children are born to unmarried women. It is certainly a reasonable hypothesis to suggest that discrimination against black men leads to unemployment among them and thereby contributes to high rates of unwed motherhood due to the scarcity of men able to support a family. But this hypothesis must also account for the fact that the illegitimacy rate was less than one-third of today's rate in the 1950s when, by all accounts, discrimination against black men was more severe than it is today. The point is that reasonable hypotheses are not the same as sound scientific explanations. In fact, it is not at all clear what factors contribute to high rates of illegitimacy among blacks. It is very clear, however, that so long as the rate of unwed motherhood remains high, so will poverty among black women and children. Policies to improve the economic prospects for blacks would do well to aim at reducing the illegitimacy rate, whatever the ultimate causes. Attributing the problem to white prejudice, even if that were the case, would not solve the problem, since it is unclear how white prejudice could be more effectively dealt with than it is today.

Some Blacks Have Succeeded

A very serious problem with the white-racism explanation is the fact that large numbers of blacks have done very well in recent decades. It is difficult to explain why a pattern of discrimination that is said to be so pervasive has been relatively ineffective in thwarting the ambitions of the many blacks who perform well in school and the many who succeed in highly desirable occupations. The large number of successful blacks argues against the notion that they are merely "tokens" to assuage white guilt. It is interesting that among the 2.4 million blacks who are Catholic (9 percent of all blacks) the high school dropout rate is lower than that of white Americans. Black Catholics are 40 percent more likely to be college graduates than other blacks. In fact, among forty- to fifty-year-olds, more black Catholics (26 percent) have college degrees than do other blacks (15 percent) and more even than whites (24 percent).

Such statistics force us to question the white-discrimination hypothesis, since it is unreasonable to suppose that whites make distinctions about blacks on the basis of religion. Similar questions arise when we are confronted with statistics comparing black Americans of Caribbean descent to those whose ancestors were born in America. Blacks of Caribbean background have higher rates of employment in professional occupations than American-born blacks and higher rates of such employment even than Americans in general.

Further Doubts About the Racism Explanation

Further reflection leads to other questions regarding the white-racism hypothesis. How is it possible for racism to be so virulent after all these years of educational and media efforts to reduce it? Have these efforts been ineffective, and if so, why? We have all been witness in recent years to highly publicized incidents of physical assaults on black individuals, and numerous reports of racial incidents on college campuses. Are these incidents newsworthy because they represent only the tip of the iceberg, as it were, or are they newsworthy because they are so atypical in America today? Perhaps the incidents receive the coverage they do because they seem consistent with the prevailing view that racism is widespread among white Americans.

When "Racism" Explains Everything

Too many brothers are content to blame everything that ails them on white racism. To a lot of black Americans, when you've said racism, you've said it all.

Actually, when you've blamed everything on white racism, you haven't said anything. Racism is paradoxically all too human a problem. Yes, it does exist—and will continue to exist probably forever among individuals of every race. Is everybody just going to sit around and wait for white racism to go away?

There are many real problems confronting the black community that have little to do with actual, identifiable, racially biased acts. We would be much more effective in improving the lot of black Americans if we turned our attention to these.

Armstrong Williams, *Washington Times*, June 15, 1994.

It is important to stress the point that questioning the hypothesis that white racism is the primary source of black problems is not the same as denying the existence of white racism. There can be little doubt that there are people who openly express antagonism to blacks, and probably many others who secretly share their antagonism. But it is simply not clear how many white Americans are avowed racists. Nor is it clear what proportion of racists there are in positions of influence who can in any major way affect what happens to blacks. So long as such questions remain unanswered, it is unwise and perhaps counterproductive to accept many common assertions as to the sources of black difficulties. I do not think it is useful to argue that many blacks fare poorly in school because American education is polluted with racism, when no evidence for such a claim can be brought forward.

On its face such a charge seems extremely dubious in light of the fact that college professors and public school teachers are generally known to be liberal on racial matters. Similar reasoning undermines the frequent claim that a disproportionate number of blacks have criminal records because of the racism en-

27

demic to the criminal justice system, when no evidence is brought forward to show that racism is common among judges, lawyers, or police officers. There are, to be sure, anecdotal reports of police misconduct and highly publicized accounts of incidents of police brutality such as the 1991 Rodney King beating, but these hardly substitute for sound evidence of widespread racism within the system. If anything, the public outcry against such incidents tends to suggest that such misconduct is, in fact, unrepresentative of the system as a whole. Also questionable is the charge that blacks suffer disproportionate health problems because racism taints American medicine. Doctors and nurses are among the least likely candidates upon whom to pin the label of bigotry.

In other words, the claim that black Americans suffer the problems they do because of the racism of white Americans requires considerable scrutiny before it is accepted as a sound explanation. On its face it seems unreasonable to assume that large numbers of white Americans, including the best educated and most influential, are as bigoted and mean-spirited as were many uneducated whites earlier in the century. If American bigotry is in fact still the primary source of black problems, then the future of black Americans is grim indeed, since it is hard to see how further efforts to eradicate bigotry can be more successful than have been those of the past four decades. Unfortunately, the prevailing orthodoxy, if closely analyzed, leads inexorably to such an unhappy conclusion. Perhaps it is time to cast aside the current view and look for alternative explanations that may produce a more useful and less pessimistic conclusion.

"Polls that grant individuals anonymity show that white Americans overwhelmingly reject the practices instituted under the rubric of affirmative action."

A Backlash Against Affirmative Action Is Growing Among Whites

Timur Kuran

American political observers for years have noted a growing opposition to affirmative action policies designed to promote the advancement of minorities and women seeking employment and educational opportunities. In the following viewpoint, Timur Kuran argues that though most whites do not support affirmative action in private, they are reluctant to openly speak out against the programs for fear of being labeled "racist." This reserve, in his opinion, masks the fact that affirmative action policies have benefited only middle-class blacks who did not need the help and that resentment is growing among whites. Kuran is a professor of economics at the University of Southern California.

As you read, consider the following questions:

1. How does the author define "white flight"?
2. According to the author, who has benefited most from affirmative action policies?
3. How will the attitudes of new generations of whites differ from older generations, according to Kuran?

Ever since the civil rights victories of the 1960s, a recurring theme in American politics has been one of an unfolding "white backlash" against policies designed to benefit blacks. When David Duke, a former grand wizard of the Ku Klux Klan, made a strong showing in the 1990 election for United States Senator from Louisiana, many commentators saw this as a signal of a growing challenge to black entitlements. Other developments commonly cited as indicators of opposition to black progress are Ronald Reagan's success in winning votes from white blue-collar Democrats; rising racial tensions on college campuses; . . . and legislative resistance to aid for communities damaged in the 1992 Los Angeles riots. . . .

There is little doubt that such events and trends reflect some dissatisfaction with established racial policies. Less clear is whether they amount, either individually or collectively, to a white backlash, if by this one means an overt mass reaction. Very few white Americans express misgivings about the prevailing racial agenda in public. Consider the so-called Reagan Democrats. Whereas many have gone on strike for better pay and protested against plant closures, they have been remarkably quiescent on matters relating directly to race. They have waged no campaign to overturn the racial quotas whites may consider obstacles to their own advancement.

The White Flight Pattern

White college students are not in the habit of holding rallies to protest the disadvantages many expect to face when they apply for employment or for admission to graduate school. They organize marches to protest tuition hikes, South African apartheid, and much else, but when it comes to race-conscious practices that could hinder their own future careers, they are extraordinarily restrained. As for politicians, only a handful have gone on record with unequivocal objections to policies that generate racial quotas. Duke is the exception that proves the rule. In an era of severe budget deficits, a vote against massive aid for minority neighborhoods hardly amounts to a repudiation of the official strategy for black progress.

Only one aspect of the official agenda has drawn a major overt response: efforts to bring racial balance to public schools through busing. Revealingly, the anti-busing demonstrations were spearheaded by parents unable to move their children into private schools or into public school districts outside the purview of busing. Wealthier parents simply fled to the suburbs, thus producing the phenomenon that came to be known as "white flight." It is the latter pattern of escapism, rather than the former pattern of open confrontation, that has been the norm. Where whites have perceived a threat to their own interests, they have generally avoided challenging the beneficiaries or promoters of the prevailing racial policies. Escaping troublesome conditions without making much of a fuss, they have kept their resentments hidden behind a facade of consent and cooperation.

The quiet resignation of whites has had several socially significant consequences. Making American race relations seem more harmonious (or less disharmonious) than they actually are, it has concealed the potential for a veritable white backlash. It has helped block the emergence of new responses to racial disparities, genuinely popular responses that would bring relief, as William Julius Wilson might put it, to the "truly disadvantaged." Finally, it has discouraged intellectuals from speaking openly and frankly on matters pertaining to race. . . .

Hidden Discontent

Although we live in an age of hypernationalism, racism has come to evoke dreadful images. Individuals to whom the charge sticks can expect to suffer social indignities, face ostracism, draw attacks from the press, even see their careers destroyed. And the possibility of being accused of racism is present in contexts as diverse as zoning, broadcasting standards, and deficit reduction. Under the circumstances, publicly professed positions on race-related issues often differ from sentiments conveyed privately to family members, trusted friends, and pollsters who promise anonymity. The resulting distortion of public discourse is more significant than that which would be caused by mere self-censorship. Self-censorship cleanses the public realm of socially disapproved sentiments, perceptions, and opinions. Lying goes further. It replaces the disapproved with approved alternatives.

The element of the agenda for black progress which induces widespread insincerity is racial affirmative action. Though established as a vehicle for ensuring that qualified minorities who might otherwise be overlooked get a chance to prove themselves, affirmative action rapidly evolved into a system of racial quotas, timetables, and standards. Polls that grant individuals anonymity show that white Americans overwhelmingly reject the practices instituted under the rubric of affirmative action.

In a 1976 Harris poll only 10 percent of the whites in the sample, as against 37 percent of the blacks, thought that a medical school should lower its standards to enroll a black candidate "who may not have the right qualifications but shows real promise." And in a 1984 Gallup poll 9 percent of the whites, but 49 percent of the blacks, supported "giving blacks preference in jobs over equally qualified whites because of past discrimination against blacks."

As with any issue, answers are sensitive to the wording of the question. The approval rate rises markedly when affirmative action is distinguished from "rigid quotas." The rate is consistently very low, however, when affirmative action is characterized as a compensatory remedy for past racial injustices or as a method for achieving racial balance in results. Yet, rarely does one hear of public objections to affirmative action. Whatever their ethnic origins, Americans generally avoid articulating their concerns even when they suspect that they themselves have been hurt by racial double standards. Not only do they refrain from complaining, but many voice support for the prevailing practices and participate in the vilification of persecuted dissenters.

Whites Are Not Free to Speak

When asked in safe—that is, private—settings to justify their stand, whites opposed to affirmative action will argue that as individuals they bear neither blame nor responsibility for present racial disparities. "We ourselves have not owned slaves," they will say, "and we have done nothing to hold anyone down. Besides, for at least a generation blacks have enjoyed great opportunities to get ahead. So offering advantages to blacks amounts to reverse discrimination against us." Whites critical of affirmative action will grumble, moreover, about being made scapegoats for all the ills that plague the black community, from high unemployment to the AIDS epidemic. Several recent books, including Andrew Hacker's *Two Nations* and Thomas and Mary Edsall's *Chain Reaction*, develop these points using data drawn from various sources, including focus-group sessions and off-the-record conversations. A common theme in the contemporary literature on race relations is that whites who have misgivings about the established racial agenda and who reject personal responsibility for racial disparities consider themselves unfree to speak their minds, to defend themselves, to be heard. . . .

Failure of Affirmative Action

What, then, is the record? Have the intended beneficiaries of racial affirmative action made tangible progress?

Educated and already well-off blacks have most certainly achieved measurable advances. The black middle class has grown appreciably in the last quarter-century, along with black representation in prestigious schools, high government offices, the most lucrative professions, and the military command. The extent to which the gains are attributable to affirmative action is, however, a matter of controversy. As Thomas Sowell has often pointed out, at the time racial guidelines and timetables began to be widely enforced, around 1970, educated and well-off blacks were already making rapid progress in various domains. Still, there is no question that in the era of affirmative action the black middle class expanded and prospered.

Equally clear is that the living standards of poor blacks have deteriorated relative to wealthy blacks, relative to poor whites, and even absolutely. As the Edsalls have documented, from 1973 to 1987 families in the bottom quintile of the black income distribution became 18 percent poorer in constant dollars—as against a smaller loss of 7 percent for families in the bottom quintile of the white distribution. In the same period, families in the top quintile of the black distribution gained 33 percent. As a remedy for black poverty, then, affirmative action programs have been a dismal failure. While blacks least in need of special help have reaped visible gains, those with the greatest need have suffered unmistakable losses.

Reprinted by permission of Mike Ramirez and Copley News Service.

The losses of impoverished blacks show up in current statistics on poverty, unemployment, family conditions, and crime. A quarter-century after the establishment of racial affirmative action, about a third of all blacks, as against a tenth of all whites, live below the poverty line. The unemployment rate of blacks is more than twice that of whites. A black child is about three times as likely to be born into poverty. More than half of all black children live in single-parent families; only one sixth of white children do. A black man is six times as likely as a white man to be murdered, and his murderer is likely to be black. Most significant for our purposes, since the 1970s racial discrepancies have all grown or held steady.

In and of themselves, such grim statistics do not establish that affirmative action has harmed black economic progress. They

suggest, however, that black poverty and its defining pathologies are rooted in factors other than contemporary racism.
Entrenched white racism might explain racial discrepancies that
have held constant, but different forces must have been at work
for those that have widened.

Yet, substantial segments of the black community, including
most civil rights leaders and elected officials, see no need for a
major change in direction. Observing the dispiriting statistics
and the troubles of black neighborhoods, they infer that the
civil rights reforms to date have been too superficial, that they
have offered minorities only the illusion of equal opportunity.
In their view, the white majority has never shown real interest
in racial equality, and it continues to prove that it cannot be
trusted. Racial disparities will persist unless blacks show a sustained determination to defend and promote black interests
through unified collective action. And behind every lamentable
phenomenon, trend, or event one may find the hand of white
racism. David Duke's political success is simply proof of mounting racism, as is every antiblack epithet scribbled on a bath-
room wall and every beating of a black man at the hands of
white police officers.

Blacks are not alone, of course, in recognizing the racial prejudices and hostilities that underlie such episodes. Most whites
condemned the 1991 beating of Rodney King by four white officers of the Los Angeles Police Department as an act of bar-
barism, and even in Ventura County, California, the site of the
first trial in which three of the four officers were acquitted, a
majority of whites found the verdict unjust. But large numbers
of blacks see additional signs of racism where most other Americans see either the irresponsibility of certain segments of the
black population or the ill effects of social policies that enjoy
the support of leading black organizations and their political allies outside the black community. . . .

A Looming Explosion?

What can be predicted is that if we stay the course on race relations the potential for a major racial confrontation will persist,
if not grow. Genuinely disadvantaged blacks—not to mention
some well-off—will continue accumulating hatreds against
whites. And whites who feel victimized by the prevailing racial
programs will continue building up resentments against blacks.
There will be substantial numbers within each race who, under
the right conditions, can be coaxed into joining some racial
movement.

Though prediction is a task fraught with hazards, there are
good reasons for believing that whites coming of age now and in
the near future will show less patience than today's adults to-

34

ward blacks threatening their interests. New generations will have no memory of the horrors of Jim Crow segregation. They will not have lived through the hostile reactions to the nonviolent marches of the mid-1960s. And they will not have been inspired by Martin Luther King's dream of a race-neutral society the way their parents and grandparents were. They will be accustomed to seeing the black leadership as an entrenched special-interest group with no special claim to the moral high ground. They will have known privileged blacks who were given special advantages in admission and employment in the name of fighting racial injustice. They will have had exposure to the bitterly anti-white edge of rap music.

Most importantly, the current emphasis on group rights, as opposed to individual rights, will have conditioned them to assign blame to groups. Sooner or later many will begin asking: "Why do blacks with no apparent disadvantages enjoy privileges from cradle to grave? And why must we endure a blanket accusation of racial bias when government is manifestly biased against us?" The consequences of such questionings are unpredictable. They could be overshadowed by hostilities—on the part of blacks and whites—toward immigrants from Latin America, successful Asian-Americans, or economically ascendant foreign nations. But the possibility of eruption of one type of conflict provides no guarantee against the aggravation of another.

"*A . . . forgetting of history has in recent years allowed some persons to argue, and argue persuasively, that affirmative action is reverse racism.*"

Opposition to Affirmative Action Among Whites Is Racist

Stanley Fish

Affirmative action policies, which were launched in the 1960s to promote the advancement of minorities and women seeking employment and educational opportunities, have been characterized by their opponents as reverse discrimination. In the following viewpoint, Stanley Fish argues that affirmative action was designed to remedy the effects of slavery and segregation that blacks and others experienced in the past, and that to equate it with reverse discrimination or reverse racism ignores this history. He contends that the growing opposition of whites to affirmative action is a racist attempt to preserve special privileges for themselves. Fish is a professor of English and law at Duke University in North Carolina.

As you read, consider the following questions:

1. How does Fish define affirmative action?
2. How is the playing field tilted, according to the author?
3. How is race a disadvantage even to those who are economically or educationally well off, according to Fish?

I take my text from George Bush, who, in an address to the United Nations on September 23, 1991, said this of the U.N. resolution equating Zionism with racism: "Zionism . . . is the idea that led to the creation of a home for the Jewish people. . . . And to equate Zionism with the intolerable sin of racism is to twist history and forget the terrible plight of Jews in World War II and indeed throughout history." What happened in World War II was that 6 million Jews were exterminated by persons who regarded them as racially inferior and a danger to Aryan purity. What happened after World War II was that the survivors of that Holocaust established a Jewish state, that is, a state centered on Jewish history, Jewish values, and Jewish traditions, in short, a Jewocentric state. What President Bush objects to is the logical sleight of hand by which these two actions are declared equivalent because they are both expressions of racial exclusiveness. Ignored, as Bush says, is the *historical* difference between them, the difference between a program of genocide and the determination of those who escaped it to establish a community in which they would be the makers, not the victims, of the laws.

It is only by thinking of racism as something that occurs principally in the mind, a falling away from proper notions of universal equality, that the desire of a victimized and terrorized people to band together can be declared to be morally the same as the actions of their would-be executioners. It is only when the actions of the two groups are detached from the historical conditions of their emergence and given a purely abstract description that they can be made interchangeable. What President Bush is saying to the United Nations is, "Look, the Nazis' conviction of racial superiority generated a policy of systematic genocide; the Jewish experience of centuries of persecution in almost every country on earth generated a desire for a homeland of their own; if you manage somehow to convince yourself that these are the same, it is you, not the Zionists, who are morally confused, and the reason you are morally confused is that you have forgotten history."

Forgotten History and Reverse Racism

What I want to say, following Bush's reasoning, is that a similar forgetting of history has in recent years allowed some persons to argue, and argue persuasively, that affirmative action is reverse racism. The very phrase "reverse racism" contains the argument in exactly the form the president objects to: it was once the case in this country that whites set themselves apart from blacks and claimed privileges for themselves while denying them to others; now, on the basis of race, blacks are claiming special status and reserving for themselves privileges they deny to others; isn't one as bad as the other? The answer is "no," and one can see why by imagining that it is not 1991 but 1955 and that we are in a town in the South. No doubt that town would contain two more or less distinct communities, one white and one black, and no doubt in each community there would be a ready store of dismissive epithets, ridiculing stories, self-serving folk myths, and expressions of plain hatred, all directed at the other community, and all based in racial hostility. Yet it would be bizarre to regard their respective racisms—if that is the word—as equivalent, for the hostility of one group stems not from any wrong done to it but from the wrongs it is able to *inflict* by virtue of its power to deprive citizens of their voting rights, to limit access to an educational institution, to prevent entry into the economy except at the lowest and most menial levels, and to force members of the stigmatized group to ride in the back of the bus; the hostility of the other group is the result of these actions, and while hostility and racial anger are unhappy facts wherever they are found, there is certainly a distinction to be made between the ideological hostility of the oppressor and the experience-based hostility of those who have been oppressed.

A Remedy for Past Injustice

Affirmative action programs were established in the United States to ensure diversity in the work place and at universities. American history is undeniably blemished with racism and sexism. And unless we are encouraged to employ fair hiring and admissions practices, discrimination against women and people of color will continue. Affirmative action seeks to remedy past injustice, while shaping policies that will deter future discrimination. Opponents of affirmative action contend that white males are now the target of discrimination. I guess that's kind of how every monopoly must feel when it gives up 100 percent of its market share.

Ironically, those who lament the entitlement and victim mentality in our country are among the first in line to claim they've been cheated of their divinely appointed supremacy.

Jennifer Coburn, *The San Diego Union-Tribune*, February 26, 1995.

Not to make that distinction is, in George Bush's words, to twist history and forget the terrible plight of Afro-Americans, not simply in World War II but in the more than two hundred years of this country's existence. Moreover, it is further to twist history to equate the efforts to remedy that plight with the actions that produced it. Those efforts, designed to redress the imbalances caused by long-standing discrimination, are called affirmative action, and it is a travesty of reasoning to argue that affirmative action, which gives preferential treatment to disadvantaged minorities as part of a plan to achieve social equality, is no different from the policies that created the disadvantages in the first place. Reverse racism is a cogent description of affirmative action only if one considers the virus of racism to be morally and medically indistinguishable from the therapy we apply to it. A virus is an invasion of the body's equilibrium, and so is an antibiotic; but we do not equate the two and decline to fight the disease because the medicine we employ is disruptive of normal functionings. Strong illness, strong remedy—the formula is as appropriate to the health of the body politic as it is to the body proper.

The Level Playing Field

At this point someone will always say, "But two wrongs don't make a right; if it was wrong to treat blacks unfairly, it is wrong to give blacks preference and thereby treat whites unfairly." But this objection is just another version of the forgetting and rewriting of history. The work is done by the adverb "unfairly," which suggests two more or less equal parties, one of whom has been unjustly penalized by an incompetent umpire or official scorer. But the initial condition of equality in relation to which the prep-school virtue of fairness might be an appropriate yardstick has never existed. Blacks have not simply been treated unfairly; they have been subjected first to decades of slavery, then to decades of second-class citizenship, massive legalized discrimination, economic persecution, educational deprivation, and cultural stigmatization; they have been killed, beaten, raped, bought, sold, excluded, exploited, shamed, and scorned for a very long time. The word *unfair* is hardly an adequate description of their experience, and the belated gift of "fairness" in the form of a resolution no longer to discriminate against them legally is hardly an adequate remedy for the deep disadvantages that a prior and *massive* discrimination has produced. When the deck is stacked against you in more ways than you can even count, it is small consolation to hear that you are now free to enter the game and take your chances.

The same insincerity and hollowness of promise infect another formula that is popular with the anti–affirmative action crowd, the formula of the level playing field. Here the argument usually takes the form of saying, "It is undemocratic to give one class of citizens advantages at the expense of other citizens; the truly democratic way is to have a level playing field to which everyone has access and where everyone has a fair and equal chance to succeed on the basis of his or her merit." Fine words, but they conceal the true facts of the situation as it has been given to us by history: the playing field is already tilted in favor of those by whom and for whom it was constructed in the first place; if the requirements for entry are tailored to the cultural experiences of the mainstream majority, if the skills that make for success are nurtured by institutions and cultural practices from which the disadvantaged minority has been systematically excluded, if the language and ways of comporting oneself that identify a player as "one of us" are alien to the lives minorities are forced to live, then words like "fair" and "equal" are cruel jokes, for what they promote and celebrate is an institutionalized unfairness and a perpetuated inequality. The playing field is already rigged, and the resistance to altering it by the mechanisms of affirmative action is in fact a determination to make sure that the present imbalances are continued as long as possible. . . .

Racial and Socioeconomic Disadvantages

Nevertheless, the case against affirmative action is not yet done; there is at least one more card to play, and it is a strong one. Granted that the playing field is not level and that access to it is reserved for an already advantaged elite, it still remains true that the disadvantages suffered by others are not racial—at least not in 1991—but socioeconomic; therefore, shouldn't it be the case, as Dinesh D'Souza urges, that "universities should retain their policies of preferential treatment, but alter their criteria of application from race to socioeconomic disadvantage" and thus avoid the unfairness of current policies that reward middle-class or affluent blacks at the expense of poor whites? One answer to this question is given by D'Souza himself when he acknowledges that the overlap between minority groups and the poor is very large, a point underscored by Secretary of Education Lamar Alexander when he said, in response to a question about funds targeted for black colleges, "98% of race specific scholarships do not involve constitutional problems"—by which he meant, I take it, that in 98 percent of the cases race-specific scholarships were also scholarships to the economically disadvantaged, to the poor.

Still, there is that other 2 percent, those nonpoor, middle-class, economically favored blacks who are receiving special attention on the basis of disadvantages they do not experience. What about them? The force of the question depends on the assumption that in this day and age race could not possibly be a seriously disadvantaging fact for those who are otherwise well positioned in the society. But the lie to this assumption was given dramatically in a recent broadcast of the ABC television program *Prime Time Live*. In a stunning twenty-five-minute segment, the reporters and a camera crew followed two young men of equal education, cultural sophistication, level of apparent affluence, etc., around St. Louis, a city where neither was known. The two differed only in a single respect: one was white, the other black; but that small difference turned out to mean everything. In a series of encounters with shoe salesmen, record store and bank employees, rental agents, landlords, employment agencies, taxicab drivers, and ordinary fellow citizens, the black member of the pair was either ignored or given a special and suspicious attention; was asked to pay more for the same goods or come up with a larger down payment for the same car; was turned away as a prospective tenant; rejected as a prospective taxicab fare; treated with contempt and irritation by clerks, bureaucrats, and city officials; and in every way possible made to feel second-class, unwanted, and inferior.

The inescapable conclusion was that alike though they may be in every other way, the blackness of one of these young men meant that he would lead a significantly different and lesser life than that of his white counterpart; he would be less well housed and at greater expense; he would pay more for services and products when and if he were given the opportunity to purchase them; he would have difficulty establishing credit; the first emotions he would inspire on the part of those he met would be distrust and fear; his abilities would be discounted even before he had a chance to display them; and, above all, the treatment he received from minute to minute would chip away at his self-esteem and self-confidence with consequences that most of us could not even imagine. As the young man in question said at the conclusion of the broadcast, "You walk down the street with a suit and tie and it doesn't matter. Someone will make determinations about you that affect the quality of your life.". . .

Newly Respectable Bigotry

Individualism, fairness, merit—these three words are continually in the mouths of our up-to-date, newly respectable bigots who have learned that they need not put on a white hood or bar access to the ballot box in order to secure their ends; rather, they need only clothe themselves in a vocabulary emptied of its historical content and made into the justification for attitudes and policies they would not acknowledge were they frankly named. So skillful have these new bigots become in appropriating vocabularies and symbols thought to be the property of their natural opponents that they can often represent themselves as the preservers of the values they are subverting. Recently a poster has appeared on a college campus that says in large letters STOP APARTHEID; it is only after you have absorbed the message that you find out that the apartheid in question involves affirmative action, minority scholarships, black dormitories and fraternities, etc. The equation of these mild attempts to afford a disadvantaged minority educational opportunities, along with such rights as voluntary association, with the totally repressive mechanisms of the South African state is a particularly egregious instance of the funny-money logic decried by George Bush, the logic by which the victims of racism become accused of racism the moment the tide turns ever so slightly in their favor. I don't know about you, but I prefer my bigotry straight. I would rather hear someone say, "I really don't believe that blacks or women or Arabs or gays should be enfranchised in every corner of our society. I really am opposed to the Equal Rights Amendment and the Civil Rights Bill of 1964 and the Immigration Act of the following year [which eliminated restrictions based on country of origin], and the various laws against discrimination that are multiplying at this very moment. I believe in the right of Anglo-Saxon American males, or in the right of those who are willing to comport themselves as Anglo-Saxon American males, to rule and to guide; and I want to institute policies that ensure the continuation of this natural prerogative." Of course, very few people are saying such things these days; instead they are prating on about fairness, merit, and individuality, and under cover of those once honorable words, they excite the fears of mainstream Americans and assure them that if they act on those fears, it will only be out of the very highest motives. You are some of those Americans, and it is your fears that are being appealed to. I hope you resist.

"Almost every poll shows a higher level of anti-Semitism among blacks than among other groups."

Black Muslims Are Engaging in Hate Speech Against Jews

Arch Puddington

In November 1993, a controversy arose around Nation of Islam spokesman Khallid Abdul Muhammad, who made derogatory remarks about Jews and others during a speech at Kean College in Union, New Jersey. In the following viewpoint, Arch Puddington argues that the speech is a signal of growing anti-Semitism among blacks, spurred by the prominence of Louis Farrakhan and his ideas. Puddington blames the promoters of multiculturalism on university campuses—who have advocated black studies and women's studies programs—for allowing hate speech in the name of diversity. Puddington, who worked for the late civil rights leader Bayard Rustin, is a frequent contributor to *Commentary*, a monthly journal published by the American Jewish Committee.

As you read, consider the following questions:

1. According to the polls cited by the author, what percentage of blacks believe Louis Farrakhan's message should be heard?
2. What is Puddington's criticism of Wellesley College professor Tony Martin?
3. According to the author, what does the multiculturalism movement actually stimulate?

What has come to be known as the Kean College incident has focused renewed attention on the problem of black anti-Semitism on the American college campus. Yet for all the uproar provoked by that incident and subsequent ones, there is still no clear recognition of the extent to which it is the imposition of an agenda of multiculturalism and "diversity" that is responsible for making open, poisonous, anti-Jewish bigotry into a veritable fixture of campus political life.

The basic facts about the Kean College incident are by now well known. On November 19, 1993, Khalid Abdul Muhammad, a prominent member of the Nation of Islam and the national spokesman of its leader, Louis Farrakhan, delivered a three-hour speech to a predominantly black audience at Kean College in Union, New Jersey, a state-funded institution which draws its student body from the declining working-class cities of northern New Jersey. From beginning to end, the address was charged with an astonishing degree of malice, contempt, and ridicule, aimed variously at whites, South Africans, homosexuals, Arabs, and black moderates—a case, if ever there was one, of equal-opportunity hate.

The Anti-Semitic Remarks

Muhammad's principal target, however, was Jews. In addition to dwelling on the traditional anti-Semitic stereotype of the all-powerful Jew, and asserting that Jews "want nothing but money," he made a special point of their crimes against blacks. He charged that Jews had dominated the slave trade in the past and that they now had black athletes, entertainers, and politicians in their grasp. He accused Jewish landlords of exploiting black tenants. He belittled Jewish participation in the civil-rights movement. And he traced the origins of Judaism to black Africa, arguing that those who today call themselves Jews are really false Jews, the genuine Jews being the descendants of African slaves.

These were some of the "truths" that Farrakhan himself subsequently endorsed at a press conference where he also announced that, because of the unfortunate "tone" in which they had been expressed, Muhammad was being temporarily removed from his position as spokesman. As to that "tone," the most frequently quoted passage, in which Muhammad accused Jews of "sucking the blood of the black community," was only one example, and by no means the most repulsive, of a rhetoric seldom encountered even on the farthest fringes of the anti-Semitic Right.

Thus, Union County, where Kean College is located, he called a "Jew stronghold," and he also referred to "Columbia Jewniversity," "Jew York City," and the "Jewnited Nations." In speaking of the Jewish people and their religion, Muhammad used the phrase "synagogue of Satan.". . . Regarding the Holocaust,

44

Muhammad suggested that the Jews had it coming:

> You see everybody always talk about Hitler exterminating six million Jews. . . . But don't nobody ever ask what did they do to Hitler? . . . They went in there, in Germany, the way they do everywhere they go, and they supplanted, they usurped, . . . and a German, in his own country, would almost have to go to a Jew to get money. . . . Now he was an arrogant, no-good devil bastard, Hitler, no question about it. He was wickedly great. . . . But they [the Jews] are wickedly great, too, brother.

And in discussing the Jewish role in the civil-rights movement, Muhammad resorted to a bit of racist mockery:

> The Jews have told us, the so-called Jews have told us, ve [sic], ve, ve suffer like you. Ve, ve, ve, ve marched with Dr. Martin Luther King, Jr. Ve, ve, ve were in Selma, Alabama. Ve, ve were in Montgomery, Alabama. Ve, ve were on the front line of the civil-rights marches. Ve have always supported you. But let's take a look at it. The Jews, the so-called Jews, what they have actually done, brothers and sisters, is used us as cannon fodder. . . .

Farrakhan's Views

This raises the question of what, exactly, are Farrakhan's views on Jews and Judaism. His apologists contend that while he did indeed call Judaism a "gutter religion" some years ago, he has moderated his attitude over time and has even made such important gestures toward the Jewish community as publicly performing the solo part in the Mendelssohn Violin Concerto (!) and meeting with a prominent Jewish journalist in Chicago. Yet to conclude that a new and unprejudiced Farrakhan has emerged requires that one not only cast aside Farrakhan's past obsession with Jews and Jewish influence, but also ignore what he and the Nation of Islam are saying and doing right now.

One must ignore the fact that the Nation of Islam publishes *The Secret Relationship Between Blacks and Jews*, a pseudo-history, with no listed author, which purports to prove that the slave trade was dominated by Jews. One must ignore the fact that the Nation of Islam continues to distribute the infamous anti-Semitic forgery, *Protocols of the Elders of Zion*. One must ignore the fact that anti-Semitism is central to the message of Khalid Muhammad and other speakers who represent the Nation of Islam at campus forums. And one must ignore Farrakhan's own words, not uttered five or ten years ago, but within the past year [1993–1994].

In the midst of the Khalid Muhammad furor, for instance, Farrakhan told an audience in Harlem that Jews "are the most organized, rich, and powerful people, not only in America, but in the world," and added that they were "plotting against us even as we speak." More telling were his comments in a *Chicago Sun-Times* interview conducted in July 1993. Presented with an ideal fence-mending opportunity, Farrakhan responded by actually reinforcing the anti-Semitic dimension of his message:

> When I talk to the Jews, I am talking to a segment of that quorum that holds my people in their grip. And I can't get to you unless I get to them first because they got a grip on you whether you want to admit it or not because they got a grip on politicians, on black preachers, on black intellectuals.

> . . . It is like the Bible. They are elders of Israel, but the elders of Israel are under the control of Pharaoh and your . . . top black leaders, your top black intellectuals, your top black professional sports and entertainers are not under our control. They are under the control of those who have done injustices to the masses of black people, so I have to go to them to get you out of their grips so you can work for your people and their salvation rather than work on a job for your enemy.

In the same interview, Farrakhan described himself as "the lone voice for black people," and left no doubt that he believed he had attained this position by refusing to knuckle under to demands that he renounce his anti-Jewish "truths."

That Farrakhan declined to disavow Khalid Muhammad's opinions, then, should have come as no surprise: Muhammad, after all, was only repeating ideas, albeit in less temperate language, taught by his leader, including most definitely the notorious proposition that Jews are "sucking the blood" of the black community. . . .

Farrakhan's Following Among Blacks

While the formal nationwide membership of the Nation of Islam is not believed to be especially impressive—most estimates fall in the 10,000 to 15,000 range—Farrakhan himself commands a substantially larger following, including many middle-class blacks. Over 30,000 admirers packed a recent Farrakhan address in New York, and over 10,000 attended a rally in Harlem where attendance was limited to black men. No other figure in black America could draw the large and enthusiastic crowds which regularly jam Farrakhan's meetings; and indeed, the Black Politics Study conducted at the University of Chicago has found that a whopping 67 percent of black respondents consider Farrakhan a positive force in the black community, with a mere 28 percent viewing him negatively. The results of a *Time*/CNN Poll are even more discouraging, with 70 percent of black respondents agreeing that Farrakhan "says things the country should hear," 63 percent agreeing that he "speaks the truth," and only 34 percent seeing him as "a bigot and a racist."

Farrakhan's appeal may stem in part from his preachments against drugs and black-on-black violence and his emphasis on black self-respect, but there is no question that racism is fundamental to his popularity. When, for instance, during one of his New York speeches, he mentioned the black man [Colin Ferguson] who, in a deranged orgy of racial vengeance, killed six non-black passengers on the Long Island Railroad on December 7, 1993, Farrakhan was greeted by sustained applause. The applause was a testimony to the level of racial resentment that pervades the Farrakhan constituency, a resentment he has labored long and hard to exploit.

KU KLUX KLAN   LOUIS FARRAKLAN

Reprinted by permission: Tribune Media Services.

So far as Jews in particular are concerned, black attitudes provide a fertile field for Farrakhan. Almost every poll shows a higher level of anti-Semitism among blacks than among other groups. In a 1992 Anti-Defamation League (ADL) survey, only 14 percent of black respondents registered no anti-Semitism, whereas 37 percent fell into the category of most anti-Semitic, more than double the level found among non-Jewish whites. Other polls have shown that better-educated blacks tend to be more anti-Semitic than blacks with less education, a reversal of the pattern in the general population.

Spreading Anti-Semitism Among Blacks

One has to conclude that this situation is likely to get worse when one considers how seriously off the mark Congressman Charles Rangel is in dismissing the Kean College incident as an isolated and therefore unimportant case. For the truth is that it is an all-too-typical example of the growing phenomenon of unconcealed, virulent black anti-Semitism on college campuses. . . .

Nor is the problem of black anti-Semitism on campus limited to the controversial personalities invited to deliver guest lectures. At City College of New York (CCNY), Professor Leonard Jeffries, Jr. continues to serve as chairman of the Black Studies Department despite a well-established record of anti-Semitism. (Jeffries, incidentally, has served as an adviser to Kean College and has spoken there on more than one occasion.) At Wellesley College, in Wellesley, Massachusetts, Tony Martin, a tenured professor in the Africana Studies Department, who has assigned his class readings from *The Secret Relationship Between Blacks and Jews*, hit back against criticism by saying that "anti-Semitism . . . has become for the privileged and powerful U.S. Jewish leadership and their unthinking Negro stooges, a bludgeon to subdue dissent, stifle discussion, deprive African-Americans of a living, and perpetuate historical lies." He also said, in a formulation quite similar to Khalid Muhammad's charge that Jews used blacks as "cannon fodder" during the civil-rights movement, that the "Jewish Establishment has concluded that a prostrate African-American population, to be oppressed or paternalized as the times warrant, will continue to be an insurance against a Euro-American reversion to European anti-Jewish activity."

The "Truth" as Seen by College Students

Of course, we could dismiss the ravings of Farrakhan and his acolytes if it were clear that their extremism and bigotry were rejected by the target audience of black students. Yet the evidence collected by journalists who have covered the controversies over black anti-Semitism on campus suggests that many black students are more than willing to give the most absurd and hate-driven views the benefit of the doubt.

This was certainly the case at Kean College. To one black student, Muhammad's speech represented "racial pride." Another said the speech was "not hate," but rather "just culture," and added that, "They come down on everyone who tells the truth." Another student asserted that it would be "wrong for me to tell him to change his thoughts because someone else might be offended by what he says."

These reactions echoed remarks made by black students on other colleges who became acquainted with Muhammad's world view. Muhammad "has a message that speaks to the black youth," commented a student at Morgan State University in Baltimore, Maryland. A law student at Howard University in Washington, D.C., called Muhammad a "freedom fighter, a staunch role model, besides being exciting, charismatic, and appealing intellectually." Similarly, a Barnard College (New York City) undergraduate found

Muhammad's opinions "very enlightening, thought-provoking, and above all true.". . .

Following upon Muhammad's speech there, Kean College officials have placed much of the blame on the growing pains of multiculturalism and diversity. To be sure, Kean College is a diverse campus, with over one-quarter of the student body black or Hispanic. By citing diversity and multiculturalism, however, college administrators were not referring to the racial or ethnic proportions within the student body, but to a broader, and much more politically loaded concept. Elsa Gomez, the college's president, alluded to this when she said that Kean was "paying the painful price of our commitment to diversity and the challenge to empower students, who often come from a disadvantaged background, to achieve their full potential."

The key word here is "empower." On campus after campus, the idea of diversity has been advanced to justify not simply extending a measure of authority to students as students—as was the case during the campus wars of the '60s—but to give authority to students as members of certain preferred groups: blacks, Latinos, homosexuals, Asians. . . .

One of the great myths disseminated by the multiculturalists is that their policies represent a way to bring harmony to institutions troubled by the problems associated with interracial student bodies. As one Kean official told a reporter, with unintended irony: "When you're a diverse, multicultural institution, you're continually working to bring people together—that's what diversity and multiculturalism are all about."

In practice, however, the diversity agenda has deepened racial, sexual, and ethnic tensions at universities all across the country. In fact, the accentuation of difference *is* what diversity is "all about," as the movement's more candid advocates will readily acknowledge. Diversity gurus reject the very notion of universal values which unite Americans as Americans, and they are using multiculturalism as a siege weapon aimed at what turns out to be America's most vulnerable institution, the university. On the ground, where the battles are fought, the diversity agenda works not to bridge differences, but to stimulate a sense of minority grievance and to enable racial minorities, homosexuals, and feminists to acquire and protect turf, secure jobs and resources, dilute standards, and reshape curriculum. . . .

Meanwhile, college officials have made it clear that they are powerless to prevent a repetition of the Kean College incident. Administrators who not so long ago were busily formulating elaborate hate-speech codes, and subjecting violators to sensitivity-training sessions, . . . now contend they are helpless to deal with genuine examples of hate speech when voiced by outside speakers or even faculty members.

"The black man will never be free until we address the problem of the relationship between blacks and Jews."

Black Muslims Are Telling the Truth About Jews

Louis Farrakhan, interviewed by Sylvester Monroe

In November 1993, Khallid Abdul Muhammad, a national spokesman for the Nation of Islam, gave a speech at Kean College in Union, New Jersey, that contained derogatory references to Jews and others. In the following viewpoint, Louis Farrakhan rebukes Khallid for his mockery of Jews, but defends the message that Khallid's speech delivered. Farrakhan argues that black people are controlled and repressed by Jews and others, and that for blacks to be independent they must have a fair and equitable relationship with other groups. Farrakhan is leader of the Nation of Islam, a movement of Muslims that preaches black nationalism. He is interviewed by Sylvester Monroe, a correspondent for *Time* magazine.

As you read, consider the following questions:

1. How does Farrakhan define white supremacy?
2. According to Farrakhan, why has he been accused of being a "black Hitler"?
3. What is the ultimate aim of the Nation of Islam, in Farrakhan's words?

T IME: *What is the message that the Nation of Islam is imparting to African Americans?*

Farrakhan: That God is interested in us, that God has heard our moaning and our groaning under the whip and the lash of our oppressors and has now come to see about us. That's the appeal.

TIME: *How does the Nation of Islam take a person who has hit bottom with drugs or alcohol or crime and remake that person?*

Farrakhan: Well, we can't do it without the help of God, and we can't do it until we can reconnect that person to the source of truth and goodness that is Allah.

So once we can reconnect him to God and show him his relationship to God, then you give him the knowledge of himself, his history. So by teaching us our history beyond the cotton fields, beyond our slave history in America, and teaching us our connection to the great rulers of ancient civilizations, the great builders of the pyramids and the great architects of civilization and teaching us our relationship to the father of medicine, the father of law, the father of mathematics and science and religion, this makes us desire now to come up out of our ignorance and achieve the best that we possibly can achieve. And this is what begins to transform the person's life.

TIME: *It has sometimes appeared that you were building this sense of self-esteem by putting down another people.*

Farrakhan: Now the truth of the matter is that white supremacists built a world on that ideology. If that system of white supremacy is based on falsehood, then the truth will attack that system at its foundation and it will begin to tumble down.

Now the truth of the matter is, whites are superior. They are not superior because they are born superior. They are superior because they have been the ruling power, that God has permitted them to rule. They have had the wisdom and the guidance to rule while most of the dark world or the darker people of the world have been, as they have called it, asleep.

Now it's the awakening of all the darker people of the world, and we are awakening at the level that the white world is now beginning to decline. And this is what Brother Khallid was talking about in his speech; I could not say he's a liar, [that] he's wrong. But this should never be taught out of the spirit of mockery.

And so to tear down another people to lift yourself up is not proper. But to tell the truth, to tear down the mind built on a false premise of white supremacy, that is nothing but proper because that will allow whites to relate to themselves as well as to other human beings as human beings.

TIME: *So what Khallid did, was that wrong?*

Farrakhan: To me, it is highly improper in that you make a mockery over people. So why should we mock them? Why should we goad them into a behavior that is so easy for them to do harm to black people? And that's why I rebuked him.

TIME: *Have Khallid's remarks damaged your relationship with the mainstream black civil rights leadership?*

Farrakhan: I don't feel that we can go down the road to liberation without a John Jacob, without a Jesse Jackson, without a Dorothy Height, without a Coretta Scott King or a Congressional Black Caucus or an N.A.A.C.P.

I mean, I have grown to the point, by God's grace, that I see the value of each and every one of these persons to the overall struggle of our people.

I feel that not only do they have something to offer me, but I have something to offer them. I'm not trying to be mainstream. I don't even know what that is. I don't know whether any black has ever achieved mainstream. But I do know this. I want the unity of black organizations and black leaders that we might form a united front and seriously discuss what we can do to better the condition of our people.

It Is Wrong to Condemn Farrakhan

Let us go back to the beginning of this sad episode, namely, Minister Louis Farrakhan's 1984 remarks abut Hitler, Judaism and the link of Jewish power to black social misery. Most Americans believe Minister Farrakhan praised Adolf Hitler and, by implication, condoned the evils done to the Jewish people. Yet this is simply wrong. As Minister Farrakhan has noted on many occasions, his statement that Hitler was "wickedly great"—like Alexander, Caesar, Napoleon and Stalin—meant that Hitler was famous for his pernicious ability to conquer, destroy and dominate others. Furthermore, Hitler hated black people with great passion. And given Minister Farrakhan's devotion to the cause of black freedom, he would not claim that Hitler was *morally* great. Nevertheless, the mainstream press portrayed Minister Farrakhan as a Nazi—that is, a devil in our midst. Surely, if we believe Minister Farrakhan was *morally* wrong to have once held that whites were devils, it is wrong of us to believe he is a devil.

Cornel West, *Time*, February 28, 1994.

TIME: *Has there been any discussion about just that?*

Farrakhan: We have never got to the point where we would sit down to open up these kinds of discussions. Unfortunately, there are those who saw in me a poison that would infect that group. And so they used their influence to push that group away from me. Even if they liked me, they could not associate with me for fear of what it would do to them professionally and economically.

So now we have to get to this talk of anti-Semitism. Am I really anti-Semitic? Do I really want extermination of Jewish people? Of course, the answer is no. Now here's where the problem is. When I am accused of being a Hitler, a black Hitler, because of my oratorical ability and my ability to move people, there is fear that I'm not under control. By the grace of God, I shall never be under the control of those who do not want the liberation of our people. I cannot do that.

The idea is to isolate me, and hopefully, through the media and everybody calling me a hater, a racist, an anti-Semite, that I would just dry up and go away.

Now they have done this for 10 years, and I have not gone away. Now fortunately or unfortunately, they have forced other black leaders into silence on the basic issues of race and color and economics, and Farrakhan now has emerged as the voice that speaks to the hurt of our people.

Now I'm going to come to something that may get me in a lot of trouble. But I've got to speak the truth. What is a bloodsucker? When they land on your skin, they suck the life from you to sustain their life.

In the '20s and '30s and '40s, up into the '50s, the Jews were the primary merchants in the black community. Wherever we were, they were. What was their role? We bought food from them; we bought clothing from them; we bought furniture from them; we rented from them. So if they made profit from us, then from our life they drew life and came to strength. They turned it over to the Arabs, the Koreans and others, who are there now doing what? Sucking the lifeblood of our own community.

Every black artist, or most of them who came to prominence, who are their managers, who are their agents? Does the agent have the talent or the artist? But who reaps the benefits? Come on. We die penniless and broke, but somebody else is sucking from us. Who surrounds Michael Jackson? Is it us?

See, Brother, we've got to look at what truth is. You throw it out there as if to say this is some of the same old garbage that was said in Europe. I don't know about no garbage said in Europe.

But I know what I'm seeing in America. And because I see that black people, Sylvester, in the intellectual fields and professional fields are not going to be free until there is a new relationship with the Jewish community, then I feel that what I'm saying has to ultimately break that relationship.

Just like they felt it necessary to break my relationship with the Black Caucus, I feel it absolutely necessary to break the old relationship of the black intellectual and professional with the Jewish community and restructure it along lines of reciprocity, along lines of fairness and equity.

TIME: *How much does this black/Jewish controversy actually wind up hurting black people?*

Farrakhan: I did not recognize the degree to which Jews held control over black professionals, black intellectuals, black entertainers, black sports figures; Khallid did not lie when he said that.

My ultimate aim is the liberation of our people. So if we are to be liberated, it's good to see the hands that are holding us. And we need to sever those hands from holding us that we may be a free people, that we may enter into a better relationship with them than we presently have.

So yes, in one sense it's a loss, but in the ultimate sense it's a gain. Because when I saw that, I recognized that the black man will never be free until we address the problem of the relationship between blacks and Jews.

TIME: *If you could tell the readers of* TIME *magazine anything you want to tell them about Farrakhan or the Nation of Islam, what would you say to them, or do you even care?*

Farrakhan: Of course I care.

I would hope that the American people and black people would give us a chance to speak to them not on a 30-second sound bite or not even through TIME magazine or any other white-managed magazine or newspaper but allow us to come to the American people to state our case.

I would hope that before the House of Representatives or the Senate will follow the advice of others to do things to hurt the Nation of Islam and our efforts in America at reforming our people, that you would invite us before the Senate or before members of the House of Representatives to question me and us on anything that I have ever said in the past.

And if they can show me that I'm a racist or an anti-Semite, with all of the legal brilliance that's in the government, and I, from that lofty place, will apologize to the world for misrepresenting what I believed to be the truth.

"The differences that separate the [black and Hispanic] communities are just as compelling as the circumstances that join them."

Blacks and Latinos Are Competing for Political Power

Rob Gurwitt

Latinos are the fastest growing population in many American cities. In the following viewpoint, Rob Gurwitt argues that as the Hispanic (Latino) community has grown in the city of Houston, Texas, and in other cities, it has begun to compete with the black community for services, jobs, and political offices. He contends that the alliance blacks and Hispanics formed during the civil rights movement is unlikely to continue in the future because the interests of the two communities are so divergent. Gurwitt is a senior writer for *Governing*, a monthly publication of Congressional Quarterly, Inc.

As you read, consider the following questions:

1. What is the racial balance in Houston, according to the author?
2. According to Gurwitt, why were Hispanics a negligible political force while Kathryn Whitmire was mayor of Houston?
3. According to Charles Kamasaki, quoted by the author, why do Hispanics see blacks as part of the majority culture?

Excerpted from "Collision in Brown and Black" by Rob Gurwitt, *Governing*, January 1993. Reprinted with permission, *Governing* magazine, copyright 1993.

The Casa De Amigos health clinic, run by the city of Houston, Texas, is located in a quiet but threadbare neighborhood on the near north side of town. Nearby, scattered blocks of tidy working-class bungalows stand amid a jumble of weed-choked vacant lots, houses that could fit in a Dust Bowl–era photograph, and a slightly rundown strip of markets, nightclubs and offices for bail bondsmen.

All but a handful of Casa De Amigos' clients are Hispanic, and many are recent immigrants from Mexico or Central America. But until 1993, the clinic had never had a fully Hispanic director. That is why, in 1992, Casa De Amigos was the scene of a brief but intense racial controversy.

The Target of Latino Activism

A small group of Latino activists, arguing that the clinic ought to be run by a Hispanic, mounted a campaign to replace the incumbent director. They made impassioned statements to the press, organized a candlelit vigil outside the clinic, and threatened to hold public officials' feet to the fire until they got some action.

What gave the whole affair its sharp edge was that the target of their effort, Eladio Reid, is black. Although his mother is Panamanian and Reid himself speaks Spanish, racially and culturally he has more in common with the city's African American community than with the clinic's users. To the protesters, he was the wrong color, just as surely as if he had been a white Anglo-Saxon.

Not surprisingly, that line of reasoning got a brusque reception from many of the city's African Americans. "How can you go in there, take jobs away from people who've been there a while, and say, 'We need to remove you and put a Hispanic in this job'?" asks Robert Newberry, a black columnist for the *Houston Post*. Reid felt no less strongly about the matter. "It would have been like deciding not to assign a black doctor to a white neighborhood," he says, "or a white police officer to a black neighborhood."

The city did not back down immediately. Reid kept his post for most of 1992 before he was shifted to another clinic and replaced by a Hispanic woman. Casa De Amigos also added some bilingual personnel, and the city's health department, under a black acting administrator, built up its Hispanic advisory groups. In the end, even some Hispanic leaders quietly allowed that the matter had been blown out of proportion, and it didn't take long for the whole affair to slip from Houstonians' memory.

Even so, the ruckus over Casa De Amigos was significant. Like a small surface tremor that signals more devastating forces at work in the earth, it hinted at a set of stresses building up in

Houston—and other cities—that are bound to unsettle urban politics in the next decade.

The Changing Demography of Houston

Houston is now, very roughly, one-third white, one-third black and one-third Hispanic. Over the past few decades, while blacks have been holding their own in population and whites have been leaving for the suburbs, Hispanics have been bursting in number; there are some estimates that the city's Mexican American population in particular has doubled every ten years. In 1990, for the first time, there were more Hispanics in Houston than there were non-Hispanic blacks. There is no sign that this growth is abating.

For years, the city's black and Hispanic political leaders worked closely in the face of a white establishment reluctant to cede either of them much influence. Over the past decade [since 1980], though, African Americans have made rapid strides in city government. Now Hispanics, the junior partner in the coalition because of their much weaker electoral presence, have begun to come into their own as a political force. As that has happened, real differences are emerging.

"There are so many city and county services that don't adequately service Hispanics, the largest minority community," says Lisa Hernandez, who directs the Houston office of the Southwest Voter Registration and Education Project. "When we start pushing for power, someone's going to have to give some up."

Many African Americans readily acknowledge the basic justice of Hispanic claims. But they also look at the fight over Casa De Amigos, or at a recent city council election in which a Hispanic woman unseated a black incumbent, and wonder why addressing those claims should cost them their own hard-won advances. "There is tension," says Sheila Jackson Lee, a young black member of the city council, "because African Americans say, 'We worked for it, we were beaten, we were spat upon. We'll work with you for it, but do you have to take it from us?'"

Growing Competition Between Hispanics and Blacks

Those sorts of arguments are beginning to rise to the surface in a wide variety of places. . . .

In Denver, where a black mayor, Wellington Webb, has succeeded a Hispanic mayor, Federico Peña, relations between the two communities have focused more on appointments and jobs. They began to sour during Peña's tenure, when blacks charged that Hispanic contractors were favored in city contracts. Now, under Webb, Hispanics complain that they are receiving a disproportionately low share of administrative appointments and only one low-level cabinet post. Matters have been made worse by a political disagreement over the makeup of the school board, with Hispanics pushing for members to be elected by district, and black leaders resisting.

These sorts of disputes are by no means limited to cities that, like Houston and Denver, have big Hispanic populations. In Detroit, where Hispanics are far outnumbered by African Americans, Hispanic leaders have nonetheless begun to agitate openly about their lack of political power. "The bottom line is that we're not a franchised community here," says Javier Garibay, associate director of the Center for Chicano-Boricua Studies at Wayne State University. "Whites have political and economic clout, African Americans have political clout, and we have no clout at all."

Garibay and others have focused their dissatisfaction on the schools. They argue that the Detroit school system recruits teachers from historically black colleges while making little effort to find Hispanic employees, and uses an Afro-centered curriculum that is as alienating to Hispanic students as European-centered studies have been to black students. "We've just been left out of the formula," says Garibay.

Blacks Affected by Latino Immigrants

The Cooke Elementary School in Washington, D.C.'s Adams-Morgan neighborhood—home to white yuppies, poor blacks and Central American immigrants—recently received a $1 million federal grant. The windfall has become a source not of celebration but of fierce dispute. The grant was awarded to make the school completely bilingual—and much of the outrage has come from black parents and teachers. (Latino parents are divided on the issue.) Black teachers fear they will be transferred because they don't speak Spanish. As for the parents, one mother told *The Washington Post*, "This is my neighborhood. My brothers and sisters and cousins went to Cooke, my kids go to Cooke, and I don't want to see the nature of the school changed."

The incident illustrates an important question about immigration that is being neglected in our emerging policy debate on the issue: How does immigration affect black Americans?

Peter Skerry, *The New Republic*, January 30, 1995.

There are other cities where trouble between blacks and Hispanics has attracted much greater publicity: Miami, where African Americans have by and large been excluded by the Cuban-American political establishment, and, of course, Los Angeles, where blacks and Hispanics have argued over everything from redistricting to whose workers will rebuild the city in the wake of the 1992 riot. Since the Los Angeles riot, black-brown tensions in the city have become a familiar story. What is less familiar is the extent to which those tensions are now a fact of political life all over urban America.

Competition for Public Services

It doesn't take much effort to understand why Lisa Hernandez would say that Hispanics in Houston are inadequately served. Walk into City Hall, and you'll find its "One-Stop Permit Center" for commercial and residential permits staffed by black clerks and white clerks, while behind them white—and a few black—managers stand talking on telephones or to each other. The same is true at other offices where citizens are likely to show up: the information desk, the business assistance center, the public works department. The brown faces are all in front of the counter, waiting for help.

The symbolism is inescapable. "If you're Hispanic, the odds are you'll get this feeling, 'This place ain't set up for me,'" says Leonel Castillo, who was the first Hispanic elected citywide, as controller, and then served as commissioner of the U.S. Immigration and Naturalization Service under Jimmy Carter.

Nowhere is that more striking than in the emergency room at Ben Taub Hospital, a county-run public hospital that sits among the more lavishly funded jewels of the enormous Houston Medical Center. At an information desk, two black receptionists strain to understand a Mexican woman holding a squalling baby as she tries to explain her child's problem. At the reception desk, a white clerk wearily looks over a long line of Mexican Americans waiting for help, while a volunteer translates their complaints. "When I walk through here," Castillo says, "I always end up doing translations."

Of Houston's 21,000 city employees, 37 percent are black and only 16 percent are Hispanic; the figure for managers is even more lopsided. Nor have Hispanics fared much better in elective office: they held only one of the city's fourteen city council seats until 1992—they now hold two—and have no seats at all on the county commission [as of January 1993]. They have done better in the state legislature, especially since redistricting in 1991, but Houston still has no Hispanic state senator.

African Americans did not get where they are in Houston politics overnight—they have been building their strength ever since they formed a citywide umbrella group, the Council of Organizations, to help mobilize black voters in the late 1940s. They began electing school board trustees in the 1950s, and sent Barbara Jordan to the state Senate in 1966 and to Congress in 1972. Now they have seats in both houses of the legislature and four seats

59

on the city council.

Just as important, the black community saw its ranks in city government grow rapidly after Kathryn Whitmire, a white liberal, became mayor in 1982. African Americans were a key part of her electoral coalition, and Whitmire placed black administrators throughout city government; they in turn helped bring in black middle managers and line employees.

Whitmire's relations with the Hispanic community were more arms-length, partly because, in spite of their absolute numbers, Hispanics were a negligible political force throughout her years in office. Where blacks had painstakingly built their electoral strength and ability to mobilize voters, Hispanics in Houston were more "politically backward," as *Houston Post* columnist Juan Palomo puts it. They lacked the institutions to organize around—the Catholic Church, for example, being far less amenable to political pursuits than individual black churches—and they lacked the cohesion imposed on the black community by the struggle for civil rights. Just as important, much of Houston's Hispanic population was made up of immigrants, and many couldn't vote. Their powerlessness became a sort of self-fulfilling condition, as both black and white political candidates learned they could ignore Hispanic neighborhoods. . . .

Political Differences Among Blacks and Hispanics

Blacks and Hispanics—especially Mexican Americans and Puerto Ricans—share a long history of discrimination and poverty in this country, and cohesion would make political sense. As Palomo puts it, "It's convenient for the white establishment to have blacks and Hispanics fighting when they could be getting together to work for change."

Over the years, the state of Texas and even the city of Houston have witnessed quite a bit of black-brown cooperation: Henry Gonzalez, now in the U.S. House, filibustered on the floor of the Texas Senate in 1957 against a set of discriminatory bills aimed largely at blacks; Mickey Leland, the black congressman from Houston who died in a 1989 plane crash, formed a close friendship with Ben Reyes, the city's preeminent Hispanic politician, during their time in the state legislature in the 1970s, and used his enormous stature within the black community to preach common cause with Hispanics. . . .

Even now, leaders in both communities still talk about the need for joining hands. "I refuse to fall into the trap of divide and conquer," says Lisa Hernandez. Sheila Jackson Lee agrees: "Coalitions are certainly the sweeter of the wine."

But the fact is, the differences that separate the two communities are just as compelling as the circumstances that join them. To begin with, there is the simple difference in the way each community sees the other. Blacks tend to see Hispanics as racially closer to whites, and thus better able to assimilate and avoid discrimination. But many Hispanics see blacks as part of a majority culture from which they themselves are excluded. "What blacks don't understand," says Charles Kamasaki, vice president at the National Council of La Raza, "is that Hispanics say of African Americans, 'They speak English, they don't have Spanish surnames, culturally they're more like whites than we are.'" Indeed, there are Hispanics in Houston who argue that black candidates have an easier time running for office, because a yard sign carrying only the name of a candidate will indicate if he or she is Hispanic, but not if he or she is black.

Advances in Officeholding and Power

That gulf carries over into political perceptions as well. There is a common—if not often expressed—conviction among Hispanics that while they may have profited from the civil rights movement as a whole, they have benefited less from the advance of African Americans into positions of power. "There is not a black leader in Houston—although Mickey Leland used to—who has appealed effectively to the Hispanic community, or who has developed close ties," says Leonel Castillo. "There's not one who speaks Spanish, not one who has a top Hispanic aide. There's a concern, in fact, that blacks who assume power act like whites: They don't share it."

But if Hispanics look enviously at how far blacks have come, what African Americans see is how far they have yet to go—which makes them especially sensitive to the notion that Hispanics are eyeing what they already have. "My community says, 'They're coming to take everything,'" comments Sheila Jackson Lee. "What 'everything'? We don't have enough!"

Franklin Jones, a political scientist at historically black Texas Southern University in Houston, notes that of the $379 million worth of contracts awarded by the city in fiscal year 1990, African American firms got 3 percent—compared with 6 percent for Hispanic firms. The city's somewhat tattered black neighborhoods, while they may now have the sidewalks and paved streets they once lacked, hardly reflect a community with great political power. And the occupants of the downtown office towers that house most of Houston's wealth-producing businesses are still overwhelmingly white.

"When you look at some of the data, blacks may have won office, but in terms of winning contracts or improving services to black neighborhoods, it hasn't been happening in the way you'd expect for people in power," says Jones. "The advance into officeholding has been greater than the advance into power."

Quite apart from cultural perceptions, there is also the simple fact that black and brown political interests don't always coincide. One of the most heated issues to consume Houston recently has been the makeup of the city council. Currently it has nine members elected by district, and five at-large. Hispanics have argued that they will never make gains in the council unless every member is elected by district, and they have been pushing for a sixteen-member council with no at-large seats other than the mayor's. The black community, which has two districts but also two of the at-large seats, has resisted.

The fight over the council, which will probably be resolved in court, has led to a widespread feeling among Hispanic activists that since their community is finally on the political map, it should above all pay attention to its own needs. "You always should form coalitions," Hispanic political consultant Mark Campos insists, "but I don't think at this point it's to our benefit to set up a permanent coalition with anybody. Right after the [1991] mayoral election [in which Hispanic voters played a large role], someone called me and said we should coalesce with blacks. I said that the Arabs are sitting down with Israel now because Israel kicks their ass. *We* ought to kick some ass. It's important we start demonstrating power, and let people come to us, not us to them."

Talk of a Coalition

Despite Campos' assertiveness, there is no question that, in Houston and other cities, many black and Hispanic political leaders still talk of coalition and of common interests. They also share a belief that, in the long run, both communities are likely to be hurt by competition. As Ron Wilson, a black state representative from Houston, puts it, "Blacks and browns have been at odds because we've for the most part been parceled out crumbs from the table, the fatback and the neck bones. When we focus on those we never get to the steak."

Wilson, in fact, argues that the Hispanic demonstrators in front of Casa De Amigos were right. "There shouldn't have been blacks running Casa De Amigos; it was a faux pas from the beginning," he says.

In the next breath, though, he admits that within the city's African American community, that is not a common sentiment. And that, in fact, is the dilemma that political leaders in both communities face. Whoever uses the rhetoric of coalition runs the risk of being outflanked, on the one hand, by a newly insistent Hispanic community, and on the other, by an increasingly resentful black electorate. "It is important for those of us in the public eye to work to create a sense that as one group grows, the other benefits," says Sheila Jackson Lee. "But at the same time, I have to work with my community, and I must acknowledge that

African Americans still hurt and suffer, and it is sometimes hard for them to envision giving something up in a coalition."

In the end, it may well be that African Americans and Hispanics will have no choice but to stick together if they are to gain greater economic and political power—and that far from being an impediment, the growing assertiveness of Hispanics will in fact pave the way for such a joint effort. "In order to work in coalition," says La Raza's Charles Kamasaki, "we have to come to the table as equals." Still, it seems safe to predict that before that happens, both sides are in for some turbulent times.

"Alliances among progressive people of color can and must help realize the dream."

Blacks and Latinos Should Form a Political Alliance

Elizabeth Martinez

In the following viewpoint, Elizabeth Martinez argues that the dominant model of racism, that of whites toward blacks, ignores the history of racism toward other groups and divides the civil rights alliance of blacks and Latinos. The growing numbers and influence of other minorities, particularly Latinos, necessitates a new model of racism and a renewed civil rights movement, in her opinion. Martinez is an instructor in ethnic studies and women's studies and author of *500 Years of Chicano History in Pictures.*

As you read, consider the following questions:

1. What does Martinez mean by the victimhood tournament?
2. What three developments does the author cite as having expanded the evil of racism in recent years?
3. What are the three reasons for the predominance of the black/white model of racism, according to Martinez?

Excerpted from "Beyond Black/White: The Racisms of Our Time," *Social Justice,* Spring/Summer 1993. Reprinted with permission.

Let me begin by admitting that I have an axe to grind. A bell to toll, a *grito* to shout, a banner to wave. The banner was fashioned during ten years in the Black civil rights–human rights movement followed by ten years in the Chicano *movimiento*. Those years taught that liberation has similar meanings in both histories: an end to racist oppression, the birth of collective self-respect, and a dream of social justice. Those years taught that alliances among progressive people of color can and must help realize the dream.

Such alliances require a knowledge and wisdom that we have yet to attain. For the present, it remains painful to see how divide-and-conquer strategies succeed among our peoples. It is painful to see how prejudice, resentment, petty competitiveness, and sheer ignorance fester. It is positively pitiful to see how often we echo Anglo stereotypes about one another.

A New Model for Racism?

All this suggests that we urgently need some fresh and fearless thinking about racism at this moment in history. Fresh thinking might begin with analyzing the strong tendency among Americans to frame racial issues in strictly Black/white terms. Do such terms make sense when changing demographics point to a U.S. population that will be 32 percent Latino, Asian/Pacific American, and Native American—that is, neither Black nor white—by the year 2050? Not to mention the increasing numbers of mixed people who incorporate two, three, or more "races" or nationalities? Don't we need to imagine multiple forms of racism rather than a single, Black/white model?

Practical questions related to the fight against racism also arise. Doesn't the exclusively Black/white framework discourage perception of common interests among people of color—primarily in the working class—and thus sustain White Supremacy? Doesn't the view of institutionalized racism as a problem experienced only by Black people isolate them from potential allies? Doesn't the Black/white definition encourage a tendency often found among people of color to spend too much energy understanding our lives in relation to Whiteness, obsessing about what the White will think? That tendency is inevitable in some ways: the locus of power over our lives has long been white . . . and the oppressed have always survived by becoming experts on the oppressor's ways. But that can become a prison of sorts, a trap of compulsive vigilance. Let us liberate ourselves, then, from the tunnel vision of Whiteness and behold the colors around us!

To criticize the Black/white framework is not simply a resentful demand from other people of color for equal sympathy, equal funding, equal clout, equal patronage. It is not simply us-too resentment at being ignored or minimized. It is not just another round of mindless competition in the victimhood tournament. Too often we make the categories of race, class, gender, sexuality, age, physical condition, etc., contend for the title of "most oppressed." Within "race," various population groups then compete for that top spot. Instead, we need to understand that various forms and histories of oppression exist. We need to recognize that they include differences in extent and intensity. Yet pursuing some hierarchy of competing oppressions leads us down dead-end streets where we will never find the linkage between oppressions or how to overcome them.

Good-Bye, White Majority

In a society as thoroughly and violently racialized as the United States, white/Black relations have defined racism for centuries. Today the composition and culture of the U.S. are changing rapidly. We need to consider seriously whether we can afford to maintain an exclusively white/Black model of racism when the population will be 32 percent Latino, Asian/Pacific American and Native American—in short, neither Black nor white—by the year 2050. We are challenged to recognize that multi-colored racism is mushrooming, and then strategize how to resist it. We are challenged to move beyond a dualism composed of two white supremacist inventions: Blackness and Whiteness.

Elizabeth Martinez, Z Magazine, May 1994.

The goal in reexamining the Black/white definition is to find an effective strategy for vanquishing an evil that has expanded rather than diminished in recent years. Three recent developments come to mind. First is the worldwide economic recession in which the increasingly grim struggle for sheer survival encourages the scapegoating of working-class people—especially immigrants, especially those of color—by other working-class people. This has become so widespread in the West that a Klan cross-burning in London's Trafalgar Square or on Paris' Champs Élysée doesn't seem hard to imagine. The globalization of racism is mounting rapidly.

Second, and relatedly, the reorganization of the international division of labor continues, with changing demands for workers that are affecting demographics everywhere. History tells us of the close relationship between capital's need for labor and racism. If that relationship changes, so may the nature of racism.

Finally, in the U.S., we have passed through a dozen years [1980-1992] of powerful reaction against the civil-rights agenda set in the 1960s. This has combined with the recession's effects and other socioeconomic developments to make people go into a defensive, hunkering-down mode, each community on its own, at a time when we need more rather than less solidarity. Acts of racist violence now occur in communities that never saw them before (although they always could have happened). An intensification of racism is upon us.

We see it in the anti-immigrant emotions being whipped up and new divisions based on racism and nativism. We see escalating white fears of becoming the minority population, the minority power, after centuries of domination. As U.S. demographics change rapidly, as the "Latinization" of major regions and cities escalates, a cross fire of fears begins to crackle. In that climate the mass media breed both cynical hopelessness and fear. Look only at that October 1992 *Atlantic* magazine cover proclaiming "Blacks vs. Browns: Immigration and the New American Dilemma" for one chilling symptom of an assumed, inevitable hostility.

Beyond the Black/White Framework

Today the task of building solidarity among people of color promises to be more necessary and difficult than ever. An exclusively Black/white definition of racism makes our task all the harder. That's the banner that will be raised here: an urgent need for 21st-century thinking, which can move us beyond the Black/white framework without negating its central, historical role in the construction of U.S. racism. We do need much more understanding of how racism and its effects developed, not only similarly, but also differently for different peoples according to whether they were victimized by genocide, enslavement, or colonization in various forms.

Greater solidarity among peoples of color must be hammered out, painstakingly. With solidarity, a prize could be won even bigger than demolishing racism. The prize could be a U.S. society whose national identity not only ceases to be white, but also advances beyond "equality"—beyond a multiculturalism that gives people of color a respect equal to whites. Toni Morrison has written eloquently in *Playing in the Dark* of this goal from an Africanist perspective: "American means white, and Africanist people struggle to make the term applicable to themselves with ethnicity and hyphen after hyphen after hyphen. . . . In the scholarship on the formation of an American character [a] . . . major item to be added to the list must be an Africanist presence—decidedly not American, decidedly other."

We need to dream of replacing the white national identity with an identity grounded in cultures oriented to respect for all forms of life and balance rather than domination as their guiding star. Such cultures, whose roots rest in indigenous, precolonial societies of the Americas and Africa, can help define a new U.S. identity unshackled from the capitalist worldview. Still alive today, they color my banner bright.

The Predominance of Black/White Relations

Let us begin that dialogue about the exclusively Black/white model of racism and its effects with the question: does that definition prevail and, if so, why?

Alas, it does prevail. Major studies of "minorities" up to 1970 rarely contain more than a paragraph on our second largest "minority," Mexican-Americans. In two dozen books of 1960s movement history, I found inadequate treatment of the Black Civil Rights Movement, but almost total silence about the Chicano, Native American, and Asian American movements of those years. Today, not a week goes by without a major media discussion of race and race relations that totally ignores the presence in U.S. society of Native Americans, Latinos, Asian/Pacific Americans, and Arab-Americans.

East Coast–based media and publishers are the worst offenders. Even a progressive magazine like *The Nation* can somehow publish a special issue entitled "The Assault on Equality: Race, Rights, and the New Orthodoxy" containing only two brief phrases relating to people of color other than African-Americans in twenty-seven pages. Outbreaks of Latino unrest or social uprising, such as we saw in the Mt. Pleasant section of Washington, D.C. [in May 1991], make little if any dent. New York, that center of ideological influence, somehow remains indifferent to the fact that in 1991, Latinos totaled 24.4 percent of its population while Asians formed 6.9 percent.

Even in California, this most multinational of the states, where Latinos have always been the most numerous population of color, it is not rare for major reports on contemporary racial issues to stay strictly inside the Black/white framework. Journalists in San Francisco, a city almost half Latino or Asian/Pacific American, can see no need to acknowledge, "This article will be about African-Americans only"—which would be quite acceptable—in articles on racial issues. At best we may hear that afterthought construction, "Blacks and other minorities."

Again, momentous events that speak to Latino experience of racist oppression fail to shake the prevailing view. Millions of Americans saw massive Latino participation in the April 1992 Los Angeles uprising on their TV screens. Studies show that, taken as a whole, the most heavily damaged areas of L.A. were 49 percent Latino, and the majority of people arrested were Latino. Yet the mass media and most people have continued to view that event as "a Black riot."

Predominantly Anglo left forces have not been much better than the mainstream and liberals. The most consistently myopic view could be heard from the Communist Party U.S.A., which has seen the African-American experience as the only model of racism. Left groups that adopted the Black nation thesis rarely analyzed the validity of Chicano nationalism in the Southwest, or advocated giving lands back to the Native Americans, or questioned the "model minority" myth about Asian/Pacific Americans. . . .

Why the Black/White Framework?

Three of the reasons for the Black/white framework of racial issues seem obvious: numbers, geography, and history. African-Americans have long been the largest population of color in the U.S.; only recently has this begun to change. Also, African-Americans have long been found in sizable numbers in most of the United States, including major cities. On the other hand, Latinos—to focus on this group—are found primarily in the Southwest plus parts of the Northwest and Midwest and they have been (wrongly) perceived as a primarily rural people—therefore of less note.

Historically, it has been only 150 years since the U.S. seized half of Mexico and incorporated those lands and their peoples into this nation. The Black/white relationship, on the other hand, has long been entrenched in the nation's collective memory. White enslavement of Black people together with white genocide against Native Americans provided the original models for racism as it developed here. Slavery and the struggle against it form a central theme in this country's only civil war—a prolonged, momentous conflict—and continuing Black rebellion. Enslaved Africans in the U.S. and African-Americans have created an unmatched history of massive, persistent, dramatic, and infinitely courageous resistance, with individual leaders of worldwide note. They cracked the structure of racism in this country during the first Reconstruction and again during the second, the 1960s Civil Rights Movement, as no other people of color have done.

Interwoven with these historical factors are possible psychological explanations of the Black/white definition. In the eyes of Thomas Jefferson and other leaders, Native Americans did not arouse white sexual anxieties or seem a threat to racial purity, as did Blacks. In any case, White Supremacy's fear of Indian resistance had greatly diminished by the late 1800s as a result of relentless genocide accompanied by colonization. Black rebelliousness, on the other hand, remains an inescapable nightmare to the dominant white society. There is also the fact that contemporary Black rebellion has been urban: right in the Man's face, scary.

There's No Mau-Mau Factor?

A relative indifference toward Mexican people developed in Occupied America in the late 1800s. Like the massacre of Indians and enslavement of Africans, the successful colonization of Mexicans in what became the Southwest was key to U.S. economic growth. One would expect to see racist institutions and ideology emerge, and so they did in certain areas. Yet even in places like the Texas borderlands, where whites have historically reviled and abused Latinos, the Mexican presence didn't arouse a high level of white sexual anxiety and other irrational fears. Today Latinos often say Anglo attitudes make them feel they are less hated than dismissed as inconsequential. "There's no Mau-Mau [intimidation] factor," observed a Black friend half-humorously about Latino invisibility.

Of course there may be an emergent Mau-Mau factor, called demographics. Anglo indifference to Latinos may be yielding to a new fear. The white response to anticipation of becoming a minority during one's own lifetime is often panic as well as hatred and those "hordes" at the gate are of colors other than Black. But the new frenzy has yet to show the same fear-stricken face toward Latinos—or Asian/Pacific Americans—as toward African-Americans. . . .

A final reason for the Black/white framework may be found in the general U.S. political culture, which is not only white-dominated, but also embraces an extremely stubborn form of national self-centeredness. This U.S.-centrism has meant that the political culture lacks any global vision other than relations of domination. In particular, the U.S. has consistently demonstrated contempt for Latin America, its people, their languages, and their issues. The U.S. refuses to see itself as one nation sitting on a continent with twenty others whose dominant languages are Spanish and Portuguese. That myopia has surely nurtured the Black/white framework for racism.

Periodical Bibliography

The following articles have been selected to supplement the diverse views presented in this chapter.

David Barsamian	"The Mind of Black America," *Z Magazine*, February 1994.
Paul Berman	"The Other and the Almost the Same," *The New Yorker*, February 28, 1994.
Valerie Burgher	"Silent Racism," *The Nation*, April 17, 1995.
Brian Duffy et al.	"Race and Rage: The Growing Split Between Black and White," *U.S. News & World Report*, May 11, 1992.
Christopher John Farley	"Enforcing Correctness," *Time*, February 7, 1994.
David Gates	"White Male Paranoia," *Newsweek*, March 29, 1993.
William Greider	"After South Central: The White Conscience," *Rolling Stone*, June 25, 1992.
Michael Kelly	"Howard's End," *The New Republic*, March 21, 1994.
Joel Kotkin	"The Difference Principle," *Reason*, February 1993.
Michael C. Kotzin	"Louis Farrakhan's Anti-Semitism: A Look at the Record," *The Christian Century*, March 2, 1994.
Dale Maharidge	"Can We All Get Along?" *Mother Jones*, November/December 1993.
Jacob Neusner	"Dissent from the Right," *Society*, September/October 1994.
The New Republic	"Race Against Time," May 25, 1992.
Time	"The Rift Between Blacks and Jews," February 28, 1994.
John Edgar Wideman	"Dead Black Men and Other Fallout from the American Dream," *Esquire*, September 1992.
Roger Wilkins	"White Out," *Mother Jones*, November/December 1992.

2 CHAPTER

Does Discrimination Persist in the American Economy?

Chapter Preface

In November 1994, Californians passed a ballot initiative (Proposition 187) that would deny most government-provided social services to illegal immigrants. (State and federal courts immediately suspended implementation of the measure until its constitutionality could be determined.) Given the measure's popularity in pre-election polls, few people were surprised that the initiative was supported by 59 percent of California voters, but many were astounded that it was favored by more than 45 percent of African American voters. African American support for the anti-immigration measure highlighted what some political observers see as the increasing conflict between blacks and immigrants (especially Latinos) over economic and political power, particularly in California but also in other gateway states, such as Florida, New York, and Texas.

According to some analysts, legal and illegal immigration has contributed to a steady increase in black unemployment. They argue that immigrants have displaced blacks from low-skill and unskilled occupations—such as janitorial, housekeeping, and gardening jobs—by accepting lower wages for such work. Even in skilled and professional occupations, some argue, immigrants with education have been able to out-compete blacks. Those who oppose current levels of immigration as too high say that poor immigrants also have crowded blacks out of social service programs. According to Gerda Bikales, president of the citizens' organization E Pluribus Unum, which proposes decreased levels of immigration, "African Americans find themselves competing for jobs, social programs, and affirmative action advantages with the new arrivals, and often end up as the losers in the competition."

On the other hand, University of California, Los Angeles, professors Paul Ong and Abel Valenzuela Jr. contend, "To focus only on immigration as the source disadvantaging African Americans would . . . constitute scapegoating." They argue that the entrance of unskilled immigrants into the job market increases the earnings of blacks, who possess relatively more skills and experience than such immigrants and can therefore merit higher wages. Ong and Valenzuela believe that discrimination against blacks and the overall shrinking of the labor market have contributed more to black unemployment than has competition from immigrants. They conclude that "other factors such as labor market discrimination and segmentation are more important in explaining African American" unemployment.

The effect of immigration on black employment is one of the issues debated in the following chapter on discrimination in the American economy.

"On the whole, the business world has not done much to expand black employment."

Racial Discrimination Limits Opportunities for Blacks

Andrew Hacker

Many people point to the accomplishments of prominent blacks to show that discrimination in American society has been reduced. In the following viewpoint, Andrew Hacker cites statistics showing that blacks (men especially) are underrepresented in many professions and in high-level positions in the private business sector as proof that discrimination persists. He argues that the reasons businesses give for not hiring more black men add up to institutional racism. Hacker is a professor of political science at Queens College in Flushing, New York, and the author of *Two Nations: Black and White, Separate, Hostile, Unequal*, from which this viewpoint is excerpted.

As you read, consider the following questions:

1. What reasons does Hacker cite for the paucity of black-owned enterprises?
2. In what occupations do blacks have the greatest representation, according to the statistics? What reasons does Hacker give for this?
3. According to the author, what are some reasons businesses prefer hiring black women to black men?

Black men and women number among the most highly paid people in the United States. Especially visible, at this time of writing [in 1992], are Bill Cosby, Eddie Murphy, Mike Tyson, Dwight Gooden, Tina Turner, Darryl Strawberry, Whitney Houston, Earvin ("Magic") Johnson, Oprah Winfrey, Bryant Gumbel, and Michael Jordan as well as Janet and Michael Jackson. All have had annual earnings in the millions, often including ownership stakes in corporate enterprises.

Also, a black physician [Louis Sullivan] served as Secretary of Health and Human Services in President George Bush's cabinet, a black physicist [Walter E. Massey] headed the National Science Foundation, while a black military officer [Colin Powell] presided as chairman of the Joint Chiefs of Staff. The Ford Foundation has had a black president for over a dozen years, while the National Baseball League is led by a black executive. A black man also heads the College Entrance Examination Board, the nation's principal testing agency. Another has the top position at Teachers Insurance and Annuity Association–College Retirement Equities Fund (TIAA-CREF), one of the nation's largest pension funds. Black women are the chief officers at Planned Parenthood and several colleges and universities.

Blacks in Business

This, certainly, is the good news. At the same time, it is apparent that all the organizations just cited are governmental or in the public service sector. In fact, three black millionaires have been on *Forbes* magazine's rosters of America's 400 richest men and women. One is John Harold Johnson, who owns *Ebony* and *Jet* magazines; and another was Berry Gordy of Motown Records. A recent addition is Reginald Lewis, who bought Beatrice Foods, and has a net worth of about $340 million. However, *Business Week*'s 1991 listing of the chief executives of America's 1,000 largest corporations had only one black chairman: Erroll B. Davis, who heads a Wisconsin utility holding company and earns a comparatively modest $269,000. Unfortunately, there are no serious signs that the other 999 firms are grooming black executives for eventual top jobs.

The so-called "small business" sector can also be a route to wealth and social status. The Census Bureau keeps count of the number of firms owned by black men and women. Its most recent survey found 425,000 such enterprises, numbering about 2.4 percent of the country's corporations, partnerships, and sole proprietorships. By and large, the black businesses are local concerns, with annual receipts averaging around $50,000, and they deal largely in products or services oriented to black clienteles. Indeed, only 70,000 of the 425,000 have any paid employees. In other words, almost 85 percent are one-person enterprises or family-run firms.

Many arguments have been given for the paucity of black-owned enterprises. There is the difficulty of getting start-up loans and capital from banks and investors stemming from biased attitudes about blacks' business abilities. Nor is it easy for blacks to get experience in corporate management as a prelude to branching out on their own. Some blacks have done well providing products and services to their own community. Still, the real challenge is to build a wider clientele. In fact, some firms have been successful in this sphere. Most whites who have bought Park's Sausages and McCall's Patterns do not know that those companies are owned and managed by blacks.

Black Culture and Entrepreneurship

It has occasionally been suggested that black Americans do not have a "culture" that encourages entrepreneurship. But it is best to be wary of such sweeping explanations, since they imply that the roots run very deep. There may be some validity to the view that youngsters who grow up in areas with few locally owned enterprises lack models for business careers. But even this need not be an obstacle, since the decision to start up on your own usually comes later in life. As it happens, in the generation following emancipation, many blacks set up businesses in Southern cities, just as others prospered in farming. Haitian and West Indian immigrants have brought entrepreneurial ambitions with them; and it will be interesting to see what becomes of the West African sidewalk vendors who have become a New York fixture.

Considering the advantages and opportunities open to white Americans, it is noteworthy that less than 8 percent of them operate enterprises of their own. Other ethnic groups are well ahead of whites in embarking on entrepreneurship. For this reason, little will be gained by asking whether blacks have a "culture" that inhibits them from establishing their own businesses. Even if that answer is in the affirmative, it also applies to white Americans, 92.6 percent of whom spend their working hours on someone else's payroll.

Representation of Blacks in Professions

Not so many years ago, entire spheres of employment were almost completely closed to blacks. As recently as 1980, the census could find only 254 black optometrists, 185 black actuaries, and 122 black auctioneers. In addition, blacks accounted for only 138 nuclear engineers, 89 theology professors, and 70 sheet metal apprentices. At present, it can be said that absolute barriers have been broken, and every occupation has some blacks among its practitioners. In many areas, however, the numbers remain exceedingly small. Table 1 gives racial break-downs for various areas of employment. Even now, blacks remain underrepresented in the professions of engineering, law, and medicine, as well as architecture and journalism. Until lately, black students felt little incentive to train for these fields, since there were few if any prospects of obtaining a job. (Paul Robeson turned to acting because no firm would hire him after he graduated from Columbia Law School.) While virtually all professions are saying they would like to have more blacks on their payrolls, it still remains to be seen whether they simply want a few faces for showcase purposes, or if they mean jobs with real responsibilities.

Table 1: Black Occupational Representation, 1980

(Blacks = 10.1% of Total Workforce)

Greatest Overrepresentation

Nursing Aides & Orderlies	30.7%
Taxicab Drivers	25.5%
Postal Clerks	25.1%
Hotel Maids & Housemen	24.8%
Bus Drivers	23.4%
Vehicle Washers	23.0%
Correctional Officers	22.8%
Janitors & Cleaners	21.8%
Social Workers	21.8%
Security Guards	21.2%
Telephone Operators	19.7%
Data Entry Keyers	19.5%
Practical Nurses	17.6%

Greatest Underrepresentation

Waiters & Waitresses	4.7%
Editors & Reporters	3.8%
Bartenders	3.6%
Engineers	3.6%
Lawyers	3.2%
Physicians	3.0%
Realtors	3.0%
Photographers	2.9%
Speech Therapists	2.8%
Biologists	2.7%
Designers	2.6%
Dental Hygienists	2.5%
Architects	0.9%

Andrew Hacker, *Two Nations: Black and White, Separate, Hostile, Unequal*, 1992.

But moving beyond the professions, how are we to account for the low percentages of blacks when it comes to waiting on tables and tending bar? These are hardly elite occupations requiring sophisticated training. The suspicion arises that proprietors of restaurants and lounges may feel that their white clienteles do not want their food and drinks handled by black employees. Or it could stem from the belief that if a place has "too many" blacks on its staff, it will drop to a lower status. (Obviously, there are exceptions: for example, New Orleans dining rooms that affect the Old Retainer Tradition.) Perhaps most revealing of all is the small number of black dental hygienists. While white patients seem willing to be cared for by black nurses, they apparently draw the line at having black fingers in their mouths.

Occupations where black workers have the strongest showing are not necessarily menial. Still, they do more than their share of janitorial chores and cleaning up after others, which have been traditional "black" positions. As Table 1 shows, the positions where blacks have greatest representation tend to be jobs that whites are reluctant to take (hotel maids and nursing aides) as well as some at lower civil service levels (correctional officers and postal clerks). Blacks now perform repetitive office chores (data keyers and telephone operators) and fill in at high-turnover occupations (security guards and taxicab drivers). In some cases, the fields offering more openings (bus drivers and social workers) are ones serving clienteles that have become disproportionately black. . . .

Black Women Are Preferred to Black Men

In recent years, black women have come to comprise a majority of the black workforce. . . . Thus black women account for 63.8 percent of all black professionals, whereas white women represent 50.6 percent of the whites holding professional positions. In the technical and managerial groups, the black women are even further ahead, while among military officers the black figure is double that for whites.

One reason is necessity. More black women must manage on their own, since they are less likely to have a housemate who brings in a second income. But even when they are married or live with someone else, they must still make a serious work commitment, since it often takes two black incomes to match what one white breadwinner can bring in. This is especially true for the middle class, where one white executive can make $100,000, but a pair of black schoolteachers hardly reach that level.

But this describes only one element in the equation. Of at least equal importance are attitudes and decisions among white employers. If and when organizations feel compelled to hire more black workers, they generally prefer to take on black women rather than black men. Black women, like all women, are perceived as being less assertive and more accommodating. Thus there is the hope that black women will show less resentment or hostility, and will be less apt to present themselves as "black" in demeanor and appearance. A further concern of white employers, albeit not one openly stated, is that having black men and white women work together might lead to familiar relationships that could either be misunderstood or have some grounding in fact.

In addition, black and white women tend to mingle more easily in workplace settings. This is partly because women tend to feel less tense about race. But there is also evidence that women can ignore racial lines in acknowledging common experiences, at least to a far greater extent than men are willing to do. At restaurants near their place of work, groups of black and white women can be seen enjoying lunch together. Far less frequently—if at all—does one encounter similar parties of men. Circumstances like these are not lost on employers, who may conclude that if they must have racially mixed workforces, things will go better if they consist largely of women.

Black Employment Opportunities Have Declined

As has been noted, public and nonprofit organizations have become havens for much of the black workforce. Over a third of all black lawyers work for government departments, as do almost 30 percent of black scientists. Blacks account for over 20 percent of the nation's armed services, twice their proportion in the civilian economy. They hold almost a fifth of all positions in the Postal Service, and have similar ratios in many urban agencies. Unfortunately, this makes middle-class blacks vulnerable to public budget cuts. Between 1979 and 1989, the average income of black college men declined by 11 percent, resulting largely from a drop in government hiring, which meant fewer opportunities for younger graduates. During this decade, however, incomes for white college men increased by 11 percent, since the private economy was expanding.

On the whole, then, the business world has not done much to expand black employment. White executives worry about how large a black presence they want to absorb within their firms. Obviously, these thoughts are not committed to paper, nor are they specified in percentage terms. At the same time, racial considerations often figure indirectly, as when companies decide to move operations to new locations or open facilities in new areas. When questioned, they usually allude to the lack of skilled people in urban areas rather than confess to racial prejudice.

Companies realize that too few black faces could lead to charges of bias, causing unpleasant publicity. At the same time, they worry lest they are seen as having "too many" black employees, or as promoting blacks too liberally. In this vein, they may fear that "too black" an appearance will jeopardize their image for competence and credibility. Firms also become uneasy if some of their products—a brand of cigarettes, for example, or a style of running shoes—seem to be attracting too large a black clientele. Perhaps projecting some of their own anxieties, they sense that white customers will shy away from items they feel have become associated with black preferences and tastes.

All the while, businesses can be expected to protest that they are "color blind" both in policy and practice, seeking only the best talent they can find, regardless of race or creed or gender. If there appear to be few black people on their payrolls, they will insist it is because hardly any have applied or not enough live near their facilities or have the necessary qualifications. What is not openly addressed is how far possessing a skin of a certain color might figure as one of those "qualifications."

Prejudice in the Workplace

Business has always been inherently conservative, waiting until other sectors take steps toward social change. In part, this attitude stems from anxieties about how their customers will react. Will they buy, or buy as much, from salespeople who are black? And can blacks join in the socializing so often needed to clinch a deal? Will users of your product feel confident that a black technician can work competently with complex equipment? Hence the tendency to play it safe, which usually means hiring as white a workforce as possible. (To combine competence and color, Asians serve as acceptable surrogates.) There is also the worry that blacks who are promoted to supervisory positions may not obtain the best performance from white subordinates, who may be resentful if not actually resistant. Chief executives may smile wanly and agree that the problem is one of prejudice. Not their own, of course, but those of customers and others who still cling to stereotypes.

In more secluded settings, white employees and supervisors may be heard to say that they find blacks hard to work with. ("We had one, but he didn't work out.") They will cite cases of coldness or hostility or chips-on-the-shoulder, compounded by a readiness to imagine racial insults. Or they will allude to an unwillingness of black men to relax in workplace relationships. Rather than inquire why this reluctance persists, or how it might be remedied, the tendency is to evade the issue by hiring and promoting as few blacks as possible. At that point, personal biases become transmuted into institutional racism.

Small wonder, then, that black Americans have always agreed among themselves that if they want to get ahead, they have to work harder and do better than white people. Given all the misgivings of white executives and supervisors, it would seem self-evident that blacks must put in a lot more effort simply to satisfy the standards their employers set. It is not as if they can simply walk in and start doing a job. All eyes are on them, as if a Great Experiment is under way.

It is not easy buckling down to a job when you have to expend so much of your energy contriving a "white" personality—or at least the appearance of one—so as to put your white workmates at ease. Nor is it easy to establish one's authority, since simply having a black face raises doubts in many white minds. Added to which is having to read nuances and allusions that whites recognize as a matter of course. All this demands much more from black workers than is ever asked of whites. If white people have any doubts on this score, they might imagine spending their entire careers with a foreign company, where they find that no matter how much they study its ways, it still refuses to grant that they can ever master the assignments at hand.

"Those who look carefully for evidence of racism—and not just for evidence of black failure—are likely to come up short."

Racial Discrimination Does Not Limit Opportunities for Blacks

Jared Taylor

Some scholars argue that statistical disparities in the economic status of blacks and whites prove that discrimination persists. In the following viewpoint, Jared Taylor cites statistics showing that blacks (women especially) have made significant gains in income in comparison to whites. If incomes of blacks are accurately compared with those of whites, he contends, differences all but disappear. Taylor argues that the remaining disparities between the incomes of blacks and whites cannot prove the existence of racism and that bias in the workplace is no longer a significant problem. Taylor is a journalist and author of *Paved with Good Intentions: The Failure of Race Relations in Contemporary America*, from which this viewpoint is excerpted.

As you read, consider the following questions:

1. Looking at Taylor's statistics, what percentage of manager jobs are held by black women compared with black men?
2. According to the business owners cited by Taylor, why aren't more blacks in management positions?
3. Why did the household income of black families fall between 1970 and 1980, according to the author?

Many people think that to show that white racism causes black failure, all they must do is show that blacks fail. The *cause* falls into place by itself. This is a common but incorrect style of reasoning. People often collect symptoms and effects, and then attribute them to a cause that suits their own argument.

In fact, it is a style of thinking that has often characterized American political thinking in the past. At various periods, and on the flimsiest evidence, Jews, Catholics, blacks, immigrants, or Communists have been blamed for everything that was wrong with the country. The historian Richard Hofstadter calls this the paranoid style in American politics. Today America is in the grip of yet another massive attack of paranoia, except that it is the majority white population that is automatically blamed for whatever goes wrong. Charges of racism can be made with the same reckless impunity as were charges of communism at the height of the McCarthy era. To ask for the facts that support the charge is only to prompt more accusations.

To make a convincing case for racism, it must be shown that America treats otherwise similar blacks differently from whites. Anecdotal evidence is insufficient. It is only in the larger sweep of society that we will find forces powerful enough to oppress an entire people. Those who look carefully for evidence of racism—and not just for evidence of black failure—are likely to come up short.

Blacks Are Achieving Income Parity

America often judges people by how much money they make. Although we assume that blacks want money as much as whites do, they make less. To show that this is the fault of racist employers, one must show that even if blacks are just as well qualified and hardworking as whites, they are still forced into bad jobs with low pay. Research by Richard Freeman, an economist at Harvard, shows that this rarely happens. Comparisons of blacks and whites who grew up in the same circumstances and went on to get similar educations show no differences in their average incomes. This was not always so. In the past, smart, qualified blacks could not get equivalent jobs. But by 1969 blacks made just as much money as whites with the same backgrounds. The trend toward parity was firmly established well before affirmative action and other special programs for minorities.

Mr. Freeman sees the big change as having taken place in the 1960s, during what he calls a "dramatic collapse" in patterns of discrimination. He summarizes the situation a decade later:

> By the 1970s black women earned as much as or more than whites [women] with similar educational attainment; black female college graduates obtained a moderate premium over their white peers; young black male college graduates attained rough

income parity with young white graduates, and all black male graduates had more rapid increases in income than whites. . . ."

Progress for Black Women

Women have made especially dramatic progress. In 1946 the median wage for black women was *only 36 percent* of that for white women. It has since climbed steadily, and by 1974 it was 98 percent. Black women with a college education have actually outstripped whites. By 1950, black women college graduates already made 91 percent of the wages paid to white female college graduates. By 1960, they earned 2 percent *more* than whites, and by 1970, the difference had grown wider still. By 1979, all black women, whatever their qualifications, earned 8 percent more than white women of equal qualifications. The reason for this advantage is that they have been steadier workers than whites. When black and white women hold similar jobs, the black woman, on average, has been on the job 38 percent longer. It is normal that she be paid more, because she has more experience.

This essential parity between the wages of equally qualified black and white women is well known in specialist circles but virtually unknown to the public at large. The economist Walter Williams, who is himself black, calls this comparative data on working women "one of the best-kept secrets of all times and virtually totally ignored in the literature on racial differences." Why do the organs of public information fail to report this powerful argument against the existence of pervasive workplace racism?

Today, 19 percent of black women in the workforce hold professional and managerial jobs, whereas only 13 percent of black men do. For whites, men are more likely to hold such higher-level jobs. Of all technical jobs held by whites, women hold 48 percent. By contrast, women hold 63 percent of the technical jobs held by blacks. If desirable jobs that have traditionally been filled by men are open to black women, what is keeping black men out of them? It is difficult to explain how white racism shackles black men but not black women—women who presumably labor under the double disadvantage of both sex and race.

Progress for Black Immigrants and Families

Another black author, Thomas Sowell, points out that some believers in racism do not merely ignore these data. "There is a positive hostility to analyses of black success," he writes, if they suggest that racism may not be the cause of black failure.

This hostility has not stopped Mr. Sowell. He has shown that in 1969, while American-born blacks were making only 62 percent of the average income for all Americans, blacks from the West Indies made 94 percent. Second-generation immigrants from the West Indies made 15 percent *more* than the average

American. Although they are only 10 percent of the city's black population, foreign-born blacks—mostly from the West Indies—own half of the black-owned businesses in New York City. Their unemployment rate is lower than the national average, and many times lower than that of American-born blacks. West Indian blacks look no different from American blacks; white racists are not likely suddenly to set aside their prejudices when they meet one.

Explaining Income Differences Between Blacks and Whites

"Once adjustments are made for factors like age, education and experience, 70 percent to 85 percent of the observed differences in income and employment between the various groups in America disappears," says economist Howard R. Bloch of George Mason University. "That's been shown by studies dating back to the mid-1960s. And you can't even be sure that the residual gap is due to discrimination. It could be due to factors we haven't controlled for."

Indeed, Harvard economist Richard Freeman found blacks and whites with the same backgrounds and education had achieved wage parity by 1969, well before quotas had America in their grip.

Peter Brimelow and Leslie Spencer, *Forbes*, February 15, 1993.

For nearly twenty years, young blacks who manage to stay married have had family incomes almost identical to those of young white couples. Until recently, the only exception had been the South, but even there the difference has vanished. Now, in families where both parents are college-educated and both work, black families make *more* money than white families. This is true in all parts of the United States and for families of all ages. In some professions, where affirmative action programs have created an artificial demand for qualified minorities, blacks may earn more than whites simply because they are black. This is the case for college professors, who can command stiff salary premiums because they help fulfill hiring goals.

Progress for Middle-Class Black Professionals

Many blacks have not let talk of racism daunt them but have instead figured out that what counts in America are brains and hard work. The number of black families that are "affluent" (earning more than $50,000 in inflation-adjusted dollars) went from one in seventeen in 1967 to one in seven in 1989. Such families increased, in actual numbers, from 323,000 to 1,509,000, a

467 percent rise. From 1982 to 1987, the number of companies owned by blacks grew by a third, and their receipts more than doubled. In 1991, the hundred biggest black-owned businesses in the country had revenues of $7.9 billion, a 10.4 percent increase over the previous year.

Between 1972 and 1991, the number of black accountants shot up by 479 percent, the number of lawyers by 280 percent, and the number of professional computer programmers by 343 percent. Preachers are virtually the only white-collar group in which the number of blacks declined during that period. From 1950 to 1990, the black population of America doubled but the number of blacks in white-collar jobs increased more than *ninefold*. Blacks, as a proportion of managers in companies with more than a hundred employees, have gone from 0.9 percent in 1966 to 3.7 percent in 1978 and 5.2 percent in 1990. If racism is such a force in our society, why did it not stop this progress?

It is true that blacks are still underrepresented in management. H.F. Henderson Industries, a small defense contractor in West Caldwell, New Jersey, is not unusual in that the proportion of whites in professional and technical jobs (80 percent) is much higher than in the company as a whole (48 percent). The only unusual aspect is that Henry F. Henderson, the company's founder, is black. He would like to have more blacks in management, but since he hires by qualifications rather than by race, most of his skilled employees are white.

J. Bruce Llewellyn, chairman of the Philadelphia Coca-Cola Bottling Company, is also black, and faces the same situation. "You have to look longer and harder to find these people [qualified minorities]," he says: "It's just obvious that the pool of talented white people is bigger than the one of talented black people."

Looking for Racism

To draw useful conclusions about racial discrimination, it is necessary to compare like with like. When this is not done, the results can suggest racism where there may be none. For example, magazines and newspapers often report that black college graduates make less money than white college graduates. The difference is said to be due to employer discrimination. The trouble with this comparison is that it includes *all* black and white college graduates. Whites are more likely to attend top-ranked colleges than blacks and are more likely to major in well-paid fields such as business and engineering. A physics graduate from Yale is likely to earn more money than a sociology graduate from Foothills Community College, whatever their races. Careful comparisons of blacks and whites who have graduated from equivalent colleges with equivalent degrees show that the blacks earn *more* than the whites.

"Racism" frequently dwindles away as analysis goes deeper. During the ten years from 1970 to 1980, the median household income for whites rose by 0.8 percent, while the median household income for blacks *fell* by 11 percent. What accounted for this? Did racism get worse? The problem in this analysis is that the income unit is households and not people. During the 1970s, many families, both black and white, broke up. Also, every time a young woman had a child and went on welfare, a new household was established.

The fact is that while individual blacks' incomes were actually rising more quickly than those of individual whites, blacks were splintering into new households at a much more rapid rate. According to one study, if black family composition had held steady during the decade, median black household income would have *risen* 5 percent. If white household composition had held steady, the white median household income would have risen by 3 percent (instead of its actual rise of 0.8 percent).

People of both races were actually making more money, but they were spreading it out over more households. In fact, the actual incomes of black husband-and-wife families rose four times as quickly as those of white families. In families in which both the husband and wife worked, the family income of blacks increased *five times* as quickly as that of whites. Black family income fell during the 1970s, not because of "racist" employers but because of disintegrating families.

Conclusions like these are the results of taking the time to compare like with like. Whenever this is done, differences that can be attributed to racism are elusive. The trouble, of course, is that the black population is not identical to the white population. The black population is less well educated, less experienced, and less qualified. Believers in racism insist that these differences are due to past racism. To some extent they undoubtedly are. But our thinking must change as America changes. Whatever effects the past may have had on the present, employers who pay qualified blacks as much as or more than they pay qualified whites are not now practicing racism.

"The values and concerns of the black middle class are virtually indistinguishable from those of other members of the middle class."

Middle-Class Blacks Have Overcome Discrimination

Peter N. Kirsanow

Many studies and polls show that the number of black families earning middle-class incomes has grown since the 1980s. In the following viewpoint, Peter N. Kirsanow argues that this growing black middle class is proof that discrimination no longer impedes progress for blacks. Members of the black middle class, he contends, reject the "victim mentality" and the demands for preferential treatment promoted by groups such as the Congressional Black Caucus and Urban League. Kirsanow is a labor lawyer and is on the advisory committee of Project 21 of the National Center for Public Policy Research in Washington, D.C.

As you read, consider the following questions:

1. According to the Heritage Foundation study cited by Kirsanow, what is the size of the black middle class?
2. Why do black leaders have an interest in expanding the welfare state, according to the author?
3. What conservative beliefs does the author cite as being held by middle-class blacks?

There are two black communities in this country. One, the black underclass, is the subject of endless commentary and analysis. Discussions concerning black America often start with the presumption that nearly all blacks fall within this group.

Lawmakers usually focus on the underclass when purporting to address the concerns of blacks in general. Predominantly black organizations such as the National Association for the Advancement of Colored People (NAACP), the Urban League, and the Congressional Black Caucus tend to advocate the underclass perspective on issues of the day. And members of the underclass are the representatives of the black community typically featured in the media.

The Silent Majority

The other group, the black middle class, is virtually invisible. Its representatives rarely surface in the popular culture; it is substantially ignored by the media. The opinions of middle-class blacks are reported as a mere adjunct to those of the underclass.

But the black middle and working classes are on the verge of becoming a new silent majority. A Heritage Foundation study found that, during the 1980s, the black middle class grew by more than 30 percent, adding more than 1 million new families to its ranks. By 1993, more than 5 million of the approximately 30 million American blacks were identified as middle class.

Moreover, the number of black-owned businesses grew by 40 percent from 1980 to 1995, to half a million. During the same period, the number of black corporate managers and officers rose by 50 percent, and the ranks of black professionals increased by more than 75 percent. The number of black households with incomes over $50,000 skyrocketed.

These figures represent encouraging progress toward Martin Luther King, Jr.'s goal of racial equality. King held that true equality means more than just the right to ride in the front of the bus, attend a decent school, and vote without impediment. According to King, it also means full participation in the economic mainstream. Civil rights without economic empowerment, he believed, is only half a loaf.

Black political progress in the years since King gave his "I Have a Dream" speech in 1963 has been astonishing, indeed. A black man [Colin Powell] has served as chairman of the Joint Chiefs of Staff and another [Jesse Jackson] has run for president. Many major cities have black mayors. Scores of blacks serve in the state and federal legislatures. The same is true of the judiciary.

Yet, despite the manifest success of a large percentage of blacks, the problems of the underclass seem to have worsened, a phenomenon that has affected relationships among blacks as well as between blacks and whites.

Thirty years after passage of the Civil Rights Act of 1964, illegitimacy, unemployment, drugs, gangs, and crime run rampant among the black underclass. It is seemingly immune to the salutary effects of Equal Employment Opportunity legislation. Billions of dollars furiously pumped into inner-city job-training programs have produced little measurable effect upon underclass employment levels.

Give Up the Victim's Mentality

The important thing is that black people have to give up the victim's mentality. Now, one thing that the media almost never talks about is the fact that more than 40 percent of blacks in this country are middle class and above. It would be a wonderful thing to talk about this group more, so that people would have a lot more role models. I can name dozens of blacks . . . who live in $500,000 to $1 million houses and who worked their way up to top jobs. It's not rare.

Ben Carson, quoted by Brian Dumaine, *Fortune*, November 2, 1992.

Since the early 1960s, the crime rate in the black community rose four times faster than in the white community. Violent crimes alone rose nearly seven times faster. The black illegitimacy rate rose from 23 percent in 1963 to 68 percent today; births to unmarried black teenagers quadrupled over the last thirty years. Fewer than half of black households have both a husband and wife present. Michael Tanner of the Cato Institute has noted that a stunning 80 percent of all black children born in 1980 will spend at least one year on welfare.

Several studies have concluded that the above-described decay is at least partly the product of the bizarre incentives offered by the welfare state. Just as a large segment of the black community took advantage of the expansion of opportunities, another became mired in dependency, with all of the pathologies flowing therefrom.

The effect of the perverse incentives of the welfare state upon the underclass are magnified by the victim mentality promoted by some black "leaders." Since these leaders receive much of their power by virtue of being the conduits through which welfare benefits flow to the underclass, they have a proprietary interest in perpetuating and expanding the welfare state. By promoting the victim mentality, they have succeeded in portraying welfare, affirmative action, and special preferences as a birthright. These benefits are viewed virtually as reparations for racial discrimination and slavery.

The mentality is readily discernible in large segments of the inner-city population. It excuses one from responsibility and holds that failure is the result of discrimination by white hegemonists. Failure is, therefore, inevitable and expected. Thus, over the years, a malaise has developed in the underclass: There is little embarrassment or shame associated with being on welfare or receiving special preferences—they are merely just recompense for the wrongs perpetrated on the race by society.

On the other hand, the members of the middle class have largely avoided the victimhood trap. They remain vigilant to the harmful effects of racism, but they also recognize that it is but one of the obstacles on the path to success—and usually not an insurmountable one.

The widening gulf between the fortunes of the black middle class and the underclass may be one of the reasons many in the latter group view the middle class with resentment. Derrick Bell, in his book *Faces at the Bottom of the Well*, quotes one cab driver's perspective on the middle class:

> I mean no offense, but the fact is that you movin-on-up black folks hurt us everyday blacks simply by being successful. The white folks see you doing your thing [and] . . . [t]hey conclude right off that discrimination is over, and that if the rest of us got up off our dead asses, dropped the welfare tit, stopped having illegitimate babies, and found jobs, we would all be just like you.

The black middle and working classes have become increasingly more conservative than their counterparts in the underclass and certain elite black "leaders"; consequently, they are somewhat alienated from their ostensible spokesmen. . . .

The Black Middle Class vs. the Elite

Many blacks maintain that the NAACP, Congressional Black Caucus, and so forth speak only for themselves or for the underclass but not for working blacks. A recent poll showed that more than half of blacks do not support the agenda of the NAACP, which is perceived as being stuck in the ideology and rhetoric of the 1960s.

The philosophical differences between the black middle class and working poor on one hand and the underclass and the black elite on the other mirror the differences between Booker T. Washington and W.E.B. Du Bois. [Washington urged blacks to seek economic advancement rather than social and political equality; Du Bois urged demands and a struggle for equality over material gains.] For their part, some in the underclass see members of the black middle class as "acting white." Educational advancement is denigrated. Dependability and punctuality on the job are "Uncle Tom" traits—evidence of being a bit too willing to please the master.

George Gilder once noted that one of the chief obstacles to addressing problems of the poor is that they are viewed by the media and policymakers as "some alien tribe, exotic in culture and motivation, who can be understood only through the channels of credentialed expertise."

The same observation may be made of the black community. In this case, the credentialed experts are social workers, certain black "leaders," and politicians who offer programs and solutions based on their unerring analysis of problems plaguing the black underclass.

These leaders portray blacks as monolithic, with the interests and opinions of the underclass as the standard. Therefore, even though members of the black middle class are not all that different from the white middle class, they are lumped together with the underclass. Consequently, all blacks are viewed as sharing the values, interests, and opinions of the underclass, as articulated by the black elite.

The Black Middle Class and White Guilt

The emergence of the black middle class has elicited mixed reactions from whites. For some whites as well as blacks, the existence of a sizable black middle class is evidence that anyone can make it in America today.

Whereas, in the past, black failures could more readily be attributed to racially discriminatory laws and practices, the growing black middle class may be viewed as proof that most of the civil rights battles have been won. The claim that racism is the chief cause of the ills of the black underclass becomes less credible in the face of multiple examples of black success: "If Joe can make it, why can't you?"

In the past, some whites felt guilty for perceived or real discrimination. But Ellis Cose, author of *Rage of a Privileged Class*, has noted that many whites today are feeling less guilty about the condition of blacks. Indeed, for the first time, whites under thirty are less sympathetic than those over thirty to the condition of blacks.

Among other things, this new attitude may pave the way for significant welfare reform. Past attempts at welfare reform, such as the Family Support Act of 1988, were met with charges of racism. The argument went as follows:

- There are a disproportionate number of blacks on the welfare rolls because their advancement out of poverty and into the middle class has been thwarted by racism and the residual effects of Jim Crow.
- Major welfare reform that would throw great numbers of blacks off the dole would penalize them simply for being

victims of racism.
- Punishing the victims of racism is racist.
- Therefore, radical welfare reform and sponsors thereof are racist.

The threat that accusations of racism might be levied against proponents of serious welfare reform may have had a chilling effect on meaningful reform proposals. But the growth of the black middle class has muted the charges of racism by challenging the presumption that racial discrimination is the principal reason for black welfare dependency.

Consequently, politicians may fashion welfare reform unburdened by racial apologia. Rather, they may freely respond to growing public discontent over an increasingly expensive system perceived as dispensing benefits indiscriminately and interminably to irresponsible individuals, regardless of race.

The Growth of White Resentment

While the growth of the black middle class may have contributed to the birth of the "guiltless white," affirmative-action programs have given rise to the "resentful white." A 1992 poll by Peter Hart and Associates shows that 48 percent of whites maintain that blacks receive too many advantages and preferences in education and employment.

The poll also found that 65 percent of young whites oppose special consideration for minority applicants. Ten to 15 percent of white males report that they have lost either a promotion, job, or other employment opportunity as a result of affirmative-action programs.

In addition, challenges to affirmative-action programs are becoming more frequent. White contractors successfully challenged minority set-aside programs in *City of Richmond v. Croson*. [Set-aside programs require federal, state, and local governments to reserve a percentage of their contracts for minority-owned businesses.] Racial promotion quotas for police and fire fighters are regularly assailed for violating the rights of more-senior whites.

The Supreme Court has revisited the issue of racial preferences in school admissions in the case of *Hopwood v. Texas*. Many whites maintain that able, hard-working whites are unfairly penalized because of their race. For example, the plaintiff in *Hopwood* alleged that she was denied admission to the University of Texas Law School in favor of black applicants, despite the fact that not one black applicant had a higher admissions index score. (In fact, only eighty-eight blacks in the entire country who took the LSAT in 1992 scored higher than the median score for whites admitted to the University of Texas Law School.)

Most black civil rights organizations continue to lobby vigorously to preserve minority set-asides and preferences. This, coupled with regular victimhood broadcasts by black "leaders," may understandably cause whites to believe that middle-class blacks are universally in favor of preferences and are preoccupied with what Senator Daniel Patrick Moynihan calls a "legacy of grievance . . . inappropriate to their condition."

The End of Race

But the fact is that most middle-class blacks also reject racial preferences. Indeed, 82 percent state that individuals should rely on their own skills and industry for success rather than depend on preferences.

The values and concerns of the black middle class are virtually indistinguishable from those of other members of the middle class. A 1993 poll conducted by Fabrizio, McClaughlin, and Associates revealed that most blacks, contrary to conventional wisdom, hold beliefs almost identical to those of whites. Furthermore, these beliefs are relatively conservative.

For example, 9 out of 10 black respondents believe that able-bodied welfare recipients should be required to work in return for welfare benefits. Three-quarters believe that English should be made the official language of the United States. Eighty-nine percent approve of voluntary prayer in the schools.

The figures also show that blacks tend to be more culturally conservative than portrayed by the popular culture. More than two-thirds of blacks maintain that the country's economic and social problems may be traced to the deterioration of the family unit. Sixty percent oppose taxpayer-funded abortions. Two-thirds disapprove of teaching children that homosexuality is a normal and acceptable life-style. More than 80 percent pray daily, and more than 90 percent pray at least once a week.

Some analysts argue that, but for the government's racial engineering noted earlier—which has done much to aggravate black-white relations—racial differences, at least between middle-class blacks and whites, would be nearly imperceptible.

This is not to say that race would be rendered irrelevant. But the real chasm is between those middle- and working-class blacks and whites who share certain values, on the one hand, and, on the other, the underclass of both races and their advocates.

The true division in society, the analysts say, would be cultural, not racial. As the black middle class grows, these observers expect its culture to prevail—the culture that prizes work, faith, intact families, and true equality; the culture that does not disparage, but rather eagerly embraces, the habits and values integral to success; the culture that is the fulfillment of Dr. King's dream.

"Despite its very evident prosperity, much of America's black middle class is in excruciating pain."

Middle-Class Blacks Have Not Overcome Discrimination

Ellis Cose

Ellis Cose has compiled many accounts by blacks of racial discrimination experienced on the job. In the following viewpoint, he argues that despite their success, middle-class blacks are still subject to discrimination in the workplace and to racially based limits on their upward mobility. He cites studies and anecdotes from which he concludes that middle-class blacks are more angry and alienated from society than are lower-class blacks. Cose is a contributing editor for *Newsweek* magazine and author of *A Nation of Strangers* and *The Rage of a Privileged Class*, from which this viewpoint is excerpted.

As you read, consider the following questions:

1. According to Joe Feagin, cited by the author, what is the white perspective on discrimination?
2. Why is it virtually impossible for blacks to believe in equality, according to Cose?
3. What statements were used by UCLA researchers, cited by Cose, to measure "Ethnic Alienation from American Society"? Which statement would you choose to describe your attitude?

Despite its very evident prosperity, much of America's black middle class is in excruciating pain. And that distress—although most of the country does not see it—illuminates a serious American problem: the problem of the broken covenant, of the pact ensuring that if you work hard, get a good education, and play by the rules, you will be allowed to advance and achieve to the limits of your ability.

Again and again, as I spoke with people who had every accouterment of success, I heard the same plaintive declaration—always followed by various versions of an unchanging and urgently put question. "I have done everything I was supposed to do. I have stayed out of trouble with the law, gone to the right schools, and worked myself nearly to death. *What more do they want?* Why in God's name won't they accept me as a full human being? Why am I pigeonholed in a 'black job'? Why am I constantly treated as if I were a drug addict, a thief, or a thug? Why am I still not allowed to aspire to the same things every white person in America takes as a birthright? Why, when I most want to be seen, am I suddenly rendered invisible?"

Struggling with Basic Assumptions About Race

What exactly do such questions mean? Could their underlying premise conceivably be correct? Why, a full generation after the most celebrated civil rights battles were fought and won, are Americans still struggling with basic issues of racial fairness? In exploring why so many of those who have invested most deeply in the American dream are consumed with anger and pain, I hope to show how certain widespread and amiable assumptions held by whites—specifically about the black middle class but also about race relations in general—are utterly at odds with the reality many Americans confront daily.

That the black middle class (and I use the term very loosely, essentially meaning those whose standard of living is comfortable, even lavish, by most reasonable measures) should have any gripes at all undoubtedly strikes many as strange. The civil rights revolution, after all, not only killed Jim Crow but brought blacks more money, more latitude, and more access to power than enjoyed by any previous generation of African Americans. Some blacks in this new era of opportunity have amassed fortunes that would put Croesus to shame. If ever there was a time to celebrate the achievements of the color-blind society, now should be that time.

Joe Feagin, a sociologist at the University of Florida, observed in a paper prepared for the U.S. Commission on Civil Rights that most whites believe that blacks no longer face significant racial barriers. "From this white perspective employment discrimination targeting black Americans is no longer a serious problem in the United States. The black middle class, in particular, has largely overcome job discrimination and is thriving economically. Only the black underclass is in serious trouble, and that has little to do with discrimination." Indeed, many people believe the tables have turned so far that whites are more likely to be victimized by discrimination than blacks.

The End of Discrimination?

At an early stage of my work, I outlined my thesis to Daniel Patrick Moynihan, senior senator from New York and celebrated scholar of ethnicity. Moynihan made the counterargument succinctly. The black middle class, he noted, was "moving along very well." And he had every expectation that it would continue to do so. Indeed, with so many black mayors and black police chiefs in place, blacks represented, to many new arrivals, America's power establishment. "The big problem," added Moynihan, "is, 'What are we going to do about the underclass?' And a particular problem is that [the] black group you're talking about [the middle class] doesn't want to have anything to do with them."

Certainly one can show statistically that black "married-couple families" with wives in the paid labor force (as categorized by the U.S. Census Bureau) do not make *that* much less than comparably stratified whites. Such households, which earn slightly over 80 percent as much as similar white households, are arguably within striking distance of economic parity. One can empathize with Moynihan's pique when he reflects on the public reaction to his famous 1970 memorandum to Richard Nixon pointing out that young two-parent black families in the Northeast were progressing nicely and suggesting that perhaps race could benefit from a period of "benign neglect." "I went through hell's own time," recalls Moynihan.

But whatever such aggregate statistics may show, they do not demonstrate—and cannot—that hiring has become color-blind. As Andrew Hacker observes in *Two Nations*, "While there is now a much larger black middle class, more typically, the husband is likely to be a bus driver earning $32,000, while his wife brings home $28,000 as a teacher or a nurse. A white middle-class family is three to four times more likely to contain a husband earning $75,000 in a managerial position." Feagin notes that he has found "*no* [emphasis his] research study with empirical data supporting the widespread white perspective that employment discrimination is no longer serious in the U.S. workplace."

In lieu of scientific research, we are offered speculation and conjecture, self-congratulatory theories from whites who have never been forced to confront the racial stereotypes routinely encountered by blacks, and who—judging themselves decent people, and judging most of their acquaintances decent as well—find it impossible to believe that serious discrimination still exists. Whatever comfort such conjecture may bring some whites, it has absolutely no relevance to the experiences of blacks in America.

Not "Racism," but Not Equality Either

I am not suggesting that most whites are "racist." The majority emphatically are not—at least not in any meaningful sense of the word. If a racist is defined as one who hates blacks (or members of any other racial group, for that matter), the number of true racists is very small, and a substantial portion of them are the pathetic sorts of people who call themselves Nazis and glorify the Ku Klux Klan. Even those fanatics tend to be motivated less by racism than by some pathology expressed in racial terms. The point here, however, is that people do not have to be racist—or have any malicious intent—in order to make decisions that unfairly harm members of another race. They simply have to do what comes naturally. . . .

This is not to say that white Americans are intent on persecuting black people, or that blacks are utterly helpless and fault-free victims of society. Nothing could be further from the truth. Nonetheless, America is filled with attitudes, assumptions, stereotypes, and behaviors that make it virtually impossible for blacks to believe that the nation is serious about its promise of equality—even (perhaps especially) for those who have been blessed with material success.

Donald McHenry, former U.S. permanent representative to the United Nations, told me that though he felt no sense of estrangement himself, he witnessed it often in other blacks who had done exceptionally well: "It's sort of the in talk, the in joke, within *the club*, an acknowledgment of and not an acceptance . . . of the effect of race on one's life, on where one lives, on the kinds of jobs that one has available. I think that's always been there. I think it's going to be there for some time." Dorothy Gilliam, a columnist for the *Washington Post*, expressed a similar thought in much stronger terms. "You feel the rage of people, [of] your group . . . just being the dogs of society."

Race Is the Bottom Line

Upon declaring her intention to leave a cushy job with a Fortune 500 company to go into the nonprofit sector, a young black woman, a Harvard graduate, was pulled aside by her vice president. Why, the executive wanted to know, was the company having such a difficult time retaining young minority professionals? The young woman's frustrations were numerous: she felt herself surrounded by mediocrity, by people trying to advance on the basis of personal influence and cronyism rather than merit; she was weary of racial insensitivity, of people who saw nothing about her except her color, or conversely of those who, in acknowledging her talents, in effect gave her credit for not really being black; she deemed it unlikely, given her perceptions of the corporate culture, that she would be allowed to make it to the top, and feared waking up in a rut several years hence to find that opportunities (and much of life) had passed her by; and she was tired of having to bite her tongue, tired of feeling that she could only speak out about the wrongs she perceived at the risk of being labeled a malcontent and damaging her career. Rather than try to explain, the woman finally blurted out that there was "no one who looks like me" in all of senior management—by which she meant there were no blacks, and certainly no black women. "What reason do I have to believe," she added, "that *I* can make it to the top?" When she related the incident to me several years later, she remained discouraged by what seemed a simple reality of her existence. "The bottom line is you're black. And that's still a negative in this society."

The Real Negro Questions

In his book *Parallel Time*, Brent Staples, an editor at *The New York Times*, describes an interview for a job with *The Washington Post* during which he was questioned intensely not just about his schooling and exemplary employment background, but about the professions, ages and whereabouts of his parents and siblings:

"These were what I'd come to call The Real Negro questions. He wanted to know if I was a Faux, Chevy Chase, Maryland, Negro or an authentic nigger who grew up poor in the ghetto besieged by crime and violence. White people preferred the latter, on the theory that blacks from the ghetto were the real thing. . . . My inquisitor was asking me to explain my existence. Why was I successful, law-abiding, and literate, when others of my kind filled the jails and the morgues and the homeless shelters? A question that asks a lifetime of questions has no easy answer. The only honest answer is the life itself."

Few African-Americans have not had such an encounter—a series of questions from an often well-meaning white person who is not just curious about you but trying to make you "fit" into some preconceived box of blackness.

Patricia J. Williams, *Civilization*, November/December 1994.

Ulric Haynes, dean of the Hofstra University School of Business and a former corporate executive who served as President

Jimmy Carter's ambassador to Algeria, is one of many blacks who have given up hope that racial parity will arrive this—or even next—millennium: "During our lifetimes, my children's lifetimes, my grandchildren's lifetimes, I expect that race will . . . matter. And perhaps race will always matter, given the historical circumstances under which we came to this country." But even as he recognizes that possibility, Haynes is far from sanguine about it. In fact, he is angry. "Not for myself. I'm over the hill. I've reached the zenith," he says. "I'm angry for the deception that this has perpetrated on my children and grandchildren." Though his children have traveled the world and received an elite education, they "in a very real sense are not the children of privilege. They are dysfunctional, because I didn't prepare them, in all the years we lived overseas, to deal with the climate of racism they are encountering right now."

Middle-Class Attitudes and the Los Angeles Riot

In 1992, a research team at the University of California, Los Angeles (UCLA) Center for the Study of Urban Poverty benefited from a fortuitous accident of timing. They were midway through the field work for a survey of racial attitudes in Los Angeles County when a jury exonerated four white policemen of the most serious charges in the videotaped beating of a black man named Rodney King. The riot that erupted in South Central Los Angeles in the aftermath of the verdict delayed the researchers' work, so they ended up, in effect, with two surveys: one of attitudes before the riot, and one of attitudes after.

The questionnaire they used included four statements thought to be helpful in measuring "Ethnic Alienation from American Society": "American society owes people of my ethnic group a better chance in life than we currently have." "American society has provided people of my ethnic group a fair opportunity to get ahead in life." "I am grateful for the special opportunities people of my ethnic group have found in America." "American society just hasn't dealt fairly with people from my background."

Responses to the statements were merged into a single score, cataloged by income level and ethnic group. The responses of blacks with a household income of $50,000 and more were especially intriguing. Even before the riot, that group, on average, appeared to be more alienated than poorer blacks. But what stunned the researchers was that after the riot, alienation among the most affluent group of African Americans skyrocketed, rising nearly a full "standard deviation"—much more than it did for those who were less well off. In reporting the findings, the UCLA team wrote: "This strong and uniform rise in black alienation from American social institutions is the single clearest and most consistent change observed from any of the items we have examined. Careful inspection of responses shows that this rising discontent occurred among black men and women, as well as across educational and income levels. With respect to the effects of income level, however, there is an unexpected twist. . . . Analysis of this 'Ethnic Alienation from American Society' measure showed, critically, that the rise in discontent was strongest among black households whose incomes were $50,000 or higher." The researchers concluded: "Our own data strongly confirm that middle-class blacks continue to feel the burdens of discrimination."

In a press release, Lawrence Bobo, a UCLA sociologist who directed the survey, added, "These are people of high accomplishment and who have worked hard for what they have achieved. As far as they are concerned, however, what happened to Rodney King can just as easily befall any of them. Given all the dues they have paid, and all the contributions the black middle class has made, these events—especially the jury verdict—came as a jolt of racial injustice."

It's quite possible that the leap in alienation recorded by Bobo and company was an ephemeral phenomenon, nothing more than a passing wave of anger generated by an extraordinary event. The entire country, after all, seemed in a state of shock over the verdict in Simi Valley. But that does not account for the sentiments registered before the verdict, when so many blacks who were doing well seemed to be so very unhappy. So many seemed in a state of raging discontent. And much of America, I am sure, has not a ghost of a notion why.

"[The] assault on affirmative action flows on a river of racism that is as broad, powerful and American as the Mississippi."

Affirmative Action Is Still Necessary to Fight Discrimination

Roger Wilkins

Affirmative action was launched in the 1960s to ensure equal opportunity for disadvantaged minorities in the workplace. In the following viewpoint, Roger Wilkins argues that affirmative action policies are still necessary because their original goal of ending discrimination has not been accomplished. According to Wilkins, many white men take for granted the everyday privileges and advantages their color provides them—an attitude that amounts to racism. Blacks continue to be affected by this attitude among whites, he contends, and must be protected by affirmative action. Wilkins is a professor of history at George Mason University in Fairfax, Virginia.

As you read, consider the following questions:

1. What have been the benefits of affirmative action, according to the author?
2. According to Wilkins, why is it important for blacks to recover their history?
3. How is racism like an addiction, in Wilkins's opinion?

Excerpted from "Racism Has Its Privileges" by Roger Wilkins, *The Nation*, March 27, 1995. Reprinted with permission from *The Nation* magazine; © The Nation Company, L.P.

Affirmative action, as I understand it, was not designed to punish anyone; it was, rather—as a result of a clear-eyed look at how America actually works—an attempt to enlarge opportunity for *everybody*. As amply documented in the 1968 Kerner Commission report on racial disorders, when left to their own devices, American institutions in such areas as college admissions, hiring decisions and loan approvals had been making choices that discriminated against blacks. That discrimination, which flowed from doing what came naturally, hurt more than blacks: It hurt the entire nation, as the riots of the late 1960s demonstrated. Though the Kerner report focused on blacks, similar findings could have been made about other minorities and women.

The Original Goals of Affirmative Action

Affirmative action required institutions to develop plans enabling them to go beyond business as usual and search for qualified people in places where they did not ordinarily conduct their searches or their business. Affirmative action programs generally require some proof that there has been a good-faith effort to follow the plan and numerical guidelines against which to judge the sincerity and the success of the effort. The idea of affirmative action is *not* to force people into positions for which they are unqualified but to encourage institutions to develop realistic criteria for the enterprise at hand and then to find a reasonably diverse mix of people qualified to be engaged in it. Without the requirements calling for plans, good-faith efforts and the setting of broad numerical goals, many institutions would do what they had always done: assert that they had looked but "couldn't find anyone qualified," and then go out and hire the white man they wanted to hire in the first place.

Affirmative action has done wonderful things for the United States by enlarging opportunity and developing and utilizing a far broader array of the skills available in the American population than in the past. It has not outlived its usefulness. It was never designed to be a program to eliminate poverty. It has not always been used wisely, and some of its permutations do have to be reconsidered, refined or, in some cases, abandoned. It is not a quota program, and those cases where rigid numbers are used (except under a court or administrative order after a specific finding of discrimination) are a bastardization of an otherwise highly beneficial set of public policies. . . .

What makes the affirmative action issue so difficult is that it engages blacks and whites exactly at those points where they differ the most. There are some areas, such as rooting for the local football team, where their experiences and views are virtually identical. There are others—sometimes including work and

103

school—where their experiences and views both overlap and diverge. And finally, there are areas such as affirmative action and inextricably related notions about the presence of racism in society where the divergences draw out almost all the points of difference between the races.

This Land Is My Land

Blacks and whites experience America very differently. Though we often inhabit the same space, we operate in very disparate psychic spheres.

Whites have an easy sense of ownership of the country; they feel they are entitled to receive all that is best in it. Many of them believe that their country—though it may have some faults—is superior to all others and that, as Americans, they are superior as well. Many of them think of this as a white country and some of them even experience it that way. They think of it as a land of opportunity—a good place with a lot of good people in it. Some suspect (others *know*) that the presence of blacks messes everything up.

To blacks there's nothing very easy about life in America, and any sense of ownership comes hard because we encounter so much resistance in making our way through the ordinary occurrences of life. And I'm not even talking here about overt acts of discrimination but simply about the way whites intrude on and disturb our psychic space without even thinking about it.

A telling example of this was given to me by a black college student in Oklahoma. He said whites give him looks that say: "What are *you* doing here?"

"When do they give you that look?" I asked.

"Every time I walk in a door," he replied.

When he said that, every black person in the room nodded and smiled in a way that indicated recognition based on thousands of such moments in their own lives.

For most blacks, America is either a land of denied opportunity or one in which the opportunities are still grudgingly extended and extremely limited. For some—that one-third who are mired in poverty, many of them isolated in dangerous ghettos—America is a land of desperadoes and desperation. In places where whites see a lot of idealism, blacks see, at best, idealism mixed heavily with hypocrisy. Blacks accept America's greatness, but are unable to ignore ugly warts that many whites seem to need not to see. I am reminded here of James Baldwin's searing observation from *The Fire Next Time:*

> The American Negro has the great advantage of having never believed that collection of myths to which white Americans cling: that their ancestors were all freedom-loving heroes, that they were born in the greatest country the world has ever

seen, or that Americans are invincible in battle and wise in peace, that Americans have always dealt honorably with Mexicans and Indians and all other neighbors or inferiors, that American men are the world's most direct and virile, that American women are pure.

Recovery of Black History

It goes without saying, then, that blacks and whites remember America differently. The past is hugely important since we argue a lot about who we are on the basis of who we think we have been, and we derive much of our sense of the future from how we think we've done in the past. In a nation in which few people know much history these are perilous arguments, because in such a vacuum, people tend to weave historical fables tailored to their political or psychic needs.

Blacks are still recovering the story of their role in America, which so many white historians simply ignored or told in ways that made black people ashamed. But in a culture that batters us, learning the real history is vital in helping blacks feel fully human. It also helps us understand just how deeply American we are, how richly we have given, how much has been taken from us and how much has yet to be restored. Supporters of affirmative action believe that broad and deep damage has been done to American culture by racism and sexism over the whole course of American history and that they are still powerful forces today. We believe that minorities and women are still disadvantaged in our highly competitive society and that affirmative action is absolutely necessary to level the playing field.

Not all white Americans oppose this view and not all black Americans support it. There are a substantial number of whites in this country who have been able to escape our racist and sexist past and to enter fully into the quest for equal justice. There are other white Americans who are not racists but who more or less passively accept the powerful suggestions coming at them from all points in the culture that whites are entitled to privilege and to freedom from competition with blacks. And then there are racists who just don't like blacks or who actively despise us. There are still others who may or may not feel deep antipathy, but who know how to manipulate racism and white anxiety for their own ends. Virtually all the people in the last category oppose affirmative action and some of them make a practice of preying upon those in the second category who are not paying attention or who . . . are simply confused.

The Politics of Denial

One of these political predators is Senate majority leader Bob Dole. In his offhandedly lethal way, Dole delivered a benediction of "let me now forgive us" on *Meet the Press* recently. After crediting affirmative action for the 62 percent of the white male vote garnered by the Republicans [in the November 1994 elections], he remarked that slavery was "before we were born" and wondered whether future generations ought to have to continue "paying a price" for those ancient wrongs.

Clay Bennett/NAS. Reprinted with permission.

Such a view holds that whatever racial problems we once may have had have been solved over the course of the past thirty years and that most of our current racial friction is caused by racial and gender preferences that almost invariably work to displace some "qualified" white male. Words and phrases like "punish" or "preference" or "reverse discrimination" or "quota" are dropped into the discourse to buttress this view, as are those anecdotes about injustice to whites. Proponents of affirmative action see these arguments as disingenuous but ingenious because they reduce serious and complex social, political, economic, historical and psychological issues to bumper-sticker slogans designed to elicit Pavlovian responses.

The fact is that the successful public relations assault on affirmative action flows on a river of racism that is as broad, powerful and American as the Mississippi. And, like the Mississippi, racism can be violent and deadly and is a permanent feature of

American life. But while nobody who is sane denies the reality of the Mississippi, millions of Americans who are deemed sane—some of whom are powerful and some even thought wise—deny, wholly or in part, that racism exists.

It is critical to understand the workings of denial in this debate because it is used to obliterate the facts that created the need for the remedy in the first place. One of the best examples of denial was provided recently by the nation's most famous former history professor, House Speaker Newt Gingrich. According to the *Washington Post*, "Gingrich dismissed the argument that the beneficiaries of affirmative action, commonly African Americans, have been subjected to discrimination over a period of centuries. 'That is true of virtually every American,' Gingrich said, noting that the Irish were discriminated against by the English, for example."

That is breathtaking stuff coming from somebody who should know that blacks have been on this North American continent for 375 years and that for 245 the country permitted slavery. Gingrich should also know that for the next hundred years we had legalized subordination of blacks, under a suffocating blanket of condescension and frequently enforced by nightriding terrorists. We've had only thirty years of something else.

That something else is a nation trying to lift its ideals out of a thick, often impenetrable slough of racism. Racism is a hard word for what over the centuries became second nature in America—preferences across the board for white men and, following in their wake, white women. Many of these men seem to feel that it is un-American to ask them to share anything with blacks—particularly their work, their neighborhoods or "their" women. To protect these things—apparently essential to their identity—they engage in all forms of denial. For a historian to assert that "virtually every American" shares the history I have just outlined comes very close to lying.

Denial of racism is much like the denials that accompany addictions to alcohol, drugs or gambling. It is probably not stretching the analogy too much to suggest that many racist whites are so addicted to their unwarranted privileges and so threatened by the prospect of losing them that all kinds of defenses become acceptable, including insistent distortions of reality in the form of hypocrisy, lying or the most outrageous political demagogy.

"Those People" Don't Deserve Help

The demagogues have reverted to a new version of quite an old trick. Before the 1950s, whites who were busy denying that the nation was unfair to blacks would simply assert that we didn't deserve equal treatment because we were *inferior*. These days it is not permissible in most public circles to say that blacks are inferior, but it is perfectly acceptable to target the *behavior* of blacks, specifically poor blacks. The argument then follows a fairly predictable line: The behavior of poor blacks requires a severe rethinking of national social policy, it is said. Advantaged blacks really don't need affirmative action anymore, and when they are the objects of such programs, some qualified white person (unqualified white people don't show up in these arguments) is (as Dole might put it) "punished." While it is possible that color-blind affirmative action programs benefiting all disadvantaged Americans are needed, those (i.e., blacks) whose behavior is so distressing must be punished by restricting welfare, shriveling the safety net and expanding the prison opportunity. All of that would presumably give us, in William Bennett's words, "what we want—a color-blind society," for which the white American psyche is presumably fully prepared.

A Color-Blind Society?

There are a number of layers of unreality in these precepts. The first is that the United States is not now and probably never will be a color-blind society. It is the most color-conscious society on earth. Over the course of 375 years, whites have given blacks absolutely no reason to believe that they can behave in a color-blind manner. In many areas of our lives—particularly in employment, housing and education—affirmative action is required to counter deeply ingrained racist patterns of behavior.

Second, while I don't hold the view that all blacks who behave badly are blameless victims of a brutal system, I do believe that many poor blacks have, indeed, been brutalized by our culture, and I know of *no* blacks, rich or poor, who haven't been hurt in some measure by the racism in this country. The current mood (and, in some cases like the Speaker's, the cultivated ignorance) completely ignores the fact that some blacks never escaped the straight line of oppression that ran from slavery through the semislavery of sharecropping to the late mid-century migration from Southern farms into isolated pockets of urban poverty. Their families have always been excluded, poor and without skills, and so they were utterly defenseless when the enormous American economic dislocations that began in the mid-1970s slammed into their communities, followed closely by deadly waves of crack cocaine. One would think that the double-digit unemployment suffered consistently over the past two decades by blacks who were *looking for work* would be a permanent feature of the discussions about race, responsibility, welfare and rights.

But a discussion of the huge numbers of black workers who are becoming economically redundant would raise difficult questions about the efficiency of the economy at a time when millions of white men feel insecure. Any honest appraisal of unemployment would reveal that millions of low-skilled white men were being severely damaged by corporate and Federal Reserve decisions; it might also refocus the anger of those whites in the middle ranks whose careers have been shattered by the corporate downsizing fad.

But people's attention is kept trained on the behavior of some poor blacks by politicians and television news shows, reinforcing the stereotypes of blacks as dangerous, as threats, as unqualified. Frightened whites direct their rage at pushy blacks rather than at the corporations that export manufacturing operations to low-wage countries, or at the Federal Reserve, which imposes interest rate hikes that slow down the economy. . . .

Seen only as a corrective for ancient wrongs, affirmative action may be dismissed by the likes of Gingrich and Dole, just as attempts to federalize decent treatment of the freed slaves were dismissed after Reconstruction more than a century ago. Then, striking down the Civil Rights Act of 1875, Justice Joseph Bradley wrote of blacks that "there must be some stage in the progress of his elevation when he takes the rank of a mere citizen, and ceases to be the special favorite of the laws, and when his rights, as a citizen or a man, are to be protected in the ordinary modes by which other men's rights are protected."

But white skin has made some citizens—particularly white males—*the special favorites of the culture.* It may be that we will need affirmative action until most white males are really ready for a color-blind society—that is, when they are ready to assume "the rank of a mere citizen." As a nation we took a hard look at that special favoritism thirty years ago [in passing the Civil Rights Act of 1964]. Though the centuries of cultural preference enjoyed by white males still overwhelmingly skew power and wealth their way, we have in fact achieved a more meritocratic society as a result of affirmative action than we have ever previously enjoyed in this country.

If we want to continue making things better in this society, we'd better figure out ways to protect and defend affirmative action against the confused, the frightened, the manipulators and, yes, the liars in politics, journalism, education and wherever else they may be found. In the name of longstanding American prejudice and myths and in the service of their own narrow interests, power-lusts or blindness, they are truly victimizing the rest of us, perverting the ideals they claim to stand for and destroying the nation they pretend to serve.

*"The struggle for genuine equal opportunity was
lost amidst the growing clamor by an ever-
increasing number of groups for special
government favors."*

Affirmative Action Is Unnecessary and Divisive

Steven Yates

Affirmative action policies—which are intended to create equal
opportunities for minorities and women—have been challenged
by white males who claim that such policies amount to "reverse
discrimination." In the following viewpoint, Steven Yates argues
that affirmative action has encouraged an increasing number of
groups to claim that they have been victims of discrimination and
has thereby produced divisiveness in society. He believes that
outright bigotry has been reduced by education, and he contends
that if affirmative action policies were eliminated, free competition among businesses would eliminate discrimination. Yates is
author of *Civil Wrongs: What Went Wrong with Affirmative Action.*

As you read, consider the following questions:

1. Who have been the primary beneficiaries of affirmative
   action, according to Yates?
2. According to the author, why will many white males not
   question affirmative action?
3. What have been the actual effects of affirmative action,
   according to Yates?

Steven Yates, "The Ethics of Affirmative Action," *The Freeman*, July 1994. Reprinted by
permission of the Foundation for Economic Education. (Original article included
documentation footnotes not included in this reprint.)

Affirmative action has troubled the American political landscape for over three decades. Sooner or later, every ethicist must confront the dilemmas it and a variety of closely related policies—multicultural education, diversity management, sensitivity training sessions—pose. The dilemmas themselves indeed seem acute. It is true, for example, that U.S. history reveals poor treatment of this country's minorities and its powerless. Native Americans were taken from their lands and forcibly relocated. Decades of enforced discrimination left blacks well behind whites politically and socioeconomically. Women were denied the right to vote for years.

The Start of Preferential Policies

The 1950s saw the start of an extensive effort to repudiate discrimination and bring about equal opportunity. Then something went wrong. The struggle for genuine equal opportunity was lost amidst the growing clamor by an ever-increasing number of groups for special government favors. Equal opportunity laws, which initially rejected preferential policies, were replaced by affirmative action programs which could not be implemented without them.

Backers of affirmative action argued that blacks and other victims of past discrimination were so far behind in the economic race that without preferential treatment, equal opportunity would never be more than a high-sounding phrase. Thus race-conscious policies emerged with a vengeance. Employers had to keep voluminous records on the race, gender, ethnic heritage, and religious background of prospective employees so they could prove they had not discriminated against those designated by the government as victims. Government agencies expanded their reach to oversee implementation. Those found not in compliance, even innocently, sometimes saw their businesses imperiled.

White males started chafing at reverse discrimination right away. Well-known cases such as *Regents of the University of California v. Allan Bakke* and *United Steel Workers v. Weber* resolved little, though, and future litigation seems inevitable. Meanwhile, special programs of all varieties not only failed to help the vast majority of those in targeted groups but left them worse off than before; the primary beneficiaries of affirmative action, after all, have not been the economically disadvantaged blacks and Native Americans, but middle- and upper-class women. The welfare state, another legacy of the 1960s, has now produced second- and third-generation dependents with no marketable skills and no incentive to acquire them. Victimology has become the country's largest growth industry—after government, of course.

The affirmative action umbrella now covers roughly two

thirds of the country's population, with the disabled and homosexuals the most recent entrants. Tensions between groups are at an all-time high, with skirmishes occurring constantly. The prevailing philosophy of multiculturalism which now underwrites much discussion of race, ethnicity, and gender has fueled division by emphasizing differences between groups.

Babin, for the Albany *Times Union*. Reprinted with permission.

What ought to concern the ethicist is the prevailing response to these problems. Instead of serious soul-searching and reexamination, an ambience of disinformation, concealment, and, when needed, outright dishonesty has protected affirmative action and its kin for years. Begin with language. *Equal opportunity* clearly does not mean equal opportunity but preferences for some at the expense of others. Newspeak surrounds preferential policies with terms like *inclusion, celebrating diversity*, and *sensitivity*. Claims that affirmative action has sometimes forced businesses and entire industries to set quotas and hire by race and gender meet with belligerent denial, along with insinuations that only racists and sexists would make such charges. This tactic serves a very specific purpose: many white males, even those in positions of authority, will not question affirmative action for fear of being labeled racists. Finally, today's "sensitivity training" seems intended to inculcate in the white male who is turned down for a job or a promotion in favor of a less qualified woman or minority that, as a member of the oppressor group, he had it coming!

If affirmative action had been the boon to women and minorities its advocates claim, I doubt there would be much debate. Its benefits would be evident to everyone. What do we see instead? We see growing populations of minorities who lack the basic skills necessary for economic advancement, and are actually slipping backward. We see an educational system which seems powerless to do anything, and rationalizes its own failings with doctrines which make achievement as well as experience a group-specific notion. In the view multiculturalists espouse, schools should give minority groups "self-esteem" instead of knowledge and marketable skills. Sometimes this means rewriting their histories to invent "achievements." Afrocentrism is the best example, with its claims that the Egyptians were black, that the Greeks stole their culture from Africa (the real origin of civilization), and that two thousand years of racism has suppressed the truth. Radical feminism, the noisy stepchild of affirmative action for women, is also shot through with bizarre claims about sex and rape, our pornography-driven culture, and the universal victimization of women by "patriarchal society." The war against "sexual harassment" has created a climate in which men are guilty if charged.

Voluntary Affirmative Action and the Free Market

Clearly we are on a downward spiral. Writers all across the political spectrum have observed that this balkanizing trend threatens not only basic Constitutional rights (such as First Amendment free speech protections) but the very fabric of representative democracy. Is there a better way? I think so. It's called the free market.

If transactions are voluntary and not coerced, businesses and other organizations will be free to hire according to their needs. This right will be *recognized* and *protected* by government. If personal responsibility is a central value, employers will *not* simply indulge base prejudices or personal whims. Rather, business necessity—the necessity to remain as competitive as possible—will require employers to "cast their nets as widely as possible" and attempt to hire the best employees. A free market will ensure that information is available where qualified members of minority groups who are alert and seeking new opportunities will see it. In this sense, what has sometimes been called "weak" affirmative action will be permitted to continue on a *voluntary basis* among those who wish to continue it. As a voluntary enterprise, it may take a variety of forms which have the potential to address and solve the problems that coercive, government-driven affirmative action has been unable to touch, and without creating the dilemmas and rifts that coercive affirmative action has created. Moreover, under conditions of genuine liberty, minorities will be freed from many constraints which have held them back: high taxes, licensure laws, zoning ordinances, etc.

Education vs. Coercion

A question is in order. Given the freedom to do otherwise, will businesses and other institutions actually reach out to minorities? The mistrust evident in the question is actually misplaced. A recent study has shown that bigotry and prejudice are no longer considered acceptable to a majority of educated people. *Education* has been and will continue to be the key. We should emphasize that racism is unfair to individuals whether directed by whites against blacks, or by blacks against whites. It is, in fact, a form of collectivism, and embodies its defects and follies in a particularly virulent form. Our tradition of individualism got rid of slavery. This tradition is still our best hope of keeping racism at bay.

At present, though, *coercion*, not *education*, is the norm. The proportioning of peoples by force is driving them apart rather than bringing them together. A new separation is loose in our society, fueled by the multiculturalist emphasis on how peoples differ instead of what they have in common.

Members of minority groups (and women) must be willing to question the dominant tendencies in what passes for education today. They need especially to question the collectivism and relativism inherent in multiculturalism, and affirm the values of liberty, responsibility, achievement, and toleration as values which hold universally, independent of race and gender. Then they will be motivated to obtain the skills they need to be employable, or to become entrepreneurs. This need not mean giving up a cultural or ethnic heritage but rather making an effort to preserve it in ways that don't undermine their capacity to prosper in a free society.

To sum up, government programs can never allocate skills where they are most needed. Lest the whole concept of "voluntary affirmative action" seem to place too much trust in human goodness, it is important to remember that government is the institution most responsible for the conditions minorities face. Slavery had foes as far back as the Revolutionary War, but continued under the support of government. Government instituted Jim Crow laws and involuntary segregation. Then, in our century, it passed minimum wage and licensure laws which effectively priced blacks out of the marketplace and created impassable barriers to their entry into many professions. Coercive preferential programs amount to government efforts to solve problems the government created in the first place—rather like using gasoline in an attempt to put out a fire.

For peaceful affirmative action to replace coercive affirmative action, though, criticisms by white males such as myself probably won't be enough. Women and minorities themselves must recognize that efforts by government to "help" them have proven futile. This means repudiating much of their current leadership. Fortunately, we have already seen the beginnings of such a trend in the writings of such black intellectuals as Thomas Sowell, Walter Williams, and Glenn Loury. If the facts presented here and in countless other places can be shouted from the rooftops long enough, there may yet be hope for general economic advancement and intergroup peace in America.

"African-Americans seem to me to be competing more directly with Latin Americans than with any other group."

Immigrants Take Jobs from Blacks

Jack Miles

During the 1992 Los Angeles riots, a great deal of attention was paid to the conflict between blacks and Koreans in South Central Los Angeles. In the following viewpoint, Jack Miles argues that the conflict between blacks and immigrant Latinos is just as important. The influx of large numbers of Latino immigrants has pushed blacks out of the labor market, he contends, because Latinos will work for less money and are perceived as less threatening than blacks by potential white employers. Poor Latinos are also competing with poor blacks for the limited amount of social services that the city can provide, according to Miles. Miles, a former editorial writer for the *Los Angeles Times*, currently directs the Humanities Center at the Claremont Graduate School in Claremont, California.

As you read, consider the following questions:

1. According to the *La Prensa San Diego* editorial cited by Miles, why did Los Angeles blacks riot in 1992?
2. According to the author, why are blacks being pushed out of jobs as social workers?
3. What is Miles's comment about the argument that immigrants are doing work that "Americans" refuse to do?

During the 1980s, according to census figures released in May 1992, the United States admitted 8.6 million immigrants. In the context of U.S. immigration history this is a staggering number—more than in any decade since 1900–1910. World-wide, half the decade's emigrants had made the United States their destination. Of them, 11 percent—more than three quarters of a million—further specified their choice as Los Angeles. By the end of the decade 40 percent of all Angelenos were foreign-born; 49.9 percent spoke a language other than English at home; 35.3 percent spoke Spanish. This is the city where, two weeks before those figures were released, the most violent urban riot in American history broke out: fifty-one people were killed, and property worth $750 million or more was lost.

Though the occasion for the riot was the acquittal of four white policemen on charges of assaulting a black traffic offender, Latinos as well as African-Americans rioted. Why? What was Rodney King to Latinos? Did a race riot, once begun, degenerate—or progress—into a bread riot? Was it a vast crime spree, as devoid of political content as the looting that followed the 1977 blackout in New York City? Of those arrested afterward—of whom more than half were Latino—40 percent already had criminal records. Was the riot a defeat of the police? If it was a hybrid of all these, was it, finally, an aberration from which, by hard work, America's second-largest city could recover? Or was it the annunciation of a new and permanent state of affairs? . . .

A Latino Riot?

We learned later that in fact many if not most of the Latino rioters were either Central Americans or very recent Mexican immigrants, and that what the riot might have been to us Anglos, it was also, to some considerable extent, to the established Mexican-American political leadership. They, too, were wondering about a huge, strange, possibly angry, Spanish-speaking population in their midst. Who were these people, and what did they want? If they had no political agenda, if they were common criminals, well, that, too—given their growing numbers and the demonstrated inadequacy of the police—was news, wasn't it? The population of South Central Los Angeles had doubled since 1965. For every black in the area there was now at least one Latino. That had to make a difference. But what kind of difference?

In the weeks following the riot, Latino leaders from East Los Angeles were concerned that the sudden spotlight on South Central Los Angeles would rob them of scarce government funds. They were on guard against the possibility that South Central Los Angeles would be rewarded for its violence and East Los Angeles punished for its good behavior. "Just because we didn't erupt in East L.A., does that translate into us being ignored or missing out on the funds that are funneling into the communities?" asked Geraldine Zapata, the executive director of the Plaza Community Center. But the more immediate challenge to Mexican East Los Angeles was coming to terms with Central American South Central Los Angeles.

African Americans vs. Immigrants

The ever-accelerating flow of immigrants has vastly complicated relations between blacks and whites in our country, to their mutual detriment. The African American leadership has been conflicted about immigration. As the country's largest minority, with the most solid moral claim upon the majority, they naturally expected that they would lead the growing non-European sector of American society and that a show of pan-minority solidarity would heighten black influence, yield greater concessions from whites, and advance the social aspirations of blacks. But the leadership must also cope with the reality that rank-and-file blacks are increasingly resentful of immigrants; in this era of dwindling distinctions between citizens and noncitizens, African Americans find themselves competing for jobs, social programs, and affirmative action advantages with the new arrivals, and often end up as the losers in the competition.

Gerda Bikales, *The World & I*, September 1994.

The mainstream interpretation had little to say about either Mexicans or Central Americans. It took the riot to be Watts II, a repetition of the 1965 black riot, touched off by the verdict in the King case but growing out of the deeper frustrations of the black population over rising unemployment, institutionalized police brutality, and eroded public assistance. That interpretation was surely right as far as it went. Those who mentally bracketed the riot between the videotaped beatings of King by a gang of white policemen and of Reginald Denny, a white trucker, by a gang of black rioters were not altogether wrong to do so. . . .

Blacks vs. Latinos

For all the compelling power of the Watts II paradigm, however, for all the relevance of white violence and black rage, something still more powerful was happening, and the Latino population of southern California was at the heart of it.

About a month after the riot a friend sent me a copy of an unsigned editorial from a Mexican-American newspaper, *La Prensa San Diego*, dated May 15, 1992. What other Latinos had begun to insinuate, *La Prensa* angrily spelled out: Blacks were not victims. Latinos were victims. Blacks were perpetrators. . . .

What occurred was a major racial confrontation by the Black community, which now sees its numbers and influence waning.

Faced with nearly a million and a half Latinos taking over the inner city, Blacks revolted, rioted and looted. Whatever measure of power and influence they had pried loose from the White power structure, they now see as being in danger of being transferred to the Latino community. Not only are they losing influence, public offices, and control of the major civil rights mechanisms, they now see themselves being replaced in the pecking order by the Asian community, in this case the Koreans.

. . . There was, to put it mildly, little in that editorial to suggest that desperately poor, fifteenth-generation African-Americans might be within their rights to resent sudden, strong, officially tolerated competition from first-generation Latin Americans and Asian-Americans. But La Prensa's anger clearly arose not just from the riot, perhaps not mainly from the riot, but from frustration at television's inability to see Latin Americans as a part of the main action at all.

An Anti-Immigrant Stance

I don't think that any clear pattern of blacks attacking Latino businesses or Latinos attacking black businesses can be established. Koreans do plainly seem to have been singled out for attack—by some Latinos as well as by many blacks. But state officials believe that at least 30 percent of the approximately four thousand businesses destroyed were Latino-owned. Both "Somos Hermanos" and "Black Owned Business" were frail armor even when those labels were honestly applied. As the police re-established control, thousands of arrests were made; more than half of the arrestees were Latinos, but the older, second-generation, law-abiding Mexican-American community resented the lack of differentiation in the label "Latino." This community insisted with some feeling that in the communities it regarded as truly and more or less exclusively its own there had been no rioting. By implication this was the beginning of an anti-immigrant stance within the community.

What counts for more, however, than any incipient struggle between older and newer Latino immigrants is the emerging struggle between Latinos and blacks. La Prensa is right to stress the raw size of the Latino population. The terms of engagement, if we take our cue from the rappers, would seem to be black versus white or black versus Asian. But the Korean population of Los Angeles County is just 150,000, a tiny fraction of the Latino population of 3.3 million. Of the 60,560 people in Koreatown itself, only 26.5 percent are Asian; more than 50 percent are Latino. Blacks are the most oppressed minority, but it matters enormously that whites are no longer a majority. And within the urban geography of Los Angeles, African-Americans seem to me to be competing more directly with Latin Americans than with any other group.

I find paradoxical confirmation for this view in the fact that some of the most responsible leaders in both groups want to head it off. A month after the riot my wife and I received the June 1992 newsletter of the Southern California Interfaith Taskforce on Central America, a group to which we have contributed a little money over the past several years. SCITCA, originally a lobby for the victims of state-sponsored violence in (principally) El Salvador and Guatemala, has more recently expanded its agenda to include the fate of Central Americans now settled in Los Angeles. It has effectively lobbied, for example, for a relaxation of the municipal regulation of street vendors.

In the wake of the riot SCITCA was worried about anti-immigrant backlash. Joe Hicks, of the Southern Christian Leadership Conference, and Frank Acosta, of the Coalition for Humane Immigrant Rights of Los Angeles, wrote in the newsletter,

> In the aftermath of the recent civil unrest. . . . Immigrants and refugees in particular have been targeted for blame, violence and civil rights abuses. . . . Fears of overcrowding, the burden on local communities, competition for scarce jobs, drainage on public resources through the education and social welfare systems are all commonly held apprehensions about the impact of immigrants in our communities. Similar fears were voiced during the migration of African-Americans from the south to the northern cities earlier this century. In the past few years, however, a growing number of social scientists, economists and researchers have concluded that the social and economic impact of immigration is overwhelmingly positive. By and large, it is the prospect of freedom and economic opportunity, not welfare, that draws immigrants to the state.

Hicks and Acosta were astute to recognize that the movement of millions of blacks from the rural South to the urban North was a migration as enormous as any from abroad, but the fate of those black immigrants and the cities that received them rather subverts the lesson the two writers want to draw. And alongside the recent, pro-immigration literature that the two cite is a small but growing body of even more recent literature suggesting that whether we will it or not, America's older black poor and newer brown poor are on a collision course.

Competition for Benefits and Jobs

A married couple, both white, both psychiatric social workers in the Los Angeles Unified School District, recently told us of several monolingual school social workers who had been let go to make room for bilingual workers. With so many Spanish-

120

speakers in the district, the rationale for requiring social workers to have a knowledge of Spanish is clear. Our friends have, in fact, been diligently studying the language to protect their own positions. And yet it struck them as tragically shortsighted that most of the dismissed social workers were black.

A member of our church administers a subsidized day-care center in northwest Pasadena, once a black neighborhood, now, like South Central Los Angeles, an extremely overcrowded black and Latino neighborhood. Black welfare mothers, our friend reports, are increasingly turned away from the center, because on the neediest-first principle they no longer qualify. Latino mothers, often with more children than the blacks and with no income even from welfare, are needier, and claim a growing share of the available places. Are the Latino mothers illegal? Are they just ill-equipped to apply for welfare? The kindly day-care people don't ask.

Hicks and Acosta exhort: "The poor communities of Los Angeles cannot get caught up fighting over the peanuts that have been given to them by the economic, political and educational institutions of America." But even if these communities make common political cause, do they have any choice about economic competition? The General Accounting Office reports that janitorial firms serving downtown Los Angeles have almost entirely replaced their unionized black work force with non-unionized immigrants.

If you live here, you don't need the General Accounting Office to bring you the news. The almost total absence of black gardeners, busboys, chambermaids, nannies, janitors, and construction workers in a city with a notoriously large pool of unemployed, unskilled black people leaps to the eye. According to the U.S. Census, 8.6 percent of South Central Los Angeles residents sixteen years old and older were unemployed in 1990, but an additional 41.8 percent were listed as "not in the labor force." If the Latinos were not around to do that work, nonblack employers would be forced to hire blacks—but they'd rather not. They trust Latinos. They fear or disdain blacks. The result is unofficial but widespread preferential hiring of Latinos—the largest affirmative-action program in the nation, and one paid for, in effect, by blacks. . . .

Labor Leaders Oppose Immigration

In July 1991 the Black Leadership Forum, a coalition headed by Coretta Scott King and Walter E. Fauntroy and including Jack Otero, the president of the Labor Council for Latin American Advancement, wrote to Senator Orrin Hatch urging him not to repeal the sanctions imposed on employers of illegal aliens under the Immigration Reform and Control Act of 1986. "We are concerned, Senator Hatch," the group wrote, that your proposed remedy to the employer sanctions–based discrimination, namely, the elimination of employer sanctions, will cause another problem—the revival of the pre-1986 discrimination against black and brown U.S. and documented workers, in favor of cheap labor—the undocumented workers. This would undoubtedly exacerbate an already severe economic crisis in communities where there are large numbers of new immigrants.

Labor leaders like Otero and another co-signer, William Lucy, of the Coalition of Black Trade Unionists, are notoriously critical of free trade, especially to the free-trade agreement between the United States and Mexico. Their opposition to lax enforcement of immigration law, which creates a free trade in labor, is only consistent. What difference is there between exporting jobs and importing workers?

The politics of labor and immigration makes strange bedfellows. On most issues the Southern California Interfaith Taskforce on Central America is an extremely liberal group, but on employer sanctions it sides with Senator Hatch. In effect, SCITCA would rather see wages go down and its Central American clients have work of some kind than see wages stay high and penniless refugees be left with nothing. La Placita, the Mission Church of Our Lady Queen of Angels, near downtown Los Angeles, became for a time a sanctuary for illegal hiring.

Latino immigrants at the bottom of the labor market often claim to be doing work that "Americans" refuse to do. Are they thinking of black Americans? It may not matter. Commenting to a *New York Times* reporter on the extremely low employment rate for sixteen- to nineteen-year-olds in New York City in early 1992—12.6 percent—Vernon M. Briggs, a labor economist at Cornell University, said, "To an immigrant willing to work two or three jobs at once, $5 an hour may not look bad. But to a kid from Brooklyn or the Bronx, it is a turnoff." To some of their parents these kids seem to be prima donnas, but in fact the influx of immigrants willing to work long hours for low wages has depressed wages and increased competition beyond anything that the parents ever faced. And the attitudinal difference between unskilled Americans of any race and their immigrant competition shrinks as the immigrants gain a clearer view of what faces them in the United States. . . .

A Cake Riot?

So, yes, Latinos compete with blacks for work at the bottom, but they also match them in rejecting $4.50 an hour as chump change. And then what? Then, among other things, readiness for a bread riot (a cake riot, if you will) in which the disappointed, by the thousands, steal what they once thought they could earn.

The question of how immigrant groups may fit into the American economy without dislodging or otherwise adversely affecting native groups is itself contained in the larger question of how an American economy carrying all these groups within it can compete against other national economies. In an article given wide distribution by the Federation for American Immigration Reform, Vernon Briggs claims that immigration accounts for 30 to 35 percent of the annual growth of the American labor force, a proportion virtually unknown elsewhere in the industrialized world. In 1989, Briggs writes, "the total number of immigrants from all sources admitted for permanent residence was 1,090,924—the highest figure for any single year since 1914 (and this figure did not include any estimate of the additional illegal immigrant flow or of the number of nonimmigrants permitted to work in the United States on a temporary basis during that year)."

The immigration story becomes the riot story by becoming a part of the labor story. And by an irony that I find particularly cruel, unskilled Latino immigration may be doing to American blacks at the end of the twentieth century what the European immigration that brought my own ancestors here did to them at the end of the nineteenth.

"[Studies] show that blacks do somewhat better in areas with a large immigrant presence."

Immigrants Do Not Take Jobs from Blacks

Thomas Muller

The belief that immigrants threaten employment opportunities for native-born Americans—especially low-skilled blacks—has produced anti-immigrant sentiment among blacks. In the following viewpoint, Thomas Muller argues that immigrants do not compete with blacks for jobs. He contends that as immigrants enter the workforce, they take jobs shunned by blacks, while educated and skilled blacks advance to better jobs. Immigrants, according to Muller, are a boon to the American economy because their consumption of goods and services creates jobs. Muller is author of *Immigrants and the American City*.

As you read, consider the following questions:

1. What is the foremost cause of poverty, joblessness, and falling wages among blacks, according to Muller?
2. According to the author, are blacks competing with immigrants for jobs in households and on farms? Why or why not?
3. With whom are immigrants competing for jobs, according to Muller?

Thomas Muller, "The Immigrant Challenge," *The Wilson Quarterly*, Autumn 1994. Reprinted by permission of the author.

Not since the Great Depression has the United States seen a tide of anti-immigrant sentiment to rival today's. So strong is public feeling that it helped drive President Bill Clinton to reverse the nation's long-held policy of welcoming any refugee who managed to escape from Fidel Castro's Cuba. Instead of a hero's welcome, the Cuban boat people received inglorious confinement in Panama or at the U.S. naval base in Guantanamo Bay, Cuba.

Two years earlier, after the 1992 Los Angeles riots, Patrick Buchanan declared that "foreigners are coming to this country illegally and helping to burn down one of the greatest cities in America." Buchanan, then seeking the Republican presidential nomination, may represent an extreme in American politics, but he was not shouted down when he made this incendiary statement. Indeed, many "moderates" simply found another way to blame the immigrants, claiming they had taken jobs from the city's poor blacks. In November 1994, Californians passed a statewide referendum on a proposition that would deny schooling and nonemergency medical care to illegal aliens. Congress may limit health and other benefits even for those entering legally, and new barriers are being erected along the U.S.-Mexico border against illegal immigrants. Even New Yorkers, heirs to one of the most liberal traditions in the nation, tell pollsters that recent immigration has hurt their city.

Anti-Immigrant Sentiments

Between 1980 and 1994, close to 14 million Mexicans, Central Americans, Asians, and other immigrants entered the United States, about two million of them illegally. Net immigration (excluding undocumented aliens) now accounts for over 35 percent of U.S. population growth, and its share will grow in the years ahead. Half or more of all workers entering the labor force during the next decade will be immigrants or the children of foreign-born families that arrived after the mid-1960s. Unlike earlier immigration waves, this one has washed over the entire nation, bringing foreign-born workers to virtually every community, large and small, from the rural South to the mountain West.

Anti-immigrant feeling is a simple sentiment with complex roots, some of them social and racial, and some seeming more practical. Immigrants are blamed for overcrowded schools, rising hospital deficits, and high welfare costs—indeed, for virtually everything that ails American society. Nothing ails this country more than the poverty of a large segment (one-third) of the black population, and stagnant or declining wages among Americans of all races and all but the highest income levels, and fingers are being pointed at the immigrants. Not too many years ago, the sight of a Korean shopkeeper or a Salvadoran construction worker would have been taken by many citizens as reassuring evidence of the American Dream's lasting power. Now such recent arrivals are likely to be seen as alien interlopers who are taking good jobs from hard-working Americans.

Immigrants vs. Blacks

These sentiments are strongest, of course, among groups with a disproportionately high share of low-wage and unskilled jobs. This has always been so. "Every hour sees the black man elbowed out of employment by some newly arrived immigrant," Frederick Douglass despaired in 1853. A century and a half later, when Congress sanctioned increased immigration in the Immigration Act of 1990, another black leader, Representative Major Owens (D.-N.Y.), warned that "we are taking one more step toward the creation of a permanent black underclass."

Immigrants and Jobs for African Americans

The presence of immigrants appears to have a direct complementary effect in increasing the earnings of African Americans who are employed, but on the other hand, the larger flow of immigrants works indirectly through joblessness to depress earnings. . . .

We argue that immigrants have a complementary effect for African Americans in public sector employment due to the increased demand in public services and agencies as a result of the growth of legal and illegal immigration. . . . As the demand for public services, programs and personnel has grown due to the population growth, a large part of which comes from immigration, African American employment in this sector has increased.

Paul Ong and Abel Valenzuela Jr., *Poverty and Race*, March/April 1995.

A certain sort of common sense suggests that such warnings may be justified. Douglass's certainly was. Free blacks who had found work in antebellum New York City as waiters, bricklayers, and servants found Irish immigrants moving into these fields while their own paths into other occupations were blocked by racism. Today, it is easy to produce anecdotes about native-born men and women who apply for a job, only to see the employer award it to a Mexican or an Asian. There even seems to be some hard data to back up this impression. Economist Donald Huddle of Rice University, a frequent critic of immigration policy, claims that for every four unskilled immigrant workers, one or two U.S.-born Americans are unable to find jobs or are thrown out of work.

But this kind of evidence tends to melt under close scrutiny. Application of Huddle's ratio to actual population figures, for

126

example, leads to the preposterous conclusion that virtually every low-skilled native-born worker in America is jobless. Representative Owens's statement overlooks, among other things, the recent experience of Western Europe, which is now watching in dismay as its own white-skinned underclass forms in the cities. And anecdotes can be found to illustrate any story. Even when they are true, they tend to ride roughshod over complex realities. Immigrants certainly do take some jobs, but they also fill jobs that nobody else will accept and which in many cases would not even exist without immigrant labor. Moreover, immigrants are consumers as well as workers, and their purchases of everything from paper towels to minivans help to create jobs in the U.S. economy.

The unpleasant reality is that persistent poverty among blacks, high rates of joblessness, and stagnant or falling real wages have complex causes. Foremost among them is technological change, which has raised the basic skill level required for a decent job above what many people possess. The evidence of this can be seen in the blighted neighborhoods of Rotterdam in the Netherlands and Liverpool in England as easily as it can in the South Bronx or on Chicago's South Side. But the immigrant explanation for what has gone wrong is attractive because it is quick, simple, and personal. . . .

The Economic Benefits of Immigration

Today, economists have at their disposal much better data and methods to measure the effects of immigrant labor. . . . During the economic recovery of the early 1990s, for example, immigrants were a major source of new housing demand, and residential construction was followed by a resurgence in purchases of appliances, furniture, and other capital goods. (If job growth was not as great as in other postwar expansions, it was not the immigrants' fault but the result of large productivity gains brought about chiefly through the use of new technology.) A Harvard University study estimates that immigrants will purchase 1.5 million homes by the year 2000. James Johnson, chairman of the Federal National Mortgage Association (Fannie Mae), believes that the recent immigrant surge will eventually create a major housing boom that will reverse urban decay in many American cities.

Immigrants also stimulate demand for public services such as education, although their impact on public finances is in dispute. Unquestionably, more teachers and other municipal workers are needed as population grows. Immigrants with low earnings cannot be expected to generate enough revenue to cover the cost of the services they receive. This is not an issue in the case of well-educated, highly trained foreign-born professionals, who typically produce a fiscal surplus. It is important to remember that some immigrants arrive with special skills. They include not only Pakistani engineers but Portuguese stonemasons and Korean wig-makers. It is chiefly because of the presence of leather workers trained in Mexico that there is a footwear industry in Los Angeles today.

Do Immigrants Compete with Blacks for Jobs?

What about the perception that immigrants compete for jobs with particular groups of native-born Americans? Among middle-class families, this concern is generally slight. While there are many foreign-born engineers in the United States, for example, there are not nearly enough native-born members of the profession to keep up with the demand. Foreign-born physicians, willing to work in public institutions and in less-than-desirable locales, have been a valuable addition to the U.S. work force. What provokes middle-class anxiety is not the job market but competition for positions whose number is fixed, notably at universities. The influx of Asian students onto the elite campuses of the University of California system, for example, has become a highly charged issue in the state.

But the American public's chief worry about aliens in the labor market is that they are competing for the same jobs as blacks with limited skills. Because average incomes in the United States have failed to rise since the early 1970s, shortly after the beginning of the current immigration wave, it is tempting to link stagnant income levels with immigrant labor. Should not blacks, who hold a higher proportion of low-paying jobs than most other groups, feel threatened by the massive flow of Mexicans, Central Americans, and emigrants from the Caribbean nations?

If the total number of low-skilled jobs were fixed, there would indeed be substantial, direct competition between the groups. But it is not. The example of two families with homes on the same suburban street in the Northern Virginia suburbs of Washington, D.C., illustrates how the pool of low-end jobs expands with supply. One of these households employs a maid from Honduras two days a week, and periodically brings in a crew of Nicaraguan nationals to work on the lawn. A neighbor has a nanny from Sri Lanka to care for the children, enabling both parents to work. These are jobs that in all likelihood simply would not exist if there were not immigrants to fill them. There are not long lines of native-born Americans waiting to work for the pay these couples can afford.

In 1983, almost 600,000 blacks in the United States, or 6 percent of all employed blacks, worked in menial jobs in households or on farms. A decade later, the number of blacks in these occupations had dropped by nearly a third, while Hispanics increased their numbers in these areas by 70 percent. Some would no doubt say that this is a case of immigrants pushing native-born workers out of their jobs. A more rational explanation is that many younger blacks have shunned these "dead-end" jobs, generally advancing to better-paid occupations as they acquire the necessary education or training, but sometimes moving laterally, into the underground economy or into unemployment. Removing immigrants from the equation makes the process easier to see: Not many people would call the change from the 1930s, when three out of four blacks in America worked as domestics, on farms, or as unskilled laborers, a defeat rather than a great triumph.

Immigrants Do Not Cause Black Unemployment

Overall, about 170,000 blacks left (or were displaced from) several categories of low-paying jobs during the 1983–93 period. At the same time, about 800,000 gained management and professional positions (a rise of more than 60 percent), and another 800,000 moved into administrative-support and sales jobs. White-collar occupations accounted for the vast majority of additions to the black labor force.

Yet even as this very positive trend was gathering strength, a disturbing schism was emerging among black Americans. As University of Chicago sociologist William Julius Wilson observed during the mid-1980s, one segment of the population was rising to prosperity while another—lacking education and marketable skills—was sinking deeper into poverty. In mid-1994, for example, the unemployment rate for black teenagers who were between sixteen and nineteen and who were not attending school was 44 percent, more than twice the rate for whites or Hispanics. Black joblessness, which has persisted at levels far above the national average since the 1960s, has both economic and social roots. Wilson places much of the blame on the loss of manufacturing jobs in the urban core and the deteriorating social climate within inner cities. Is rising immigration another underlying cause?

Studies comparing cities with differing percentages of immigrant workers find no significant variation in black income, earnings, unemployment rates, or other economic indicators. Indeed, they show that blacks do somewhat *better* in areas with a large immigrant presence. Thus, in the immigrant magnets of Los Angeles, New York, and San Francisco, about one out of every four blacks in 1992 was employed as a professional worker or as a manager, almost 50 percent above the national average for blacks. These gains reflect, in part, rising educational attainment among blacks in these cities and nationally. By 1990, 36 percent of all black adults across the nation, but only 28 percent of all Hispanics (and an even smaller share of Hispanic immigrants), had some college education. Immigrants *do* have a modest adverse impact on the wages of one group: native-born Hispanics. That is because the two groups are more likely to compete for similar jobs.

Sophisticated econometric models confirm these findings. Kristen Butcher and David Card at Princeton University found in their 1991 study little indication of an adverse wage effect of immigrants "either cross-sectionally or within cities over time." A study by Julian Simon and several co-authors released in 1993 concluded that "there is little or no observed increase in aggregate national unemployment due to immigration." Extensive research by Robert LaLonde and Robert Topel at the University of Chicago found that "immigration has a small effect on wages but virtually all of this burden falls on immigrants themselves." In other words, the surfeit of immigrants competing for jobs as nannies or in apparel factories keeps wages down in these fields.

Competition for Political Advantages

While there is scant evidence that immigrants are hurting the chances of blacks and other minorities today, there is reason to worry about the future. One of the main avenues of black upward mobility in America during the past thirty years has been government employment. In Los Angeles, 30 percent of all black jobholders—but only 6 percent of employed Hispanics—work for the federal, state, or local government. Today, blacks are more than twice as likely as Hispanics to hold jobs in the public sector. And these jobs typically pay better than comparable ones in the private sector. It is not hard to see what is going to happen. As Hispanic (and Asian) political strength grows—and the two groups together recently passed blacks in sheer numbers—so will the demand for a "fair share" of these desirable jobs. This is already occurring. A recent report by the U.S. Postal Service's Board of Governors concludes that blacks dominate the agency, while Hispanics are under-represented—not particularly surprising since blacks, finding other doors closed to them, began flocking to the Post Office Department during the 1930s. In Los Angeles, the report notes, 63 percent of all Postal Service employees are black, even though blacks constitute only 11 percent of the city's work force. Unless large numbers of blacks begin moving into the private sector, bitter political struggles are likely, some of them on Capitol Hill and in courtrooms, but many of them in the furnace of big-city electoral politics.

Meanwhile, the flow of immigrants seeking low-skilled jobs is not going to slow any time soon. As long as there are help-wanted signs in the nation's restaurants, hotels, and suburban shopping centers, foreigners seeking a better life will continue to come to the United States. Although there has been a shift toward work that requires greater skill and more education, one study projecting job growth in the coming decade includes occupations such as janitor, food counter worker, and waiter among its top 10. Because both legal and illegal entry are expected to rise above current levels in the years ahead, there will be plenty of applicants for these jobs.

No measure now contemplated, including a national identity card, will stop or substantially slow the immigrant influx. Instant global communications, easy transportation, and the high U.S. standard of living keep the dream alive of coming to America. Only draconian steps that American society is unwilling to consider—such as mandatory confinement of undocumented workers and their employers—could conceivably keep immigrants out. For black youngsters and others looking for jobs near the bottom of the occupational ladder, the message is clear. It is futile to compete directly with immigrants who will keep coming and keep working for low wages and it is vitally important to acquire enough education and training to qualify for jobs that aliens cannot get. There will be many more such jobs in the future and for many of them we will doubtless have the foreign-born workers themselves—and their paychecks—to thank.

Periodical Bibliography

The following articles have been selected to supplement the diverse views presented in this chapter.

Derrick Bell	"The Freedom of Employment Act," *The Nation*, May 23, 1994.
Marc Breslow	"The Racial Divide Widens: Why African-American Workers Have Lost Ground," *Dollars & Sense*, January/February 1995.
Peter Brimelow and Leslie Spencer	"When Quotas Replace Merit, Everybody Suffers," *Forbes*, February 15, 1993.
Sara Diamond	"Blaming the Newcomers," *Z Magazine*, July/August 1992.
Brian Dumaine	"Blacks on Blacks," *Fortune*, November 2, 1992.
Leonce Gaiter	"The Revolt of the Black Bourgeoisie," *The New York Times Magazine*, June 26, 1994.
Andrew Hacker	"The Myths of Racial Division," *The New Republic*, March 23, 1992.
Darrell Y. Hamamoto	"Black-Korean Conflict in Los Angeles," *Z Magazine*, July/August 1992.
Reed Irvine and Joseph C. Goulden	"The 'Blame Whitey' Media," *USA Today*, January 1994.
Alex Kotlowitz and Suzanne Alexander	"Tacit Code of Silence on Matters of Race Perpetuates Divisions," *The Wall Street Journal*, May 28, 1992.
Seymour Martin Lipset	"The Politics of Race," *Current*, June 1992.
Toni Morrison	"On the Backs of Blacks," *Time*, Fall 1993.
Scholastic Update	"Sociology: Culture Clash," March 20, 1992.
Thomas Sowell	"Middleman Minorities," *The American Enterprise*, May/June 1993.
Paul Starr	"Civil Reconstruction: What to Do Without Affirmative Action," *The American Prospect*, Winter 1992.
Richard Vedder and Lowell Gallaway	"Declining Black Employment," *Society*, July/August 1993.
Elizabeth Wright	"Black Men: They Could Be Heroes," *Issues & Views*, Summer/Fall 1993. Available from PO Box 467, New York, NY 10025.

Is America's Justice System Biased?

Chapter Preface

In April 1992 in Los Angeles, California, four white police officers who had been videotaped beating black motorist Rodney King were acquitted of using excessive force by a jury with no black members. In November 1992 in New York City, a black teenager on trial for stabbing and killing a Jewish man during the 1991 Crown Heights riot, having been identified by the dying victim, was acquitted by a jury that included no whites. These verdicts are among many in recent years that have proven controversial for the seeming reluctance of jurors to convict those of their own race. A few legal theorists have proposed racially balanced juries as a remedy to such racial voting by juries.

Some lawyers and legal experts consider racially balanced juries necessary for achieving fair verdicts, especially in racially charged criminal cases. A jury that contains representatives of different races is more likely to render a fair verdict, believes Peter Arenella, a criminal law professor at the University of California, Los Angeles, because members of different racial groups perceive the fairness of the criminal justice system differently. "We live in a racist society, and people experience different social worlds as a result of race," states Arenella. "Certainly, [jurors'] race, as well as their class, will affect their judgment."

Other legal experts discount the need for racially balanced juries, expressing doubt that the race of jurors is a determining factor in their ability to render an impartial verdict. Alexander H. Williams III, a Los Angeles Superior Court judge, maintains, "People are not knee-jerk voters in the jury room on the basis of their color." Williams and others feel that if a jury represents a cross-section of the community it is drawn from—a standard the Supreme Court has long upheld—even if it is all-white or all-black, the verdict it renders will be fair.

Verdicts in racially charged legal cases, such as the ones in Los Angeles and New York, become controversial when there is a perceived pattern of racial voting. The viewpoints in the following chapter present differing views on the necessity of racially balanced juries and differing perceptions of fairness in America's justice system.

"Because of racism in the criminal justice system, Blacks are more likely to be arrested, convicted, and given stiffer sentences."

America's Justice System Discriminates Against Blacks

Gerald Horne

African Americans constitute a disproportionate share of the American prison population. In the following viewpoint, Gerald Horne argues that this is a legacy of the system of slavery and a result of racism. He contends that despite a decrease in crime, young black men are stereotyped as criminals, are imprisoned and punished harshly, and are feared and discriminated against. Horne is the author of *Reversing Discrimination: The Case for Affirmative Action*.

As you read, consider the following questions:

1. According to Horne, what percentage of young black men are incarcerated, on probation or parole, or under indictment?
2. According to the Bureau of Justice statistics cited by the author, by what percentages did personal and household crimes fall between 1973 and 1990?
3. How much did imprisonments increase between 1980 and 1990, according to statistics cited by Horne?

Excerpted from "On the Criminalization of a Race" by Gerald Horne, *Political Affairs*, February 1994. Reprinted with permission.

It is useful to recall that the settling of North America by Britain was not as idyllic as many have been led to believe. As in the case of Australia, it began as a dumping ground for convicts and not just religious dissenters. This was particularly true of the state of Georgia and to a greater or lesser extent for most of the original colonies. Though Australia continued on this infamous path for some time to come, in colonial North America, the labor of convicts was supplemented, then supplanted, by that of African slaves.

Slavery itself was an atrocious form of imprisonment. But, according to Charshee C.L. McIntyre in her arresting book *Criminalizing a Race: Free Blacks During Slavery*, the newly independent government saw no other use for non-slave Blacks except imprisonment and, to an extent, the animus that motivated that policy continues to persist to this very day.

Consider the demographics in the prison population of the antebellum U.S., cited by McIntyre:

> The statistics for 1790 reveal Blacks representing about 44 percent of the male and 75 percent of the female inmate population in major northern (New York, Pennsylvania, Massachusetts, and New Jersey) penitentiaries. Incredibly, in the year 1820 in Virginia, Blacks comprised 100 percent of the female inmate population. In other words, according to the records that year in Virginia, no white women committed prisonable crimes.

These figures are even more stunning when one considers the relatively small percentage of the population constituted by non-slave Blacks in the North.

From Slavery to Chain-Gangs

After slavery the sight of African Americans in chain-gangs became part of the landscape of the deep South, as the authorities sought to force former chattel into another form of bondage. The convict-lease system was used by plantation owners and entrepreneurs, who "rented" the imprisoned for their own profit-making ventures. "Debt peonage" was utilized to maintain the formerly enslaved in a disguised form of slavery. Black sharecroppers were cheated constantly by plantation owners and if they sought to flee, were imprisoned and, at times, "leased" to that very same owner.

In 1994 it appears that a trend first marked two hundred years ago continues to persist stubbornly. New York Governor Mario Cuomo, who is often praised for his soaring rhetoric about the "family of New York," also brags incessantly about the prison construction binge that has characterized his reign. Strikingly, in many of these prisons upwards of 75 percent of the inmates are either Black or Latino (the latter hailing predominantly from

Puerto Rico and the Dominican Republic). Most formerly resided in a few neighborhoods in the Bronx, Brooklyn and Manhattan.

Though the title of Nils Christie's *Crime Control as Industry: Towards Gulags, Western Style?* seeks to associate this nagging aspect of capitalism with the former Soviet Union, his evidence overwhelmingly indicts a system of production based wholly on profit as the culprit that produces such horribly racist results.

Imprisonment of African Americans

The figures he presents are staggering. Though African Americans are little more than 12 percent of the population, they constitute half of the inmate population nationally. Half a million Black males are now in prison or jail, according to Christie:

> This means that 3,400 per 100,000—or 3.4 percent—of the male Black population are in prison just now. How extreme this is, internationally, can be seen when it is compared with South Africa, where 681 per 100,000 Black males—or 0.7 percent—are incarcerated. With 3.4 percent in prison, one and a half times as many are probably on probation or parole, which means that between 7 and 8 percent of Black males are under some sort of legal constraint.

There is an aspect of age discrimination embedded in this race and gender bigotry, for overwhelmingly it is younger African Americans who run afoul of the criminal justice system. By some estimates, approximately one in four Black males in their twenties and younger are either incarcerated, on probation, on parole, or under indictment.

Needless to say, those areas of the nation with heavily Black populations have astounding rates of imprisonment. Washington, D.C., where Blacks comprise about 70 percent of the population, "leads the nation with the unbelievable figure of 1,168 prisoners sentenced to one year or more per 100,000 resident population," states Christie. Of the top five states heading this dubious category, four are either in the deep South or border states with relatively high African American populations.

Increasingly, the nature of imprisonment is becoming ever more fiendish and diabolical. Pelican Bay prison in California is seen by some as the prison of the future. It is entirely automated and designed so that inmates have virtually no face-to-face contact with guards or other inmates. For 22.5 hours a day, inmates are confined to their windowless cells built of solid blocks of concrete and stainless steel so that they won't have access to materials with which to fashion weapons. Prisoners shower alone and exercise alone. Cell doors are opened and closed electronically by a guard in a control booth. Similar prisons are in place in Florida and Oklahoma—they are becoming quite the rage from coast to coast. With this form of imprisonment, the idea of rehabilitation—paid mere lip service in the best of times—has been tossed aside. Now the idea is revenge. . . .

A Crime Wave?

It would be simple to surmise that fear of a "crime wave" has motivated such draconian punishments; however, such a notion is mistaken. Bureau of Justice figures indicate that rates of victimization continue a downward trend that began in the early 1980s. There were approximately 34.4 million personal and household crimes in 1990, compared with 41.4 million in 1981. From 1973 to 1990 the rate of personal crimes (rape, robbery, assault, personal theft) fell by 24.5 percent and the rate for household crimes (burglary, household theft, motor vehicle theft) fell by 26.1 percent. The number of serious offenses reported to the police also shows a slight decrease. The FBI statistics on serious offenses started at 5.1 million in 1980 and ended at 4.8 million in 1989—as the overall population continued to increase.

Blacks and Imprisonment

Blacks make up 12 percent of America's population but make up an increasing share of prison admissions with nearly one-fourth of black men between the ages of twenty and twenty-nine in jail, on parole, or on probation.

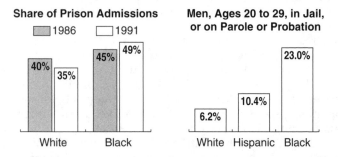

Source: Federal Bureau of Investigation, The Sentencing Project, Department of Justice, National Center on Institutions and Alternatives.

Yet the severity of punishment for these crimes has increased. In 1980, 196 offenders were sentenced to prison for every 1,000 arrests for serious crimes. In 1990 the number of imprisonments for such crimes had increased to 332, according to Bureau of Justice figures. In other words, severity of sentences and the rate of imprisonment are going up as the number of crimes goes down—with an increasing percentage of those imprisoned being of African descent.

Why? It is obvious that racism is not a negligible factor in explicating this process. When *Business Week* devoted their December 13, 1993, cover story to "The Economics of Crime," a major focus was "Blacks and Crime." With every passing day it seems that the face of the criminal is the face of the Black—or at least that is the image the mainstream news media conveys. "Reality" TV shows like *COPS* often feature live shots of police breaking down doors in urban areas with cameras broadcasting these images into living rooms across the nation; all too many of those roused out of bed are Black.

In New York City, fear of "Black crime" often causes taxi drivers to avoid picking up African Americans or causes stores to refuse to admit Black customers. When queried, those responsible justify their action by pointing to statistics allegedly showing a disproportionate number of robberies committed by African Americans. Often this form of discrimination by statistical reasoning or collective punishment is justified by the bourgeois press (this is the same bourgeois press that rails at the idea of using statistical reasoning to show underemployment of Blacks as a basis for affirmative action!).

However, if one were to suggest not to employ an Italian American contractor because allegedly this ethnic group is disproportionately found in the ranks of organized crime, justifiably the accusation of bigotry would be hurled. Yet, some of the same people who easily detect bigotry when non-Blacks are involved, are not as sensitive when Blacks are at issue. Understandably, this is viewed by African Americans and their allies as a form of racism.

The fact is that because of racism in the criminal justice system, Blacks are more likely to be arrested, convicted, and given stiffer sentences. This end result, their overrepresentation in prisons, is considered a basis for averring that Blacks are prone to crime. Clearly this ignores the fact that the racism in the system leads to their incarceration in the first place.

"Race is only weakly related to whether a defendant is arrested, convicted, prosecuted, or sentenced severely."

America's Justice System Does Not Discriminate Against Blacks

Patrick A. Langan

Polls show that African Americans, perceiving disparities between conviction and imprisonment rates of blacks and others, believe the criminal justice system is biased against them. In the following viewpoint, Patrick A. Langan cites a study that shows no significant disparities between the rates of prosecution and conviction of blacks and whites. Although the study found that more blacks than whites were sentenced to prison, Langan argues that this disproportion is attributable to factors other than race. Langan is senior statistician at the U.S. Department of Justice's Bureau of Justice Statistics.

As you read, consider the following questions:

1. According to Langan, since what year has America's criminal justice system not shown a bias against blacks?
2. According to the statistics Langan cites, by what percentage are blacks convicted of crimes less often than whites?
3. What three legitimate factors, according to the author, explain the difference in sentencing between blacks and whites?

Patrick A. Langan, "No Racism in the Justice System." Reprinted with permission of the author and *The Public Interest*, No. 117 (Fall 1994), pp. 48-51, ©1994 by National Affairs, Inc.

Whether or not America's criminal justice system is biased against blacks today, it clearly was in the past. Between 1930 and 1964, for example, six southern jurisdictions—Louisiana, Mississippi, Oklahoma, Virginia, West Virginia, and the District of Columbia—put to death 67 men for the crime of rape. Not one of the 67 was white. All were black. Is it conceivable that not a single white man committed rape in any of these places? Over a thirty-five-year period? Surely not.

The bulk of the evidence amassed since then on justice system bias is far less conclusive. Plenty of studies exist showing no bias in arrest, prosecution, adjudication, and sentencing. While plenty also exist that show possible evidence of bias, the general consensus among criminologists is that the evidence is not strong.

Race in the Justice System

Compared to legitimate factors affecting decisions, such as the defendant's prior record or the seriousness of the offense, race is only weakly related to whether a defendant is arrested, convicted, prosecuted, or sentenced severely. Moreover, criminologists are divided over how to interpret the weak relationship. Some believe it proves the existence of a lingering, small amount of bias in the justice system, while others are not satisfied that the studies rule out the alternative explanation: when blacks and whites are treated differently it is because the races differ on legal factors that legitimately influence the decisions of justice system officials.

Racial bias studies never completely take into account all of the legitimate factors that determine how a case is handled. Consequently, these unmeasured factors might explain a racial disparity if the factors are ones on which the races differ. Given the small disparity in the first place, such unmeasured factors become potentially important.

Existing racial bias studies share another limitation. They do not tell us how all or even most black defendants in the United States are handled at each of the major stages of the justice system. Instead, they tell us how blacks are treated at a single stage, or in one jurisdiction, or for particular offenses.

Surveying Prosecution, Adjudication, and Sentencing

That limitation is not present in new data from a 1993 survey sponsored by the Justice Department's Bureau of Justice Statistics. For one year, the survey tracked samples of adult felony defendants as their individual cases proceeded across major criminal justice stages, from the filing of state court charges in May 1990, through prosecution, to adjudication, and finally to sentencing. (The survey is based on a sample of 10,226 defendants [out of] 42,538 defendants in the nation's 75 largest counties.)

Felony charges of all kinds were included—murder, rape, robbery, burglary, theft, drug trafficking, etc. However, what makes the survey especially relevant to black Americans is the places from which defendants were sampled.

There are over three thousand counties in the nation, but to learn how the U.S. justice system treats most black defendants, we need examine only the 75 most populous urban jurisdictions. The 75 are where most black Americans live (59 percent compared to 33 percent of whites). They are also where blacks have the majority of their contact with the criminal justice system as criminal defendants. In 1990, for example, 62 percent of black arrests for violent crime and 67 percent for drug trafficking occurred there.

The Justice System's Treatment of Blacks

	Blacks	Whites
Percentage of defendants *prosecuted* after being charged with a felony:	66%	69%
Percentage of defendants *convicted* after prosecution:	75%	78%
Percentage of convicted defendants *sentenced* to prison:	51%	38%

Pheny Z. Smith, *Felony Defendants in Large Urban Counties, 1990*, Washington, DC: Bureau of Justice Statistics, 1993.

By design, felony defendants in the Justice Department survey were all from the 75 largest counties. The survey, therefore, gives us a close look at the justice system's treatment of blacks in the places where most of their contacts with the justice system occur. Such information has never before existed.

Here is what the survey reveals, first about whether blacks were prosecuted more vigorously than whites; second, about whether they were convicted more often; and third, about whether they were sentenced more harshly.

Prosecution. Following the filing of felony court charges, 66 percent of black defendants were subsequently prosecuted (the rest were dismissed). Yet that is slightly *less*, not more, than the 69 percent of whites. Looked at another way, at the stage where felony court charges were filed, black defendants comprised 53 percent of all defendants, but they comprised 51 percent of those actually prosecuted.

Adjudication. Among blacks prosecuted in urban America's

courts during the study period, 75 percent were subsequently convicted of a felony offense. Again, this figure is slightly *less*, not more, than the 78 percent of whites. Despite the small difference, blacks comprised 51 percent of those prosecuted and also 51 percent of those convicted of a felony.

Racism in Sentencing?

Sentencing. Results at the sentencing stage are mixed. On the one hand, the average state prison sentence received by blacks convicted of a felony was five and one-half years. That is one month longer than what whites received, a small difference not of statistical significance.

On the other hand, among black defendants convicted of a felony, 51 percent received a prison sentence, substantially more than the 38 percent of whites. As a result, the racial mix changed from adjudication to sentencing, with black defendants comprising 51 percent of those convicted of a felony but 58 percent of those sentenced to state prisons.

Curiously, prosecutors did not prosecute black defendants at a higher rate than whites, courts did not convict black defendants at a higher rate than whites, and judges did not give longer prison sentences to convicted blacks than whites, yet judges sent to prison relatively more convicted blacks than whites. However, before concluding that judges are biased, we should check whether the different sentences may have been justified by racial differences in legal factors that judges legitimately take into consideration when deciding on a sentence.

First is whether more black defendants were convicted of any of the violent crimes, since judges imprison violent offenders at the highest rate. The answer is yes. Ten percent of blacks had robbery as their conviction offense versus 5 percent of whites. Moreover, blacks least often had as their conviction offense one of the least severely punished crimes, a public-order offense (18 percent of blacks versus 24 percent of whites), which include possession of stolen property, repeatedly driving without a license, and possession of a concealed weapon.

Next is whether more black defendants were repeat offenders, since judges sentence repeat offenders more harshly than first-timers. Again, the answer is yes. Fifty percent of convicted black defendants had one or more prior felony convictions versus 38 percent of whites.

Jurisdictions with Tougher Sentencing

Another question—one that frequently arises in racial bias studies that combine or "aggregate" samples from different states and different counties—is whether black defendants were more heavily represented in jurisdictions where sentences were possibly tougher, not just for blacks, but for whites as well. If so, combining the jurisdictions would create the appearance of a sentencing disparity even when no disparity actually exists. Because America's races are scattered differently across jurisdictions, and jurisdictions sentence differently from one another, aggregating has an effect that is easily mistaken for racially disparate sentencing.

A simple check confirmed the presence of an aggregation effect. Jurisdictions with above-average imprisonment rates for convicted *whites* were identified, and the concentration of the different races in them was then compared. One in five convicted whites, but one in three convicted blacks, were in these tough-sentencing jurisdictions.

Blacks were convicted of more serious offenses, had longer criminal records, and were convicted in places that generally meted out more prison sentences. These three differences explain why 51 percent of convicted blacks but only 38 percent of convicted whites were sent to prison.

The Justice Department survey provides no evidence that, in the places where blacks in the United States have most of their contacts with the justice system, the system treats them more harshly than whites. Yet, black Americans widely perceive bias. Asked in a 1993 survey, "Do you think the American criminal justice system is biased against black people?" two-thirds of blacks polled said yes.

John DiIulio argues that black Americans have the most to gain from his call for vastly more cops on inner-city streets and tougher courts to lock up inner-city criminals. He is right to be pessimistic about prospects that his reforms will be adopted. Whether or not the justice system is biased against them, black Americans widely perceive that it is. So long as they do, we can hardly be surprised if they fail to embrace justice system solutions to some of their enduring problems.

===

*"Just being black and being there automatically
constitute grounds for frontier justice."*

===

Racism Against Blacks Taints America's Justice System

Wanda Coleman

The 1991 shooting of black teenager Latasha Harlins by Korean
store owner Soon Ja Du, occurring within months of the beating
of Rodney King by Los Angeles police officers, contributed to the
tensions which precipitated the Los Angeles riots of 1992. In the
following viewpoint, Wanda Coleman contends that Harlins's
shooting was perceived by blacks in Los Angeles as yet another
example of how black victims of crime receive less attention
than victims of other races. She argues that racism toward blacks
in American society and in the justice system has allowed many
black children to be killed while their killers go unpunished.
Coleman is a poet, writer, and author of *Hand Dance*.

As you read, consider the following questions:

1. How does the author describe the events leading to the
   shooting of Harlins?
2. What expectations lead to misunderstanding between blacks
   and immigrants, according to Coleman?
3. What was the effect of the King verdict, in Coleman's words?

Excerpted from "Blacks, Immigrants, and America," *The Nation*, February 15, 1993.
Reprinted by permission from *The Nation* magazine; © The Nation Company, L.P.

I am terrorized by the murder of a child. Intermittently, dramatic images of her death unreel. Two years hence, I'm still enraged, upset, unable to sleep. I'm haunted by her murder and by the thousands of murders of black youths since 1955, when a brutally bludgeoned Emmett Till [a black youth who was killed for whistling at a white woman] rose from the autumn waters of Mississippi's Tallahatchie River. Each afternoon, as I wait for my fourteen-year-old son to return from school, I pray. I'm not a religious woman. But when I hear him coming through that door, I'm overjoyed. How long, I wonder, will America allow him to live?

It allowed Latasha Harlins barely fifteen years. In March and April 1991, a year before South Central Los Angeles erupted, local residents repeatedly witnessed news broadcasts of the videotaped Empire Liquor Market killing of fifteen-year-old Latasha Harlins by fifty-one-year-old Soon Ja Du. Central to black-Korean tensions that fueled the 1992 riots, this incident was scarcely a footnote in national media coverage of the riots.

The Shooting of Latasha Harlins

The video, filmed by an in-store camera, was painfully graphic: We saw Latasha approach Du, alone behind the counter, with money in her hand. We watched Du accuse her of stealing a $1.79 bottle of orange juice. We saw Latasha turn to show Du the juice in her knapsack, then wave the $2. There was a heated verbal exchange, and Latasha threw the orange juice down on the counter. We watched the angry Du grab for Latasha's pack, then catch the flap of her jacket. We saw Latasha slap the shit out of Du, who immediately let go. We saw Latasha turn and walk away. We watched Du fumble for the .38 caliber, firing once. We saw Latasha pitch forward and drop to the floor as the bullet struck the back of her head. . . .

Initial newspaper accounts of the incident were careful to describe Latasha as "studious and self-assured." But the slant of so-called objective coverage betrayed tacit sympathy for Du. She had lived every bigot's fantasy. She had shot *one of them*.

The fear that motivated Soon Ja Du was couched in statistics designed to justify her killing of Latasha: "In the surrounding 32 blocks, 936 felonies reported last year . . . 5 murders . . . 9 rapes . . . 184 robberies and 254 assaults." The fact that Du's son was the victim in one of those assaults was subtly emphasized. The nasties of ghetto life were responsible, not the "feeble and overwhelmed" grocer forced to work fourteen-hour days, at the mercy of shoplifters, street hoodlums and chronic migraines, and certainly not white society.

Incredibly, in one article Crystal Harlins, Latasha's mother, dead six years, was retroactively indicted, because of her "boisterous behavior," for Latasha's death and for her own during an argument at an after-hours bar. The chilling implication? Like mother, like daughter.

Other Black Children Shot

This troublesome reportage was eerily reminiscent of the open support expressed by whites for acquitted New York City subway vigilante Bernhard Goetz, who gunned down four black youths in 1984 because he thought they *might* attack. The Goetz case is a notorious demonstration of white loathing of anyone big and black. To parents like me, it was clear that open war had been declared against our children.

Black Anger over Crime Victimization

The acquittal of four white Los Angeles police officers in the beating of black motorist Rodney King is incomprehensible and frightening. The wanton violence and destruction in Los Angeles following the verdict are inexcusable. But one can understand the rage that has fueled the rampage without condoning the rioting itself. Today, much as in the 1960s, it is vital that we as a nation resolve to eliminate the causes of these explosions of anger. . . .

One aspect of black experience that white Americans tend to appreciate only imperfectly involves the uneasy terms on which so many millions of black Americans exist with the forces of official authority. . . .

One particularly difficult aspect of that uneasiness is the fear of unfairness in the criminal justice system, whether one is the victim or the accused. Study after study has confirmed that sentences for identical offenses tend to be more lenient when the victim happens to be black. Consequently black Americans, who stand a far greater chance than white Americans of being victims, are underprotected by the system.

Stephen L. Carter, *The Wall Street Journal*, May 1, 1992.

In underreporting these incidents (Michael Donald, beaten and strangled by Klansmen in Mobile, Alabama; Melvin Eugene Hair, asphyxiated by chokehold during an altercation with Tampa, Florida, police; Loyal Garner Jr., who was beaten and died while in police custody in Hemphill, Texas), the media serve themselves and society by ignoring, distorting and/or understating acts of violence against blacks, as in the November 1992 Bay Area slaying of Jerrold Hall. Hall, nineteen, was killed by a transit cop's shotgun blast to the back of his head. He was "under suspicion" for stealing a Walkman. Fred Crabtree, the white officer involved, was a seventeen-year veteran. The only detailed account of this fantastic tragedy was reported by Tim Redmond in the *San Francisco Bay Guardian*. No mainstream California newspaper has, as of this writing, touched the Hall story, nor has it hit the international wire services.

Like Harlins's, Hall's story initially appeared in a tiny column barely two paragraphs long. The Hall case received the similar treatment of guilt by insinuation. Blame/responsibility for the incident is placed on the victim (as with Emmett Till, for whistling and looking). She or he had to be doing *something*. This "doing" justifies any violent means or ends. Just being black and being there automatically constitute grounds for frontier justice. The victim, in effect, becomes the victimizer. And all the news that was news was told.

Redmond surmises that Hall's story is being deliberately ignored for fear it may cause blacks to riot. Five days before L.A. burned, a young white male asked me if blacks would riot should Laurence Powell, Stacey Koon, Timothy Wind and Theodore Briseno [defendants in the Rodney King beating trial] walk. I hesitated, thought of Harlins, then stammered that *we* probably wouldn't but that I wished we would. "Will y'all riot?" was the tiresome question posed after every incident involving blacks, from Jonestown to the death of Harold Washington. The smug implication was that blacks were so impotent, all we could do was tear up our own surroundings. It angers me that the assumption is stingingly correct.

Furthermore, I contend that if such lynchings received even minimally fair media coverage, we would witness a numbing tableau of violence and bloodshed. Our national psyche, always in denial about race, would collapse under the onslaught. By relegating stories like Hall's to the back-page boonies, the media help to perpetuate the illusion of a "kinder, gentler America." Loudly voiced community outrage is necessary to dispel this illusion, and to command the media's attention.

The Protest over the Shooting

Local protests over the Harlins shooting were swift and raucous, the culmination of complaints by black community leaders about "the Korean invasion" and lack of dialogue between the two groups. For nearly a decade the local media, alternative and mainstream, had refused to investigate the problem initially brought to their attention by a handful of concerned black writers, including myself.

During that period, I had had three especially infuriating run-ins with Korean merchants. One was a fight at a hamburger stand, when the Koreans across the counter refused to accept my newly minted $20 bill. They'd been burned before, and they thought the bill was bogus. I was guilty of the crime someone else, also black, had committed. Using my own stubby fuse and lofty blood pressure as a gauge seemed unfair. But when even my demure sixty-year-old mother complained of abuse by "some Koreans because I'm black," I saw that violence was inevitable in my community.

Black protest over the Harlins-Du incident increased, but was unexpectedly dissipated when attorney Charles Lloyd was hired for Du's defense. Lloyd is black. As with the Anita Hill versus Clarence Thomas fiasco, many were reluctant to go against one of our own. A "wait and see" attitude was adopted toward the previously hotly disputed case. When Soon Ja Du's bail was set at $250,000 and her release made imminent, the courtroom, crowded with Korean-Americans, broke into applause. The black community was virtually silent. It would remain so until after the verdict in the Rodney King beating trial. . . .

Tension Between Blacks and Immigrants

In his October 1992 *Atlantic* article "Blacks vs. Browns," Jack Miles sidesteps black-Korean conflicts to trace black-Latino clashes underscoring "Watts II" [the repeat of the 1965 riots in the Watts neighborhood of Los Angeles]. (A June 1983 issue of *Time* estimated that 90 percent of illegals come from Mexico. The 1986 Census Bureau reported a 16 percent increase in America's Latino population since 1981, making one out of four-teen Americans Latino.) Miles observes that Latinos, even when foreign, seem native and safe while blacks, who are native, seem foreign and dangerous. Miles implies that blacks are so "nihilis-tic, so utterly alienated" that white Americans cannot "make a connection" with us. It's "just easier with the Mexicans." But the point is that the prejudice of white America has promoted the very attitude among blacks that whites like Miles find so discom-forting. No matter how many immigrants white America puts between itself and blacks, this national dilemma will persist.

Furthermore, as a price of entry, the majority of immigrants buy into the lie of American apartheid: Black people are inferior. To fail to accept this tenet of American life is to jeopardize what is already a tenuous existence for the newly arrived. When mer-chants like Soon Ja Du mimic whites' fear of blacks, their behav-ior is condoned, if not rewarded, by our society. Alliances be-tween blacks and immigrants are troubled because the two groups profoundly misunderstand each other: While the immi-grant populations (Koreans, Latinos, et al.) expect rational behav-ior from blacks driven mad by poverty and racism, blacks expect immigrants to empathize with our plight the minute they set foot on our turf—when too many of us don't grasp it ourselves. Newly arrived immigrants often do not understand that what may be in-terpreted as a mere inconvenience or slight by whites may be in-terpreted as disrespectful, even life-threatening, by blacks. "Objectivity" is impossible because racism prevents it. . . .

Why the Violence?

Why violence after the verdict in the King beating case, and not after the verdict in the Harlins case? Was it because Soon Ja Du was represented by Lloyd, a skilled black professional adept at squelching any mischaracterizations of himself as Uncle Tom or traitor to his race? Or was it, perhaps, because the racism that operated in the Harlins case was considerably less apparent?

The videotape of the King beating received instant national and international distribution, while circulation of the Harlins video was largely local. The whopping of a black man by racist whites went straight to the core of black experience. Our abuse at the hands of vigilantes, law enforcement and the criminal justice system runs generations deep. For the first time, irrevocably we thought, the white man was caught dead-to-rights—by his own technology and media. Any fool could *see*. But no one, outside the savvy few, anticipated the blow the Simi Valley jury would deliver [when they acquitted the defendants in the Rodney King beating trial].

Our very eyes had lied. Not our eyes alone—those of the nation, the world. Whites who couldn't embrace blacks could embrace their own ideal; could recognize the failure of an institution they believed in: benevolent American democracy, grounded in the Constitution. The King verdict angered and disillusioned *all* subscribers to this faith because it rendered American justice the figment of a collective imagination, black and white. . . .

In November 1991 Soon Ja Du was convicted of voluntary manslaughter. Judge Joyce Karlin sentenced Du to 400 hours of community service, a $500 fine, reimbursement of funeral costs to the Harlins family and five years' probation. A stunned black community's campaign to oust Karlin from office followed but failed. Karlin was overwhelmingly re-elected by the majority of Southern California voters, mostly white. Ironically, her victory came with the June 1992 municipal elections, in the wake of the South Central uprising, the largest civic unrest in the history of the United States. The resounding message to black America was emphatic: The lives of your children are less than the lives of ours. Under the circumstances of race prejudice, material things—a bottle of orange juice or a Walkman—are worth the same as a black child's life. You are under suspicion at birth, you are born guilty. And sooner or later, you will pay for the crime.

"The anti-Korean aspect of the riots was the culmination of years of escalating violence against Koreans."

Racism Against Blacks Does Not Taint America's Justice System

William F. Jasper

The sentencing of Korean American grocer Soon Ja Du to five years' probation in the 1991 shooting of black teenager Latasha Harlins led to protests by black community leaders of Los Angeles, who felt she should have been sentenced to prison. In the following viewpoint, William F. Jasper argues that the facts of the case justify the light sentence given to Du. The sensationalizing of the case by the media, he contends, exacerbated anti-Korean bias in Los Angeles and contributed to the attacks on Korean businesses during the 1992 riots. Jasper is senior editor of the *New American*, a conservative biweekly.

As you read, consider the following questions:

1. According to K.W. Lee, cited by the author, how have Korean Americans been characterized?
2. How did the court, quoted by Jasper, describe the events of Harlins's death?
3. According to Jasper, how did the media portray the shooting?

William F. Jasper, "Victims of Hate," *The New American*, June 29, 1992. Reprinted with permission.

In the arson, looting, and destruction that accompanied the 1992 rioting in Los Angeles, business people of all colors were victimized. But there is no question that Korean-American merchants bore a disproportionate share of the damage. According to statistics compiled by Radio Korea in Los Angeles, nearly 1,900 Korean-American businesses were looted or burned, with losses totaling almost $350 million.

K.W. Lee, editor of the Los Angeles–based *Korea Times*, lays much of the blame for this destruction and the rising black-on-Korean violence on the news media. "The mainstream media's ignorance and sensationalism in black-Korean coverage," says Lee, "has had a life-threatening impact on many fearful Koreans, contributing to the Lebanonization of the City of Angels, polarizing the two misunderstood groups, rather than healing and calming tensions."

Racist Stereotyping

Korean-Americans, says Lee, have been unfairly cast as villains in a campaign of racist stereotyping. "Ironically," wrote Lee in an angry May 4, 1992, editorial, "it is a growing number of African-American opinion leaders . . . who voice this new form of racism in symbiotic alliance with the guilt-ridden white media. In their selective outrage, these so-called leaders have chosen to ignore the fact that killings, robberies, fire bombings, burglaries, gang terror, shopliftings, and racial threats afflict these frightened merchants routinely."

Benedict B. Yim, an attorney who represents Korean business groups, says that Korean-Americans are "being falsely portrayed as exploiters of the black community." Korean-American merchants "didn't go into south central Los Angeles to exploit black people," Yim told *The New American*. "They went there because that was the cheapest area where they could afford to set up business." Far from being exploiters, says Yim, "they risk their life savings and their lives and work long hours providing goods and services that no one else is providing" to many of these high-crime, inner-city areas. Indeed, unless many of these Korean-American merchants rebuild, many black and Hispanic communities will be without vital services for a long time.

The anti-Korean aspect of the riots was the culmination of years of escalating violence against Koreans. Eui-Young Yu, professor of sociology at California State University, Los Angeles, noted in June 1992 that "since January 1, 1990, at least 25 Korean-American merchants have been killed by non-Korean gunmen."

This background, together with the mob violence and lack of police protection during the three days of rioting, led many Korean-American merchants to arm themselves to protect their lives and property. Even that was misrepresented. "On TV screens the scenes of armed Koreans defending their property were shown again and again," wrote Professor Yu in a commentary for the *Los Angeles Times*. "Some of them were seen aiming at would-be attackers. The attacking mobs were not shown. Why? The defenders were portrayed by the mainstream media, particularly KABC [the ABC network affiliate in Los Angeles], as gun-toting hoodlums. They just wanted to scare away the mobs."

The belief that they are being victimized by criminals, activists, politicians, and the media is a charge that has been made repeatedly by Korean-Americans throughout the charred, riot-torn areas of Los Angeles. One doesn't have to look far to see that they have a valid point. There have been several highly charged black-Korean incidents, but by far the most explosive, and the one that continues to give rise to heated passions, is the Latasha Harlins/Soon Ja Du case.

Sensationalized Tragedy

On April 30, 1992, the day after the King verdict [acquitting the four Los Angeles police officers accused in the beating of Rodney King] was handed down, the *Los Angeles Times* compared the Simi Valley jury's rendering "with that of a Korean-born grocer [Mrs. Soon Ja Du] who recently was granted probation after being convicted in the shooting of a fifteen-year-old black girl she had accused of attempting to steal a bottle of orange juice." Similarly, *Washington Post* writer David Mills referred to Mrs. Du's shooting of "teenager Latasha Harlins in a dispute over a bottle of orange juice." Over and over again that line has appeared in countless printed and broadcast reports: Korean grocer kills black girl over bottle of orange juice. Who wouldn't be outraged over such an egregious injustice?

On the morning of March 16, 1991, one day after the arraignment of four Los Angeles Police Department officers for beating Rodney King, fifteen-year-old Latasha Harlins was shot and killed at the Empire Liquor Market in south central Los Angeles. She was shot by Mrs. Soon Ja Du, who, together with her husband, Billy Du, and son, Joseph Du, owned and operated the market. Miss Harlins was black; Mrs. Du is Korean-American. Those are the bare facts.

Like the Rodney King incident, the Harlins/Du affair was also caught on video—by the store's own video security camera. Like the King video, it was replayed many times on television news programs. Also, like the King video, many of the replays would be edited to show only the dramatic shooting segment, without showing the violence that precipitated it. But, as in the Rodney King case, there is much that the video does not tell—even if the entire, unedited version is shown.

The Dus were experiencing about forty shoplifting incidents a week at the Empire Market. Joseph Du, who usually ran the market, said that often when he would try to stop shoplifters, "they show me their guns." The store had been burglarized over thirty times and robbed twice. Joseph Du testified at his mother's trial that his life had been threatened more than thirty times, and that on more than twenty occasions people had come into the store and threatened to burn it down. The situation, said Joseph, was like "having to conduct business in a war zone."

Koreans Are Targets of Crime

Inner-city retailing, for all its risks, can be profitable. California State University sociologist Eui-Young Yu found in a 1990 survey in Los Angeles that Korean firms that sold to blacks and Hispanics earned more than those catering to other Koreans or whites. Still, the price has been high: In L.A. alone, 12 Korean merchants were killed by thieves between November 1990 and May 1992. Another Korean was killed and about 1,600 Korean stores were burned or ransacked in the L.A. riots. Some stricken shop owners say they will now return to Korea, as some 7,000 Korean-Americans did in 1991 [the year before the riots]. Racial conflict is a major reason.

Emily MacFarquhar, *U.S. News & World Report*, May 18, 1992.

In December 1990, Joseph Du was robbed while working at the store. He incurred the wrath of local gang members when he agreed to testify against one of the gangsters whom he identified as the robber. He testified at his mother's trial that on December 19, 1990, ten to fourteen black persons entered the store, threatened him, and robbed him again. Because of the escalating threats of violence and the increasing incidence of attacks on Korean merchants in the Los Angeles area, the Du family closed the store for two weeks while they tried to come up with some plan to placate the gangsters.

Fatal Visit

The store had only recently reopened when the shooting occurred. Since Joseph was a gang target, his mother, Soon Ja, had traded places with him and he was operating the family's other store in Saugus. Mrs. Du was alone in the store when Latasha Harlins and two other youngsters entered the premises on the fateful day of March 16th.

Quoting from the Second District Court of Appeal's opinion:

Defendant [Soon Ja Du] had observed many shoplifters in the store and it was her experience that people who were shoplifting would take the merchandise, "place it inside the bra or any place the owner would not notice," and then approach the counter, buy some small items and leave.

Defendant saw Latasha enter the store, take a bottle of orange juice from the refrigerator, place it in her backpack and proceed to the counter. . . . Defendant concluded that Latasha was trying to steal the juice. . . .

Defendant began pulling on Latasha's sweater in an attempt to retrieve the orange juice from the backpack. Latasha resisted and the two struggled. Latasha hit the defendant in the eye with her fist twice. With the second blow, defendant fell to the floor behind the counter, taking the backpack with her. . . .

Defendant testified that she thought if she were hit one more time, she would die. Defendant also testified that Latasha threatened to kill her. . . .

After being knocked down by a violent punch to the eye, Mrs. Du grabbed her husband's gun from under the counter. The court decision continued:

As Latasha turned to leave, defendant shot her in the back of the head from approximately three feet, killing her instantly. . . .

At defendant's trial, she testified that she had never held a gun before, did not know how it worked, did not remember firing the gun and did not intend to kill Latasha. Defendant's husband testified that he had purchased the .38-caliber handgun from a friend in 1981 for self-protection. He had never fired the gun, however, and had never taught defendant how to use it.

A ballistics expert testified that the gun had been altered (apparently by a previous owner) and that the trigger pull necessary to fire the gun had been drastically reduced.

Selective Media Coverage

The picture most people got repeatedly from television and their newspapers was of a cold, heartless Korean murdering a little black child. But the tragedy of the incident is vastly compounded by such sensational misrepresentation. A more accurate picture might show a small, frightened fifty-one-year-old immigrant woman from Korea whose family and livelihood were under siege from local thugs. Thievery and robbery had them on the brink of economic ruin. She was on medication for her nerves, which were shot from worry over death threats against her son. In a frightened, confused daze after suffering a violent pummeling, she grabbed a hair-trigger gun (that she had never used before) and pointed it at her attacker (who had just turned away).

First- and second-degree murder charges were rejected. The jury convicted Mrs. Du of voluntary manslaughter. After considering the circumstances, Mrs. Du's background, and the unlikelihood that she would commit any criminal acts, the judge gave her five years of probation.

As in the King case, after reviewing all of the evidence, reasonable people may disagree on the verdict. So far, the media have kept most people from seeing the evidence. On May 11, 1992, the *Los Angeles Times* rehashed the story, leaving out the critical part about the blows struck by Latasha Harlins: "As the fifteen-year-old walked away from the scuffle, the grocer fatally shot her in the back of the head."

Are major organs of the Establishment media trying to promote racial hatred? It certainly looks like it.

"*Race-conscious jury selection procedures may be needed to achieve more diversity than the current antidiscrimination approach allows.*"

Juries Should Be Racially Balanced

Tanya E. Coke

High-profile court cases such as the Rodney King beating trial have focused attention on the racial composition of juries. In the following viewpoint, Tanya E. Coke argues that the Supreme Court's position that jury pools, but not actual juries, need to be racially balanced does not go far enough to promote public confidence in the justice system. Racially balanced juries, in Coke's opinion, are necessary to represent a cross section of the communities' experiences of crime and law enforcement, which can differ between races and classes of people. Ensuring this cross section of experience can produce verdicts that both appear and are fairer, she believes. Coke is editor of the *New York University Law Review*.

As you read, consider the following questions:

1. In Coke's opinion, why should courts tinker with the jury selection process to ensure representative juries?
2. According to studies cited by the author, how does "in-group bias" manifest itself?
3. According to the author, how did some jurors in the King beating trial defend their verdict?

Excerpted from "Lady Justice May Be Blind, but Is She a Soul Sister?" *New York University Law Review*, vol. 69, May 1994. Reprinted by permission.

Conventional wisdom has it that Los Angeles burned in the spring of 1992 because of a damning videotape and a verdict of not guilty. The more precise source of public rage, however, was that the jury which acquitted four white police officers of beating black motorist Rodney King included no African Americans. Public protest following that and other verdicts in recent race-related trials has highlighted again the longstanding disjunction between what Americans popularly conceive as a "jury of peers" and what the legal system actually delivers. Indeed, more than sixty years after the infamous trial of the Scottsboro boys [in which eight black teenagers were convicted of raping two white women by a jury that included no blacks], the all-white jury remains a prominent feature of the American judicial system, even in cases involving cross-racial crimes.

A Jury of Peers

Just what should a "jury of peers" mean in twenty-first century America? The phrase itself never actually appears in our Constitution. The text of the sixth amendment speaks only of an "impartial jury," drawn from residents of the vicinity in which the crime occurred. Most recently in 1990, the Supreme Court reiterated that this language requires only that the pool of *eligible* jurors constitute a "fair cross-section" of the community; there is no constitutional requirement that the *actual* jury hearing a case reflect the racial composition of the district or include members of the defendant's race or gender. Because the Court has held fast to its position that "it would be impossible to apply a concept of proportional representation to the petit jury in view of the heterogeneous nature of our society," the sixth amendment has been little help in seating racial minorities on trial juries. As long as a state's jury list is "reasonably representative" of all cognizable classes in the jury pool, the Court has said, there is no sixth amendment violation if a defendant's actual jury is racially homogeneous or of a single gender.

Defense attorneys have not had much better luck pressing complaints of unrepresentative trial juries under the equal protection clause of the fourteenth amendment. That is because courts have defined the equal protection jury right narrowly as an equal opportunity for all races to *serve*, holding that the fourteenth amendment requires only that non-discriminatory procedures be used in jury selection, not a jury of any particular racial composition. As Albert W. Alschuler wryly noted just before the Rodney King verdict: "If the luck of the draw gives you five successive juries of wealthy Republican women golfers, there's no constitutional problem."

Doctrinal impediments aside, the logistics of securing proportional representation in the present system are themselves daunting. Once local officials summon a pool of eligible citizens for jury duty, known as the venire, lawyers for the parties seat six to twelve individuals, the petit jury, by alternately excluding jurors they deem unsuitable. Lawyers may exclude jurors for legally recognized reasons (challenges "for cause") or intuitive reasons ("peremptory challenges"). Because juries are seated through this process of exclusions, a primary rationale behind the Supreme Court's refusal to mandate "representativeness" has been the practical impossibility of assuring, after exclusions, a petit jury of any particular racial or gender makeup. Indeed, given the doctrinal and practical difficulties of assuring representative panels, why should courts bother tinkering further with an inherently unpredictable process of jury selection?

The state trial verdict in *People v. Powell* [the Rodney King beating trial] and its aftermath provide a partial answer. The rebellion following the acquittal of four police officers in the Rodney King beating is an unusually dramatic but nonetheless familiar example of how non-representative tribunals erode public confidence in the legal system. Even the least controversial interpretation of the conflagration in Los Angeles—that the public believes that all-white juries put minority defendants and victims at a disadvantage—is reason to worry about prevalence of non-representative trial juries. There is, however, an additional and perhaps more important reason for concern: the racial composition of juries implicates the substance, as well as the appearance, of justice. Mixed race juries help to vindicate the defendant's interests in a fair trial and the courts' interest in promoting thorough, unbiased adjudications. . . .

Why Race Matters in Jury Trials

Contrary to the Supreme Court's position in cases like *Powers v. Ohio* and *Georgia v. McCollum* [which prohibited the defense from excluding jurors because of race], race does indeed matter in the delivery of criminal justice. Defendants and the public are right to demand racially diverse juries—not because diversity always affects verdicts, but because it is very likely to enhance the quality of deliberations. Additionally, the judicial system has a legitimate interest in fostering representative juries because many members of the public equate diversity with fairness. The courts' long-term interest in institutional integrity rests on more than a procedurally "fair" system: preserving the *appearance* of fairness is an important ingredient of public confidence and legal justice. This viewpoint discusses reasons why race-conscious jury selection procedures may be needed to achieve more diversity than the current antidiscrimination approach allows.

The Supreme Court's opinions in *Batson v. Kentucky* and

Strauder v. West Virginia [which prohibited prosecutors from excluding jurors because or race] were important because they recognized that a criminal defendant has a legitimate interest in impaneling members of his or her race on the jury. Years of empirical studies of mock and actual juries show that racially mixed panels minimize the distorting risk of bias. This occurs in part because the presence of members of other racial groups suppresses the expression of prejudice.

Integrated juries also affect verdicts because sympathy is often racially selective. Researchers consistently find evidence of this "in-group bias": black and white subjects of studies find defendants of different races more culpable than defendants of their own races, especially when the evidence is not particularly strong and thus open to greater subjective interpretation. White jurors are more likely than blacks to convict black defendants and to acquit defendants charged with crimes against African-American victims. Non-Latinos tend to find defendants guilty at a higher rate than Latinos when the defendant testifies in Spanish. Overall, black jurors tend to acquit more frequently, regardless of the defendant's race.

Social scientific research also supports the conclusion that racially mixed juries adjudicate cases against non-white defendants and victims differently than do all-white tribunals. A 1984 review of jury verdicts in Dade County, Florida, for example, found that juries with at least one African-American juror were less likely than all-white panels to convict black defendants.

Differing Attitudes Toward Crime

Some commentators reject the notion that the racial composition of juries still affects outcomes in the post–civil rights era, even if empirical evidence indicates a strong correlation. Certainly, it would be wrong and dangerous to ascribe juror sympathies based on racial or gender identity alone. The varied class, political, and religious backgrounds of Americans mean that sweeping generalizations about any race's point of view in a given case will frequently be inaccurate. Attitudes toward crime and criminal defendants often differ widely between rural and urban populations and among nationalities and socio-economic classes. In fact, studies suggest that in some instances—particularly in cases where both the victim and the defendant are black—African-American jurors are *more* predisposed than whites to convict. Moreover, as Justice Thurgood Marshall once observed, "members of minority groups frequently respond to discrimination and prejudice by attempting to disassociate themselves from the group, even to the point of adopting the majority's negative attitudes towards the minority."

Nevertheless, viewing race as an always fictional or illegitimate classification ignores the fact that certain experiences are specific to racial identity. Mono-racial juries (like juries of a single gender) will therefore summon only a limited range of social experiences to interpret the facts before them. One can accept this intuitive premise without adhering to essentialist generalizations about the sympathies of jurors of different races. African Americans, Latinos, Asian and Native Americans are not merely citizens "who happen to be" racial minorities, but are members of historically defined communities that more often than not retain a cultural specificity. In some instances, an all-white jury simply may not have access to the language or cultural experiences important to understanding the facts in cases involving minority defendants or witnesses.

Differing Experiences of Law Enforcement

In the trial context, one shared and highly relevant aspect of the lives of many dark-skinned Americans is their experience of discrimination in formal and informal law enforcement settings. While discrimination frequently occurs at the hands of police and security guards, it also occurs when African Americans, Latinos (and in some communities, Native Americans) come into contact with storekeepers, landlords, and cab drivers, who may just as readily deny them entry on the assumption that they are likely to steal or raise hell. Rare is the African American who cannot relate a tale of having been stopped by police in an affluent neighborhood or followed closely at the heels around a clothing store. As one black law professor, Charles Ogletree, put it, "If I'm dressed in a knit cap and hooded jacket, I'm probable cause." One consequence of such treatment is that the attitudes of blacks and whites toward police diverge markedly. A recent study of 800 former jurors reported in the *National Law Journal* found that forty-two percent of whites believed that, given a conflict between a law enforcement officer and a defendant, the police officer should be credited. Only twenty-five percent of African-American jurors interviewed felt that the police officer's testimony should be believed.

To understand that race and culture play a role in jury deliberations does not compel the conclusion that minority jurors are "biased" against law enforcement or in favor of defendants. It may well be the case that in some instances minority jurors have a fuller, more realistic picture of the criminal justice system and its vagaries than do members of the white mainstream. Given their disparate experiences of law enforcement, middle-class white jurors are more inclined than African Americans to believe that police officers always tell the truth, act with integrity, and protect the innocent. . . .

Thus, one fundamental reason why the racial composition of

juries matters, quite apart from the issue of in-group partiality, is that a jury that draws upon the varied experiences of its members is less likely to rely upon complacent but uninformed assumptions in its deliberations. This view admits that impartiality is not embodied in a single "ideal" juror but achieved through the cross-pollination of a range of views and experiences. The issue is not whether whites, blacks, or Latinos have a greater or lesser capacity for impartial decisionmaking, but whether the optimum conditions for that deliberative process exist. Given the experiential boundaries of neighborhood, job, race, gender, sexual orientation, and social station, most of us fail to recognize the false assumptions that underlie racism, sexism, and homophobia until others challenge them. Virginia Loya, the lone Hispanic juror to deliberate in the state criminal trial in *People v. Powell*, told reporters after the verdict that the white jurors "wanted to see what they wanted to see. . . . They already had their minds made up." The defense attorney for Theodore Briseno, one of the police officers charged in the King beating, later corroborated Ms. Loya's perception that the racial composition of the jury affected deliberations. The venue change to Simi Valley helped the white officers' case tremendously, Briseno's attorney explained, because politically, racially, and culturally, Simi Valley is as different from downtown Los Angeles "as Manhattan is from the moon." Although it is impossible to say whether a more diverse jury would have rendered a different verdict on the same charges, it might have challenged the kind of hardened assumptions about the use of force by police and black motorists in white neighborhoods that Ms. Loya described. [White jurors interviewed after the verdict said they believed the beating was justified; jurors also reportedly believed King "asked for" the beating by being in a white neighborhood.] . . .

Fair Representation for Defendants

At least to the public, the "fair representation" claim applies with equal force to victims of crimes as it does to defendants accused of them. Some of the most sustained public protests of jury verdicts in recent years have, like the Los Angeles rebellion, involved juries that did not include members of the *victim's* ethnicity.

For example, on February 11, 1992, an all-white jury in New Jersey acquitted Gary Spath, a white police officer from Teaneck, of murder charges in the killing of Philip Panell, a sixteen-year-old black youth. The verdict provoked criticism and several organized protests by local black leaders, who complained that the racial composition of the jury made an acquittal a foregone conclusion. In October 1992, a jury of six blacks, four Hispanics, and two whites acquitted a black teenager named Lemrick

Nelson of murdering a Hasidic scholar during three nights of race-related violence in the Crown Heights neighborhood of Brooklyn, New York. The verdict prompted a night of street protests by Jewish residents, who in a telling correspondence adopted the familiar civil rights refrain, "No Justice, No Peace."

Cultural Confusions

The presence of jurors who share the background of a defendant or plaintiff is useful in pointing out to other jurors cultural differences and confusions. Paul Igasaki, executive director of the Asian Law Caucus in San Francisco, California, recalls a lawsuit heard by a jury containing only one Asian American. The panel was puzzled by the failure of the plaintiffs to demonstrate sufficient passion over the damages they claimed to have suffered. More Asian Americans on the jury might have illuminated matters by pointing out that the plaintiffs came from a Chinese-Filipino culture that frowns upon public displays of emotion.

"We don't all see things in the same way," observes Beth Bonora of the National Jury Project, a trial consulting firm. "That's why the jury system exists in the first place."

Richard Lacayo, *Time*, Fall 1993.

Even if one doesn't buy the link between diverse juries and impartiality, this second aspect of institutional legitimacy is incontrovertible: confidence in the criminal justice system rests as much on the *appearance* of fairness as on the delivery of "accurate" results. As the Powell, Panell, and Nelson cases illustrate, the public is more likely to question the accuracy of verdicts when a non-representative tribunal delivers them, especially when the issues are controversial or the crime is race-related. At some level, it does not really matter how diligently the jurors deliberated if the tribunal itself is considered illegitimate. Several of the jurors in the *Powell* case argued steadfastly in defense of their verdict that, had critics been present in the courtroom and heard the evidence, they too might have voted to acquit. These jurors felt unfairly maligned after having devoted weeks to reviewing evidence and then several more days struggling to come to a verdict. Unfortunately, this criticism—echoed by others who did in fact watch the trial—misses the point. Given what the public *thought* it knew about the facts of the racially explosive case, an acquittal rendered by a predominantly white jury was destined to be branded illegitimate. Authorities responded by convening a second grand jury almost immediately after the verdict to indict the officers on federal

163

civil rights charges. One wonders whether any of this would have been thought necessary had a racially mixed jury, rather than a predominantly white one, delivered the same verdict.

The *Powell* trial in Los Angeles and the *Nelson* trial in Brooklyn furnish especially compelling evidence of the link between race and legitimacy in the public consciousness, for together they suggest that the link is as true for juries with few or no whites as it is for juries with few or no racial minorities. The crisis of faith inures in non-representativeness, whether the lack identified is the absence of blacks, Koreans, whites, or another significant ethnic group in the community. The Supreme Court clearly understands this need for legitimacy, but implausibly seeks a solution in race-neutral procedures rather than in racially diverse tribunals. Ever since its landmark 1986 opinion in *Batson*, the Court has insisted that it is discriminatory selection *procedures* that undermine public confidence in the system. Writing just weeks after the Los Angeles riots, Justice Harry Blackmun warned that "'the harm from discriminatory jury selection extends beyond that inflicted on the defendant and the excluded juror to touch the entire community.'. . . [P]ublic confidence in criminal justice is undermined by a conviction in a trial where racial discrimination has occurred in jury selection."

The opinions in *McCollum* and *Powers* stress that race-based peremptory challenges threaten institutional legitimacy. "The overt wrong, often apparent to the entire jury panel, casts doubt over the obligation of the parties, the jury, and indeed the court to adhere to the law throughout the trial of the cause," the Court wrote in *Powers*. While it is certainly true that animus against race might undermine the fairness of any tribunal, the exclusive emphasis on jury strikes seems misplaced. Since the public at large generally is not privy to what occurs in the courtroom during jury selection, it is less the deployment of peremptory strikes than the composition of the resulting panel that is the focus of mass interest. Even in high-profile cases, newspapers rarely report how many minority or white venirepersons counsel for the parties strike in a single trial. They do, however, typically report the racial composition of the petit jury ultimately impaneled. The significant question for the public is whether the resulting jury is actually racially mixed, not how legitimate were the means by which racial minorities were excluded. The Supreme Court, however, evidently believes that recognizing a defendant's interest in the actual racial composition of his or her jury would send the lower courts hurtling down an impossible course of competing claims. It thus continues to settle for less than justice and the public demand.

"We should hope that the courts will avoid saying that institutionalized racial quotas are permissible, whether for jury lists or for juries themselves."

Juries Need Not Be Racially Balanced

Andrew Kull

Trials such as that in which a nearly all-white jury acquitted four Los Angeles police officers of beating Rodney King have prompted some to question the ability of racially homogeneous juries to render impartial verdicts. In the following viewpoint, Andrew Kull contends that courts should not require that juries be racially balanced (the Supreme Court now requires that pools of potential jurors be racially representative). He argues that attempts to draw racially balanced juries are not only problematic but are based on the improper assumption that people of one race cannot represent the interests of those of another race. Kull is the author of *The Color-Blind Constitution*.

As you read, consider the following questions:

1. What was the negative standard imposed by constitutional doctrine, according to Kull?
2. According to the author, why is the fair cross-section standard applied only to the jury list and not the jury itself?
3. What is the "implication", according to the author, of upholding the DeKalb County or Hennepin County jury systems?

Andrew Kull, "Racial Justice," *The New Republic*, November 30, 1992. Reprinted by permission of *The New Republic*; ©1992 by The New Republic, Inc.

Was there a single news report on the Rodney King verdict—setting off the 1992 Los Angeles riots—that failed to mention the racial composition of that jury in Simi Valley? The universal assumption was that ten whites, one Asian, and one Hispanic could not fairly decide a case in which white police officers were accused of beating a black man, or at least that a verdict of acquittal rendered by such a jury could never be accepted as fair. Even if we indignantly reject the first assumption, events might force us to concede the second.

Suppose you had the job of choosing the people called for jury duty in the court . . . where the "L.A. Four" were tried for their part in the televised attack on Reginald Denny, the truck driver dragged from his vehicle at the start of the Rodney King riots. Or just suppose your court handles run-of-the-mill cases in any multiracial, multiethnic community. Current political sensibilities virtually demand that the pool of potential jurors show a good racial and ethnic mix. The closer you can get to proportional representation, the better people will like it.

A Fair Cross-Section in the Jury Pool

Supreme Court rulings on the composition of juries pull in the same direction. In 1975 the Court announced that the Sixth Amendment guarantee of an "impartial jury" in criminal cases required that jury lists (though not the jury actually seated in a particular case) reflect a "fair cross-section" of the communities from which they were drawn. This was a new requirement, and it changed the law more radically than might at first appear.

Earlier constitutional doctrine had imposed a negative standard—no discrimination—drawn from the Fourteenth Amendment. States could not exclude blacks, women, or any other significant group from jury service, either overtly or by the discriminatory application of a neutral standard. But a rule of nondiscrimination does not require any particular result: states were free to draw potential jurors exclusively from lists of registered voters, for example, so long as voter registration was open to all on equal terms. By contrast, a constitutional requirement of "fair cross-section" imposes an affirmative duty to put together a jury list in which significant groups are appropriately represented. As criminals began to get their convictions reversed on the ground that women or blacks (or, in later cases, Hispanics or young adults) were underrepresented in local jury lists, court administrators moved swiftly to rectify any imbalance.

Achieving Fair Cross-Sections in Georgia

DeKalb County, Georgia, where I happen to live, offers an extreme example of the procedures adopted in some jurisdictions. The traditional source of potential jurors in Georgia is the list of registered voters. Because various groups within the population are not equally likely to be registered, however, a jury list drawn at random from the voter list underrepresents some categories by comparison with census figures—notably blacks, males, and people aged eighteen to thirty-four. In the aftermath of the Supreme Court's "fair cross-section" decision, county officials tried first to supplement the voter list with other sources of potential jurors. They also tried to encourage non-voters to volunteer for jury duty. These efforts were notably unsuccessful. Faced with the choice between balancing its jury list and losing its ability to convict criminals, DeKalb County decided to adopt the desired results directly.

Representative Juries

Even backers of multiracial juries have doubts about forcing courts to create them. "People are not knee-jerk voters in the jury room on the basis of their color," says Los Angeles Superior Court Judge Alexander H. Williams III. "If an African American commits a crime in a city that is all white, is there something wrong with him going to trial with a white jury? It's not a much further step to say that if I'm an African American, I have a right to representatives of my race on any jury that tries me.". . .

If the goal is better justice and greater legitimacy, American juries certainly need to be more representative. But in a just society, the process of creating a true assembly of peers need not be reduced to a systematic gathering of the tribes.

Richard Lacayo, *Time*, Fall 1993.

The method is straightforward. By an analysis of census data, the entire voting-age population of the county is broken down into those groups treated as "cognizable." The relevant groups at present are black males, black females, white males, white females, "other" males, and "other" females, each subdivided into age groups 18 to 24, 25 to 34, 35 to 44, 45 to 54, 55 to 64, and 65 plus. Taken together, these categories yield a grid of thirty-six squares: each square is assigned "requested quota totals" by percentage and, for a jury list of given magnitude, by head count. The computer fills the quotas by a random draw from the list of registered voters in the various categories. (Yes, Georgia records the race of registered voters. This long-standing practice, once arguably unconstitutional, is now welcomed by the Justice Department as a means of facilitating its review of the state's compliance with the Voting Rights Act [of 1965, which abolished discriminatory voter registration laws].)

The computer selection is necessarily less random for some classes of voters than for others. Any black male aged 18 to 24 who registers to vote is virtually guaranteed a spot on the jury list. By contrast, the chance that someone in my own group (middle-aged white male voters) will find his name on the most recent list is just over one in eight. The disparities are less pronounced for other sectors of the grid, but black voters overall are still nearly 40 percent more likely to be drawn than white voters. Jury duty is commonly thought to be one of the burdens of citizenship, not one of its benefits, and its uneven incidence along racial lines appears to deny equal treatment to black voters—subjecting them, in effect, to a racially discriminatory tax on suffrage.

The jury list that results from this process is, moreover, a statistical artifact, not a cross-section of anything. It reflects neither the voting population nor (since non-voters are excluded) the county as a whole. But that's not the objective. What DeKalb County gets for its trouble is a bulletproof jury list, one in which each "cognizable group" enjoys near-perfect proportional representation. As I was told at the courthouse, "When people want to challenge our jury list, we show them these figures. They challenge something else."

From Non-Discrimination to Racial Proportionality

The case in which the Supreme Court announced the fair cross-section requirement involved a law affecting the jury participation of women. A Louisiana statute (already repealed when the Court declared it unconstitutional) required that women be left off jury lists unless they filed a notice of their wish to be included. Plainly, an "opt-in" provision like this could have been held unconstitutional under the old non-discrimination standard. (If an optional exemption for women strikes you as a quaint but well-meaning accommodation of the burdens of motherhood, imagine an identical "opt-in" requirement for black jurors.) The Court chose to invalidate the law on the very different ground that it infringed a criminal defendant's affirmative right to a jury drawn from "a representative cross-section of the community." The announcement of a new constitutional test, in a case that could easily have been decided on the basis of an old one, signaled an important change in the way the Court conceived the underlying problem.

The shift from non-discrimination to fair cross-section as a standard for jury lists paralleled the redefinition of other, more visible aspects of the law of race during the early 1970s. School desegregation turned into racial balancing; "no discrimination" in employment under the Civil Rights Act came to mean "no disparate impact"; "voting rights" became a claim to proportional representation. The transition in every case was from a prohibition of racial discrimination to a demand for race-specific results. The social ideal reflected by the legal rules was no longer a world in which racial distinctions were irrelevant, but one in which racial groups achieved representation in proportion to their numbers.

The Problems with Quotas

The discovery that a criminal defendant had a Sixth Amendment right to trial by a cross-section of the community made a problematic addition to the list, because it imposed a requirement that the Court was not prepared to address in logically coherent fashion. "Fair cross-section," the Court has insisted, concerns only the jury list. Neither the group summoned to jury duty on a particular day, nor the panel of prospective jurors assigned to a particular case, nor the jury ultimately seated needs meet the test. But this crucial limitation is practical, not logical. Once the consensus of "a representative cross-section of the community" is deemed necessary to produce a just verdict (or a verdict publicly perceived as just), then there is no way to explain why the panel from which each jury is selected should not present a representative cross-section; or, for that matter, why the twelve jurors who hear the case should not reflect in obtainable proportion the "cognizable groups" within the community. If we accept the underlying premise of "fair cross-section" but stop short at the jury list, we give the defendant no more than a sporting chance at a trial meeting what is implicitly the constitutional standard.

Some court officials not only accept this logic but propose to do something about it. Instead of summoning potential jurors at random, some Georgia counties have tried programming their computers to summon jurors in groups that mirror the carefully constructed proportionality of the master list. (The practice has been criticized by the Georgia Supreme Court, and its present extent is difficult to ascertain.) In Hennepin County, Minnesota—commonly regarded as one of the nation's most progressive, reform-minded jurisdictions in matters of criminal justice—a task force has recommended that at least two seats on every twenty-three-member grand jury be reserved for members of racial minorities. . . . If a minority quota can be adopted for grand juries, comparable procedures for trial juries are the logical next step.

The social and political forces favoring some degree of race-conscious jury selection are nearly irresistible at present, and to discuss the constitutionality of the practice without recognizing these practical constraints would be idle. Yet when the question arises—as it will, sooner or later—we should hope that the courts will avoid saying that institutionalized racial quotas are permissible, whether for jury lists or for juries themselves.

The old aspiration that government deal with individuals without regard to race has a particular force where it touches the voting booth or the jury box. The argument for proportional representation in legislatures and courtrooms rests on the unmistakable premise that a person can neither represent another's interests effectively nor judge him fairly unless he is of the same race. That is the repulsive implication of the modern law of "voting rights," which—since both political parties have apparently decided that it serves their own interests—we are plainly stuck with for the foreseeable future. We now run the risk of extending the same destructive premise to modify our official conception of what constitutes a fair and impartial jury.

Grant, for the sake of argument, that raw racial nerves perceive potential unfairness in *any* decision rendered these days by an "all-white jury." This is a reason to try to avoid seating many such juries. It is still not a reason to admit, at a constitutional level, that a juror's race can be of any consequence. If either the DeKalb County jury list or the proposed Hennepin County grand jury quota were upheld against a constitutional challenge, the implication would be that the judgment of citizens of different races is so fundamentally different that a fair and impartial jury cannot be constituted without offering to each group, in effect, a racial veto. This comes close to denying that Americans of different races share a common citizenship. Some people might deny that we do. Yet a Constitution even acknowledging such a proposition would describe a political system far less attractive than the one to which we ought to aspire.

Alternatives for Maintaining Non-Discrimination

We still have a choice in the matter. If the ideal of non-discrimination were thought to be important enough, DeKalb County could pursue racially mixed juries the hard way: supplementing voter registration as a source of jurors with lists of licensed drivers, taxpayers, welfare recipients, and every other source of adult citizens' names. Georgia counties don't do it this way, for two reasons. One is the additional time, trouble, and expense. But the second reason is probably the decisive one: trying to come up with a fair cross-section jury list simply by spreading the net wider will never yield quota-perfect results. No judge has ruled that jury lists must match census data to a tenth of a percentage point, the way they do here, but from the standpoint of a court administrator it's impossible to err on the side of proportionality. The only countervailing consideration—other than the burden on the black voters, which anyone can avoid by not registering—is the distaste people once felt for the government's sorting people by race.

170

The alternative to race-specific measures, in jury selection as in everything else, is the long, costly process of constructing a system whereby race-neutral procedures produce socially acceptable results. The country has been unwilling to undertake that burden in any other context, and on the issue of jury composition—where the pressure for a suitably proportional result is, if anything, more intense than elsewhere—a return to the constitutional standard of non-discrimination is plainly not foreseeable. That is not to say, however, that the resort to racial quotas in the selection of juries—directly or indirectly—should be constitutionally permissible.

Recent Supreme Court decisions prohibiting the use of peremptory challenges to exclude prospective jurors on racial grounds—widely hailed by civil rights advocates—carry necessarily different implications about race and the jury system from those that underlie "fair cross-section." In one of the peremptory-challenge cases, Justice Anthony Kennedy wrote that "if race stereotypes are the price for [public] acceptance of a jury panel as fair, the price is too high to meet the standard of the Constitution." The standard of the Constitution confounds the assumptions of every newspaper story and television newscast about the high-profile trials by which the issue of jury composition comes to public notice. The news media are surely not wrong about this, but neither is the Constitution. We stand caught between what we can't realistically deny and what we can't afford to admit. Better to live with such a contradiction than to resolve it, however, because it preserves for future use a charter for a better society than the one we now inhabit.

Periodical Bibliography

The following articles have been selected to supplement the diverse views presented in this chapter.

Eric Breindel — "Race and Riots in New York," *The Wall Street Journal*, November 18, 1992.

Nina Burleigh — "Preliminary Judgements," *ABA Journal*, October 1994. Available form 750 N. Lake Shore Dr., Chicago, IL 60611.

John J. DiIulio Jr. — "The Question of Black Crime," *The Public Interest*, Fall 1994.

Bruce Fein — "Racism Taints Districting, Jury Selection," *Insight*, April 12, 1993. Available from 3600 New York Ave. NE, Washington, DC 20002.

Robert I. Friedman — "The Color of Rage," *Vanity Fair*, January 1995.

Chad G. Glover — "Still Second-Class Citizens," *Essence*, September 1994.

Stephanie Goldberg — "Fault Lines," *ABA Journal*, June 1994.

Philip J. Gourevitch — "The Crown Heights Riot and Its Aftermath," *Commentary*, January 1993.

Elizabeth Kadetsky — "Jews, Blacks, and Justice: Racial Politics in New York," *The Nation*, November 30, 1992.

Randall Kennedy — "Blacks and Crime," *The Wall Street Journal*, April 8, 1994.

Richard Lacayo — "Whose Peers?" *Time*, Fall 1993.

Emily MacFarquhar — "Fighting over the Dream," *U.S. News & World Report*, May 18, 1992.

Eric Pooley — "The City Politic," *New York*, April 18, 1994.

Larry Reibstein et al. — "Justice: Playing the Race Card," *Newsweek*, February 20, 1995.

Jeffrey Rosen — "Jurymandering," *The New Republic*, November 30, 1992.

Jeffrey Rosen — "Court Watch: Gerrymandered," *The New Republic*, October 25, 1993.

Jim Sleeper — "Psycho-Killer," *The New Republic*, January 10 and 17, 1994.

Jill Smolowe — "Race and the O.J. Case," *Time*, August 1, 1994.

Jack E. White — "A New Civil Right," *Time*, June 13, 1994.

Robert L. Woodson — "Blacks Who Use 'Racism' as Their Excuse," *The Wall Street Journal*, March 20, 1992.

How Should America's Political System Respond to Minorities' Interests?

Chapter Preface

The Voting Rights Act of 1965 abolished the discriminatory electoral laws, used particularly by southern states, that since the days of Reconstruction had impeded blacks from registering and voting and had effectively prevented blacks from being elected to political office. Because no southern blacks had been elected to Congress in nearly one hundred years, some supporters of the Civil Rights Act sought the election of black representatives as the goal of reform in order to guarantee that blacks' interests were adequately represented. As a way of ensuring that more blacks would be elected, activists promoted the expansion of the Civil Rights Act in 1982 to allow gerrymandering, the redrawing of electoral districts to encompass a majority of blacks.

Advocates of majority-black districts contend that it is next to impossible for black voters to elect a black person to represent their interests in majority-white districts. Because whites form a permanent majority in most electoral districts, they argue, whites can consistently outvote blacks. According to Allan J. Lichtman, a professor of history at American University in Washington, D.C., and a proponent of majority-black districts, "As a result of white bloc voting, black candidates had (and still have) minimal prospects in majority-white districts, despite cohesive support from black voters." With the creation of majority-black districts, Lichtman points out, the number of black members of the U.S. House of Representatives has increased, advancing the representation of blacks' interests.

Abigail Thernstrom, a senior fellow at the Manhattan Institute in New York City, opposes the creation of majority-black districts by gerrymandering and argues that politicians, regardless of their color, must represent the interests of voters of all races. She points to the number of black mayors, governors, and House members who do not come from majority-black districts as proof that black candidates can gain the support of white voters. "Safe black districts, which exist to protect black candidates from white competition, are unnecessary," she maintains. "Blacks can win without them."

On June 29, 1995, the U.S. Supreme Court ruled that a Georgia voting district drawn to maximize black voting power was unconstitutional, opening the door for all such gerrymandered districts to be challenged. The necessity and effectiveness of gerrymandering are among the issues debated in the following chapter on the political representation of minorities' interests.

> *"Cumulative voting . . . allows representation of substantial minority viewpoints, while assuring that the majority gets most of the power."*

Elections Should Guarantee Minority Representation

Lani Guinier

In an attempt to increase the representation of minorities in Congress, the Voting Rights Act of 1965, which was amended in 1982, allowed the drawing of congressional districts to include a majority of blacks or other minorities. These majority-minority districts have been criticized by the Supreme Court and others on the grounds that they violate the rights of voters to participate in color-blind elections. In the following viewpoint, Lani Guinier discusses possible alternatives to race-conscious districting and their potential to ensure adequate representation for minorities. She advocates "cumulative voting," which would give each voter multiple votes based on the number of open congressional seats in the state. Guinier is a law professor at the University of Pennsylvania and author of *The Tyranny of the Majority: Fundamental Fairness in Representative Democracy.*

As you read, consider the following questions:

1. How does Guinier describe majority-black districts?
2. What does the author say is the problem with race-conscious electoral schemes?
3. How do district elections in North Carolina compare with the Israeli electoral system, according to Guinier?

Lani Guinier, "When the Shoe's on the Other Foot," *The Washington Post National Weekly Edition*, April 11-17, 1994. Reprinted with permission.

Nicetown, Fishtown, Germantown. These are neighborhoods in Philadelphia, Pennsylvania, the city in which I now live. Names from a distant century, they barely capture the checkerboard city Philadelphia has become. The City of Brotherly Love now ranks in the top ten of the country's most racially segregated municipalities.

Sharing Public Space in Politics

But within this city of racially distinct neighborhoods, there are a few racially neutral spaces. These are public areas in which no group feels it owns or controls the space. Here people of different racial and ethnic identities come together to enjoy public festivals or leisurely Sunday afternoons. Here blacks, whites, Asians and Latinos leave their homogeneous neighborhoods behind and enjoy and celebrate their identity as Philadelphians.

From the example of Philadelphia's public spaces we might learn how to rethink one of the trickiest legal and racial issues facing the federal courts and state legislatures: how to draw the lines for congressional districts. And in doing so, we might find a useful model for transcending other aspects of America's racial division.

The imperative for rethinking the nature of congressional districts comes from the Supreme Court and the Congress. In enacting the Voting Rights Act in 1965 and subsequently amending it in 1982, Congress said the courts must act affirmatively to assure all citizens the opportunity and capacity to participate in their own government. But in the court's *Shaw v. Reno* decision handed down in June 1993, a bare majority of justices called into question congressional districts that are drawn with the purpose of increasing black representation.

These majority-black districts are the political equivalent of the ethnically homogeneous neighborhood. They are a safe haven for members of that group, a bit of turf that one ethnic group controls, a place where its voice is pre-eminent. In her majority opinion, Justice Sandra Day O'Connor said that race-conscious gerrymandering, however well-intentioned, smacked of "political apartheid" and was thus constitutionally suspect.

The legal reasoning of O'Connor's opinion (signed by four of her colleagues, including the court's only African-American member, Clarence Thomas) is certainly open to criticism. But the political implications of the decision are clear: The high court is challenging elected officials, lower courts and the American people to do for their democracy what the city planners have done for Philadelphia: define and design racially neutral space.

The difficulties of this task should not be underestimated. Take the example of North Carolina, where the *Shaw v. Reno* case originated. The white majority had dominated every congressional district in every election in the state from the beginning of the century until 1990. The state's population is 24 percent black but had been represented by an all-white congressional delegation since Reconstruction. No blacks were elected to many statewide or local offices, even where blacks were a sizable minority of the voters. Ten years ago, the Supreme Court found voting in the state to be so racially polarized that 82 percent of white voters would not vote for a black candidate. Political campaigns, the court noted, had been dominated by explicit racial appeals, in which black candidates were targeted because of, not in spite of, their race.

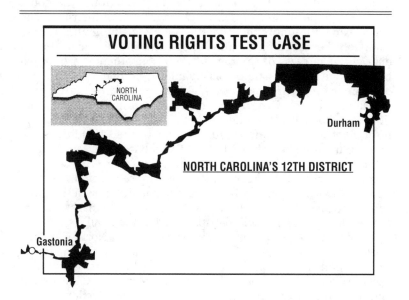

Source: Richard Furno, *The Washington Post National Weekly Edition*, July 5-11, 1993.

The traditional answer to remedying such voting rights abuses is to acknowledge the exclusion and then to give those whom the court finds to have been excluded their own safe space—in short, race-conscious districting. The 12th Congressional District in North Carolina, the subject of *Shaw v. Reno*, was one result. The district snakes around the state to create a constituency that is 54 percent black and 46 percent white. The district proved offensive to the court in large measure because of its bizarre shape.

Lawyers for black voters in North Carolina acknowledged the district's strange outline but said it was a justifiable way to redress previously exclusionary practices. Shouldn't we be more worried, they asked, about the composition of North Carolina's congressional delegation than the appearance of any one district?

In *Shaw* the Supreme Court seemed to answer this question in the negative. The court said race-conscious districting may stigmatize blacks and violate the rights of whites to participate in colorblind elections. Such an approach, the court implied, won't lead us to race-neutral political space comparable to Philadelphia's public parks.

Race-Conscious Districts

In discovering this new right (previously undetected in the Constitution) to participate in colorblind elections, the court overlooked the reality of drawing congressional districts. The court seemed to imply that there is some racially neutral way to establish the geographic boundaries of voting districts. But all districts, regardless of the race of their constituency, are drawn by someone to eliminate or disadvantage the political influence of someone else. Using race as a criterion in drawing up congressional districts is no more arbitrary than using party affiliation, a practice as old as the Republic itself, which the court did not object to. More important, the court failed to address the harsh but unmistakable reality that without some government intervention, public spaces like the North Carolina congressional delegation have been, in fact, racially segregated.

In its unwillingness to bless race-conscious districting, the court neglected to tell us how else to integrate the parks, i.e., to create racially neutral political space accessible to all.

One alternative would be not to district at all in North Carolina, to elect all members of Congress at-large. There is nothing in the Constitution that requires the states to create congressional districts; in fact, congressmen were elected at-large in Alabama and Hawaii in the early 1960s. At-large congressional elections would eliminate the race-conscious districting that the court is skeptical about. The problem, of course, is that if voting is racially polarized then this option is effectively "racially neutral" for only one group: the group with the most votes. Where whites won't vote for blacks, and whites are a majority, this option would effectively assure the white majority control of all congressional seats. For the racial minority, not to district at all is not to be represented at all.

Still another choice might be to make as many as possible of the twelve congressional districts competitive, which is usually defined as a district in which no group has more than 55 percent nor less than 45 percent of the voters. In a competitive district, the outcome of the election cannot be predicted based simply on the relative numerical strength of the more dominant group. In a competitive district, the majority is fluid or majority status is at least within reach of the minority if it plays its cards right. The minority can presumably attract defectors from the majority and become part of the next governing coalition.

This approach is race conscious. Indeed, the 12th Congressional District in North Carolina is drawn to maximize the possibility of black representation in the district while at the same time creating maximum incentives for candidates from the majority to appeal to white voters. This attempt was not sufficient for the white plaintiffs, or for the five justices. The white minority, according to depositions taken of some of the plaintiffs in the case, does not feel it can win over members of the black majority. In their eyes, the black majority of the district is monolithic and likely to remain so, even if only by a narrow margin.

In other words, the problems with the race-conscious solution is that it simply reproduces the racial polarization at the heart of North Carolina politics, this time to the disadvantage of a white, not a black, minority. The political justification for the disadvantaged position of whites in this district is that whites, as a majority in ten of the twelve other districts, have the advantage in electing the congressional delegation statewide.

Cumulative Voting

Yet another alternative, the subject of my much-maligned writings, is cumulative voting. This is a non-districted racially colorblind solution that lowers the threshold for representation by giving each voter multiple votes to cast based on the number of open seats. If North Carolina elected twelve representatives statewide, each voter would get twelve votes. Voters could put all their votes on one candidate or spread their votes out among any number of the other candidates. If all the members of a politically cohesive minority cast votes for the same candidate, that candidate could get elected even under the most adverse circumstances. Women, environmentalists or Republicans could all vote strategically to form "districts of the mind."

Some will fear the empowerment of politically cohesive minorities. Citing the example of Israeli politics, skeptics will worry about the possibility of reinforcing group identities in ways that lead to political paralysis and disproportionate influence of narrow interests. The Israeli electoral system, though, is an extreme example, because parties with as little as 1.5 percent of the vote are entitled to seats in the legislature. North Carolina's current system of district elections is another extreme, because any majority with 51 percent of the vote gets total power, potentially excluding even substantial 49 percent minorities. Cumulative voting is a compromise between these two extremes. It allows representation of substantial minority viewpoints, while assuring

179

that the majority gets most of the power.

In some ways this cumulative voting alternative is ideal because it responds to the issues raised by both black and white voters in North Carolina at the same time that it is colorblind. It does not arbitrarily label voters by drawing districts based on assumptions about race or ethnicity. People are represented based on the way they cast their ballots, not on where they happen to live. Finally, although 60 percent of North Carolina black voters do not live in either of the two currently designated majority black districts, under this alternative every African-American voter would have a chance to elect representatives of their choice.

Whatever the preferred alternative, it should be measured by its ability to remedy—and not to reproduce—the prior discrimination in which majority rule became majority tyranny. The larger challenge is to make sure that collective decision-making about our common destiny occurs within a legislative body or political space in which all voters feel represented. If we fail to meet this challenge we shall never design racially neutral political spaces comparable to Philadelphia's parks. And if we fail, we shall be hard pressed to ask those who feel consistently excluded to keep faith with our democracy.

"The Voting Rights Act has . . . brought several unintended consequences that have impeded progress toward a color-blind society."

Elections Need Not Guarantee Minority Representation

Carol M. Swain

The 1982 amendment of the Voting Rights Act of 1965 gave impetus to the creation of majority-black and majority-Hispanic congressional districts, which were drawn to give these minorities a numerical advantage in electing representatives of their choice. In the following viewpoint, Carol M. Swain argues that majority-minority districts are not necessary to elect black representatives, that they have diluted the voting strength of blacks in other districts, and that they have devolved into proportional representation schemes that are politically divisive. Swain is a professor of politics and public affairs at Princeton University and author of *Black Faces, Black Interests: The Representation of African Americans in Congress.*

As you read, consider the following questions:

1. What are the drawbacks of majority-black districts, according to Swain?
2. How do majority-black districts waste black votes, according to the author?
3. What does Swain see as the shortcomings of proportional representation?

Excerpted from "Some Consequences of the Voting Rights Act" by Carol M. Swain, in *Controversies in Minority Voting*, edited by Bernard Grofman and Chandler Davidson. Copyright 1992 by The Brookings Institution. Reprinted by permission of the publisher, Brookings Books.

African Americans have made substantial progress in getting themselves elected at all levels of government. Rather than rejoicing, however, voting rights advocates—those people who make it their business to testify and litigate for the creation of minority districts—often seem threatened when an election sees no racial polarization or when black voters choose to elect white candidates instead of black. If blacks from local communities testify for defendants in voting rights cases, the advocates may even dismiss that testimony and call the witnesses Uncle Toms and Aunt Janes. Such attitudes are typified by a voting rights advocate whom I heard say, "Unfortunately for our case, we did not find the expected pattern of racial voting."

Progress Under the Voting Rights Act

No one can deny the remarkable contribution of the Voting Rights Act of 1965 to the empowerment of racial minorities. Not only have minorities been elected at all levels of government since the passage of the act, but white elected officials have shown greater responsiveness to minorities in the South and throughout the nation. Today there are few places where white politicians, especially Democrats, can afford to ignore their black constituents. Even long-time segregationists changed in response to the act. In 1963 Governor George Wallace told the people of Alabama, "I draw the line in the dust and toss the gauntlet before the feet of tyranny, and I say: Segregation now—segregation tomorrow—segregation forever." Ten years later he was actively courting black voters, crowning a black homecoming queen at the University of Alabama, and telling a biracial conference of mayors, "We're all God's children. All God's children are equal." In 1982 Senator Strom Thurmond of South Carolina, the man who led the filibuster against the 1957 Civil Rights Act and who had previously opposed all such legislation, cast votes for extending the Voting Rights Act and making the birthday of Martin Luther King, Jr., a national holiday.

In spite of such positive changes, however, the Voting Rights Act has also brought several unintended consequences that have impeded progress toward a color-blind society. One of these has been an overemphasis on the creation of majority-black political units, which despite evidence to the contrary, many assume are needed to elect black politicians. The drawbacks of this strategy for increasing the number of black elected officials are obvious. Blacks are not concentrated enough geographically to create a significant number of new majority-black political units. Indeed, population losses threaten existing minority enclaves: the 1980 census revealed that thirteen of the seventeen districts represented by blacks in 1980 had lost more than 10 percent of their population in the 1970s, and five had lost more than 20 percent.

182

George Crockett's Detroit-area district lost 37 percent of its population, more than any other in the country. Although population losses in districts represented by blacks were lower between 1980 and 1990, those with the greatest losses were in the Northeast and Midwest, the regions currently producing the most black representatives. Illinois, Michigan, New York, Ohio, and Pennsylvania lost congressional representation after the 1991 redistricting.

Racial Districts Are a Distortion of the Law

Safe black districts, which exist to protect black candidates from white competition, are unnecessary. Blacks can win without them.

Race-based districting has been unprincipled, unnecessary—and (to top it off) a gross distortion of the law. Equal electoral access, not proportional racial and ethnic representation, was the point of the Voting Rights Act of 1965 and all its amendments. In the hearings on the 1982 amendments, key civil rights advocates argued that there was no "precisely correct racial mix" (as one lawyer put it) for a district with a single representative—no entitlement to a district that was, say, two-thirds black. The law simply promised an electoral process that was fluid—open to racial change—and not frozen. Reassured, Congress unequivocally rejected the notion of guaranteed legislative seats for members of certain protected minorities, as well it should have. Jim Crow arrangements—separate districts for whites and blacks—have no place in American law.

Abigail Thernstrom, *The New York Times*, December 7, 1994.

Another unfortunate consequence is an overemphasis on creating safe black districts. This strategy has meant redrawing some majority-white districts that had already elected black representatives. Atlanta's Fifth District (1972), Tennessee's Ninth (1974), and Illinois's Seventh (1970) elected blacks to Congress before being redrawn to have black majorities. Increasing the black population in such districts wastes black votes that might have had greater impact in districts not already sending blacks to Congress. The fact of black representatives from majority-white districts flies in the face of the conventional wisdom that majority-black political units, preferably 65 percent black or more, are needed to elect black politicians. As Charles Bullock has pointed out, thresholds lower than that give black candidates a reasonable chance of winning elections without squandering black votes.

183

For many advocates of voting rights a reasonable chance of winning is not good enough when a minority victor can be guaranteed by the creation of an overwhelmingly minority electoral district, a view supported in effect by a number of court rulings. Such developments led Abigail Thernstrom to complain that recent interpretations of the Voting Rights Act have gone beyond the goal of ensuring blacks the right to vote to that of insisting on proportional representation. But proportional representation has serious shortcomings for increasing black political influence. Even if black Americans, who are 12 percent of the population, held 12 percent of the political offices in this country, they would be unable to implement their legislative goals without help. No doubt proportional representation systems could be devised that would increase the number of black officeholders in the short run, but in the long run these electoral arrangements could be a barrier to building black strength: they could hold the proportion of black legislators to the proportion of blacks in the population. Proportional representation could also deprive white legislators of a sense of obligation to blacks. At present many white officials consider representing blacks and other minorities a significant part of their duty. In doing so they may even support controversial minority rights issues opposed by many of their white constituents, something they might not do if the electoral system were changed.

Furthermore, race relations suffer when electoral remedies favor one minority group or create environments in which candidates can engage in racially or ethnically polarizing tactics without fear of defeat. This is true whether one is discussing former Klansman David Duke, whose racist insinuations garnered him 55 percent of the white vote in his 1991 gubernatorial race in Louisiana, or Chicago's Gus Savage, whose stock-in-trade seems to be anti-Semitism.

Building Coalitions

Political and racial majorities show much ingenuity in resisting unwanted changes. In some areas of the country, for example, states are moving toward deciding important policy questions by referendum on a statewide ballot, that is, toward government by unalloyed majority rule, which can harm minorities if their preferences differ from those of the majority. For example, California's passage by referendum of Proposition 13 (cutting property taxes) and Proposition 98 (stipulating the percentage of state funds to be allocated to public schools) pitted racial and political minorities against majorities. Referendums and government by initiative can doom the coalition building by elected officials that is the essence of compromise and harmony.

Whether to form biracial coalitions has been intensely debated since the 1960s, when Stokely Carmichael and Charles Hamilton wrote *Black Power*, in which they argued that such coalitions would be detrimental until African Americans had developed independent bases of power that would allow them to become equal partners. That time has come. Since the 1960s, African Americans have become far more politically effective. They have shown white politicians that they expect something in return for their votes. As a consequence, more and more white elected officials are responsive to minority concerns.

All of this suggests a number of conclusions. First, proponents of voting rights should acknowledge the growing number of elections in which racial polarization does not occur. Its absence may mean that the laws have done their jobs well. Second, we should not second-guess the choices black voters have made among candidates. Sometimes, white politicians are simply better than their black alternatives. Third, advocates should stop denigrating those blacks who testify for defendants in voting rights cases. No one is in a position to deny the reality of another person's experience. Finally, people must move beyond entrenched positions that require them to resist the logic of opposing arguments.

So, the knowledge of how majority rule works should push America toward greater creativity in finding ways to remove not-so-obvious barriers to minority influences: overly restrictive registration laws, resistance of party leaders to the recruitment of black candidates in majority-white areas, the absence of a system of financing political campaigns that could encourage challengers to incumbents. A focus on removing such barriers is a more efficient use of time and energies than fighting old battles and refusing to recognize the signs of progress.

3

VIEWPOINT

"Californians . . . have responded to the plummeting indicators in almost every measure of quality of life by turning their bitter gaze toward the nation's undocumented immigrants."

Anti–Illegal Immigration Measures Are Racist

Elizabeth Kadetsky

In the November 1994 election, Californians passed a ballot measure (Proposition 187) that would deny educational, non-emergency medical, and welfare services to illegal immigrants, and several other states have considered or are considering similar measures. Because such federally mandated benefits have been upheld in previous legal decisions, the measure was immediately suspended by state and federal courts. In the following viewpoint, Elizabeth Kadetsky argues that Proposition 187 was promoted by racists who capitalized on a popular sentiment that erroneously blames illegal immigrants for the economic problems of California. Kadetsky is a freelance writer in Los Angeles.

As you read, consider the following questions:

1. What do advocates of the California ballot measure hope it will do, according to Kadetsky?
2. According to the author, what has lent the movement for the ballot measure a racist patina?
3. What is the percentage of support for the measure among whites, according to Kadetsky?

Excerpted from "Bashing Illegals in California" by Elizabeth Kadetsky, *The Nation*, October 17, 1994. Reprinted with permission from *The Nation* magazine; © The Nation Company, L.P.

186

Parrish Goodman had just saved a burdened shopper the trouble of returning her grocery cart and was back at the expanse of sidewalk outside Ralph's supermarket in West Los Angeles competing with the whoosh of the electric doors. Goodman greeted all who passed in such a friendly way that they tended to thank him for his cryptic, millionth-generation photocopies that were equal parts longhand and typewriter script. "You'll be voting on this in November," he'd say, winking, all courtesy and ambiguity.

California's Proposition 187

Goodman was campaigning for Proposition 187, the grandiosely titled "Save Our State" (S.O.S.) ballot initiative that, if . . . validated by the courts, will use strict verification requirements to prevent California's estimated 1.7 million undocumented immigrants from partaking of every form of public welfare including non-emergency medical care, prenatal clinics and public schools. The measure would require employees at public health facilities, welfare offices, police departments and schools to demand proof of legal residency and to report those who can't produce it to the Immigration and Naturalization Service (I.N.S.); it also calls for stiff penalties for creating or using false documents. While conceding that the measure actually does nothing to deter immigration at its source—at the border and with the employers who encourage workers to cross it—advocates say S.O.S. responds to California's economic downturn by making life so difficult for the undocumented that they will either go home or never show up to begin with.

The opposition runs the gamut from those who dispute the premise that immigrants contribute to hard times to those who argue that the initiative scapegoats children, lets employers off the hook, inefficiently enlists public employees to do the work of the I.N.S. and violates several federal mandates as well as a Supreme Court decision granting all children the right to free education. That several of the state's major newspapers and a cross section of city governments, school districts, health associations and law-enforcement officials have opposed Save Our State as racist, xenophobic, ineffectual, costly—and just mean-spirited—would seem enough to disqualify the avuncular Goodman from its sponsor's ranks.

But Goodman is not alone among Californians, who have responded to the plummeting indicators in almost every measure of quality of life by turning their bitter gaze toward the nation's undocumented immigrants, 43 percent of whom land in California. It's no news that California—strapped by the country's second-weakest economy, years of budget shortfalls, the most crowded classrooms in the nation and pockets of the worst smog and traf-

fic—is no longer the "golden door" the Grateful Dead still sometimes sing about.

Blaming Immigrants

Discontent at the condition of the Golden State has exploded in
the faces of immigrants, particularly those from Latin America.
The American Friends Service Committee border monitoring project investigates two or three incidents of anti-immigrant violence
per month. This atmosphere of panic owes its fire to a network
of several dozen mostly new grass-roots organizations whose
work, fanned by the goading rhetoric of politicians like Governor
Pete Wilson, has culminated with S.O.S. The authors of S.O.S. so
successfully tapped into a popular sentiment and movement that
the group's P.O. box collected as many as 1,000 pieces of mail a
day. S.O.S. had no trouble recruiting volunteers, and those volunteers had an equally easy ride gathering 400,000 of the signatures
needed to qualify the initiative for the ballot. . . .

S.O.S.'s core supporters are a ragtag movement replete with
registered Greens, Democrats, Perotists, distributors of New Age
healing products and leaders of the Republican Party. The participants have little in common, but their rhetoric of invasion—a
kaffeeklatsch in the Southern California town of Bellflower calls
itself We Stand Ready—and the virulence of their wrath. One
S.O.S. organizer, Bette Hammond, drove me through her town's
immigrant quarter ranting about an imagined "stench of urine"
and pointing to clusters of streetside day laborers who, she asserted, surely defecated in the nearby bushes. "Impacted, impacted, impacted," Hammond spit out as she glanced toward
apartment complexes in various states of disrepair. "They come
here, they have their babies, and after that they become citizens
and all those children use those social services." Barbara Kiley, a
Prop 187 backer who is also mayor of the Orange County town
of Yorba Linda, described such children to one reporter as
"those little fuckers.". . .

The Proposition's Supporters

Richard Mountjoy, a finger-jabbing right-wing Republican state
assemblyman from east L.A. County, took up the anti-immigrant
torch when, he told me, he foresaw "a heated campaign" for reelection in 1992. He has since become the movement's most tena-
cious government spokesman, introducing ten mostly unsuccessful bills in the state legislature that foreshadowed Prop 187 (one
would make it a felony to use a false ID). Mountjoy one-upped
even Prop 187 with a pending bill that would disqualify native-
born children of undocumented mothers from their Fourteenth
Amendment right to U.S. citizenship. A self-proclaimed "expert"
on immigration, Mountjoy told me he wanted a crackdown on il-

legal immigration from countries other than Mexico, such as Puerto Rico, where, unbeknownst to the assemblyman, everyone is a U.S. citizen. Mountjoy, who has contributed $43,000 to S.O.S., has cynically blamed immigrants for the state's budget crisis after having built his own career campaigning for Proposition 13, the 1978 antitax initiative that is now acknowledged by experts on all sides as the *actual* cause of that crisis. Other top backers include Don Rogers, a state senator from outside Palm Springs who kicked in $20,000 and is perhaps best known for his association with the white supremacist Christian Identity movement.

Mountjoy and Rogers are not alone in lending the movement for S.O.S. a racist patina. The measure is backed by the Federation for American Immigration Reform (FAIR), an outgrowth of the environmentally leaning Zero Population Growth that has received at least $800,000 from the Pioneer Fund, a notorious right-wing philanthropy that sponsors studies on topics like race and I.Q. . . .

Proposition 187 and Racism

Proponents of California's Proposition 187, including its drafter, former INS [Immigration and Naturalization Services] Commissioner Alan Nelson, deny that racism played a part in the vote and point to what actually was a relatively close vote in the African American and Asian American communities. But without a doubt, race was the linchpin that drove this issue. In a state where minorities are 45% of the population (Latinos 25%, Asians 10%, Blacks 8%, Native Americans 2%), immigrant-bashing has increased tremendously. In addition, with the downturns in the economy, including military base closures in California that have thrown many workers into unemployment, many have found it convenient to blame the problems on the increasing number of non-white immigrants.

Bill Tamayo, *Poverty & Race*, January/February 1995.

If S.O.S.'s visible advocates personify either fringe populism or cynical manipulation of public sentiment for political gain, their movement has crossed over to the mainstream. Sixty-two percent of Californians supported S.O.S. in a September 1994 *Los Angeles Times* poll; however, voters' visceral reaction fades when asked in other polls about the particulars of the proposition, such as yanking children from public schools or denying medical care, which are opposed by 54 percent and 74 percent, respectively. Still, the initiative passed.

Despite the verbiage about immigrants' economic impact, polls show supporters span the political and economic spectrums and are not more likely to have been adversely affected by the recession. Most of S.O.S.'s support, as well as its most vocal advocates, is actually concentrated in areas least affected by the recession or by the state's shifting multicultural composition.

S.O.S. is most popular in Orange County, the sterile midzone of low-slung shopping malls between border San Diego and multicultural Los Angeles. It's the region that brought us Richard Nixon, Disneyland and S.O.S.'s ten authors. Here, only 7 percent live in poverty, as opposed to 17.5 percent in Los Angeles.

Bette Hammond lives in San Rafael, where she moved from a Boston suburb in 1981, bought a motorcycle and planned "to get the freedom that one hears about from California." For her the dream is this Marin County enclave that is 84 percent white, enjoys the well-above-average median family income of $54,000, the well-below-average unemployment rate of 6 percent—and probably has more hot tubs per capita than any place in the world.

These demographics suggest that Ron Prince, the vampirishly charming chairman of the Save Our State Committee, was disingenuous in recommending as a representative volunteer Parrish Goodman, who is African-American. Goodman likewise planned to illustrate "how the African-American community is organizing around S.O.S."—though he was unable to conjure up one other African-American S.O.S. volunteer besides himself. In fact, anti-immigrant sentiment is concentrated among whites: 59 percent of white people in California believe that children of undocumented immigrants should be turned away from the schools. This contrasts with 41 percent of African-Americans and Asians, and 22 percent of Latinos, according to a Field Institute poll.

A former Black Panther who hails from New York City and is now a union computer technician for the telephone company, Goodman nevertheless exploits black/Latino tensions by harping on a "fight over jobs" in the ethnically volatile African-American and Latino South Central district. Cruising down Venice Boulevard in his white Camaro, Goodman speed-surfed the AM talk-radio channels as his placid surface cracked into little slivers of invective: "These people want you to be like them, poor and mumbling in half-Spanish and half-English." Then Goodman, who came to California in 1980 in search of a "change of attitude," turned calm, almost wistful. "I thought California was supposed to be palm trees and beautiful girls on the beach. Instead we got a gang war. You almost have an enemy presence in your midst.". . .

Costs and Benefits of Immigration

As the rhetoric flies, California does wrestle with the confounding fact that immigrants strain a social and physical infrastructure already burdened by slow economic expansion and a growing population. None of the dozens of wildly contradictory studies circulating among participants in the immigration debate can adequately estimate the real numbers and costs of undocumented immigrants in California, but several concur that while low-wage immigrants contribute to and are even crucial to the state's long-term economic vitality, those immigrants are a short-term burden on state and city governments that cannot, as one study from the RAND Corporation puts it, "borrow against their future." The most resonant of several studies, by Los Angeles County, reported that immigrants (legal and illegal) and their children cost the county $954 million a year in public services but give back far more, $4.3 billion—albeit in taxes paid to the federal government. That discrepancy has led to bipartisan railing against federal mandates—the same mandates that S.O.S. violates—that require states to provide social services without the federal dollars to pay for them. In any case, while S.O.S. ostensibly un-does that burden to the state, the state's legislative analysis has calculated that the measure would actually cost billions in the long run.

Even the cost-benefit equation, however, fails to address the fact that immigration from Mexico is a logical outgrowth of the economic interdependency of Mexico and the United States. State Assembly Speaker Willie Brown did, however, call for seizing the assets of employers such as hoteliers who are found to depend on underpaid and poorly treated undocumented immigrants. This proposal elicited an amusing silence from Republican fist-thumpers like Governor Wilson, who have done everything in their power to see that employer-sanction provisions in the 1986 Immigration Reform and Control Act remain unenforced. After eight years, Los Angeles saw the first major criminal employer sanction doled out in the fall of 1994.

That a poorly conceived initiative sponsored by fringe activists with a persecution complex won the support of a majority of voters in November 1994 points to the willingness of politicians to play the immigration card in a volatile social climate.

"California must be allowed to devote our limited resources to those people who have come to our country through the legal process."

Anti–Illegal Immigration Measures Are Not Racist

Pete Wilson

In 1994, several states—including California, Florida, Arizona, and Texas—filed lawsuits against the federal government to recover the costs of illegal immigration (though none of the lawsuits has succeeded to date). In the following viewpoint, Pete Wilson, governor of California, argues that the costs of providing federally mandated services and benefits to illegal immigrants hurt the economy of California and limit its ability to provide services to its legal residents. He believes that forcing the federal government to reimburse the states for these costs will compel the government to stem illegal immigration. Wilson won reelection as governor of California in November 1994.

As you read, consider the following questions:

1. How much does Wilson estimate California spends providing services to illegal immigrants?
2. How does the author counter charges of racism?

From Pete Wilson's speech "Securing Our Nation's Borders," given at the Los Angeles Town Hall, April 25, 1994. Reprinted with the author's permission.

The federal government's immigration policy is broken and the time to fix it is now.

It's hard to blame people who day after day pour across our borders. They're coming to find a better life for themselves and their families. It's easy to sympathize with them and even admire their gumption. It is those in Washington that we should condemn—those who encourage the illegals to break the law by rewarding them for their illegal entry.

A Nation of Legal Immigrants

We are a state and a nation of immigrants, proud of our immigrant traditions. Like many of you, I'm the grandchild of immigrants. My grandmother came to this country in steerage from Ireland at age sixteen. She came for the same reason any immigrant comes—for a better future than she could hope for in the old country. And America benefited from her and millions like her.

But we, as a sovereign nation, have a right and an obligation to determine how and when people come into our country. We are a nation of laws, and people who seek to be a part of this great nation must do so according to the law.

The United States already accepts more legal immigrants into our country than the rest of the world combined—1.8 million in 1991 alone.

We are a generous people. But there is a limit to what we can absorb and illegal immigration is now taxing us past that limit.

Thousands come here illegally every day. In fact, the gaping holes in federal policy have made our borders a sieve. President Clinton has used that very word to describe their porous condition.

The results are, in Los Angeles, there's now a community of illegal residents numbering a million people. That's a city the size of San Diego. Alone, it would be the seventh largest city in the nation—half again the population of our nation's capital, Washington, D.C.

Two-thirds of all babies born in Los Angeles public hospitals are born to illegal immigrants.

Paying for Illegal Immigration

As we struggle to keep dangerous criminals off our streets, we find that 14 percent of California's prison population are illegal immigrants—enough to fill eight state prisons to design-capacity.

And through a recession that has caused the loss of one-third the revenues previously received by state government, as we have struggled to maintain per-pupil spending and to cover fully enrollment growth with classrooms around the state bursting at the seams, we're forced to spend $1.7 billion each year to educate students who are acknowledged to be in the country illegally.

In total, California taxpayers are compelled *by federal law* to spend more than $3 billion to provide services to illegal immigrants—it's approaching 10 percent of our state budget.

To ignore this crisis of illegal immigration—as some would have us do—is not only irresponsible, but makes a mockery of our laws. It is a slap in the face to the tens of thousands who play by the rules and endure the arduous process of legally immigrating to our country.

Steve Kelley/Copley News Service. Reprinted with permission.

It's time to restore reason, integrity and fairness to our nation's immigration policy. And we need to do it now. California can't afford to wait.

First, the federal government must secure our border. That's the first step in securing our future. They must devote the manpower and the technology necessary to prevent people from crossing the border in the first place.

Second, the federal government should turn off the magnetic

lure that now rewards people who successfully evade the border patrol and cross the border illegally.

And finally, until our representatives in Washington do act, until they secure the border and turn off the magnetic lure, they should pay the full bill for illegal immigration. The states shouldn't be forced to bear the cost for a failed federal policy that gives a free pass to those who breach our borders, then passes the buck to us.

Those who oppose reform invariably cry racism. They want to stifle even any discussion of the issue.

But this debate isn't about race, it's about responsibility and resources. Washington must accept responsibility for this strictly federal issue, and California must be allowed to devote our limited resources to those people who have come to our country through the legal process.

Holding Washington Accountable

This isn't a partisan issue, or even simply a California issue. Washington's failure to bear responsibility for illegal immigration is forcing states around the nation to bear enormous costs. . . .

Immigration and control of our nation's border are, by virtue of the Constitution, a strictly federal responsibility. But today, there is no fiscal accountability for that policy.

The Congress is writing blank checks on other people's bank accounts—and one of those accounts belongs to the taxpayers of California.

Congress must be forced to bear the fiscal consequences for its immigration policy. If they have to pay the bill for that policy, if they feel the pinch in the federal budget for which they alone are accountable to the voters, then and only then will they have the incentive to fix this policy that simply doesn't work.

President Clinton has acknowledged as much himself. In summer 1993 he said, "One of the reasons the federal government has not been forced to confront this . . . is that the states of California, Texas and Florida have had to bear a huge portion of the costs for the failure of federal policy."

It's a fundamental element of democracy—a government must be held accountable for its actions.

And if the federal government were held accountable, they would quickly discover that the cost of ignoring the real and explosively growing problem of illegal immigration is far greater than the cost of fixing it.

They would see that the federal resources necessary to secure our nation's border are dwarfed by the billions that California and other states spend today in making massive illegal immigration to America a safety-net for the world. What's more, by compelling California to provide this safety-net for illegals, the feds are tearing gaping holes in the safety-net we seek to provide for our own needy legal residents.

For 1995, the Clinton Administration proposed increasing spending on border enforcement across the country by just $180 million a year. We'll spend nearly ten times that amount just educating illegal immigrants in California schools. . . .

Our goal, though, is larger than simply seeking reimbursement—as important and as urgently needed as it is.

Our goal is to force the federal government to accept responsibility for the crisis of illegal immigration. Only when they accept responsibility will Congress finally adopt the reforms necessary to restore integrity and fairness to our immigration laws.

Once Congress is forced to confront this problem, I'm sure it will waste no time in doing what's necessary to secure our nation's borders.

Periodical Bibliography

The following articles have been selected to supplement the diverse views presented in this chapter.

Jan Adams — "California: Proposition 187 Lessons," *Z Magazine*, March 1995.

Bruce E. Cain — "Voting Rights and Democratic Theory: Toward a Color-Blind Society?" *The Brookings Review*, Winter 1992.

Ruth Conniff — "The War on 'Aliens,'" *The Progressive*, October 1993.

Ellis Cose — "The Voting Rights Act: A Troubled Past," *Newsweek*, June 14, 1993.

Arthur C. Helton — "Anti-Immigration Laws: Closing the Golden Door," *The Nation*, October 18, 1993.

Lewis R. Jones — "Admissions Omission," *The American Prospect*, Winter 1993.

Elizabeth Kadetsky — "Bashing Illegals in California," *The Nation*, October 17, 1994.

John Meacham — "Voting Wrongs," *The Washington Monthly*, March 1993.

John J. Miller — "Asian Americans Head for Politics," *The American Enterprise*, March/April 1995.

Daniel D. Polsby and Robert D. Popper Jr. — "Racial Lines," *National Review*, February 20, 1995.

Peter H. Schuck — "The New Immigration and the Old Civil Rights," *The American Prospect*, Fall 1993.

Peter Skerry — "Not Much Cooking: Why the Voting Rights Act Is Not Empowering Mexican Americans," *The Brookings Review*, Summer 1993.

Dana Y. Takagi — "The Retreat from Race," *Socialist Review*, October–December 1992.

Abigail Thernstrom — "Guinier Miss: The Jurisprudence of Lani Guinier," *The New Republic*, June 14, 1993.

Roger Wilkins — "Absent by Design," *Sojourners*, November 1992.

What Should Society Do to Improve Race Relations?

Chapter Preface

In May 1954, the U.S. Supreme Court ruled in the case of *Brown v. Board of Education of Topeka, Kansas*, that the existence of separate public educational facilities for blacks and whites was inherently unequal. The Court's decision marked the start of an often contentious social struggle to desegregate America's schools and universities. That is why some educators are dismayed to find in the 1990s that some black (and other) university students are choosing to resegregate themselves by living in separate dormitories, joining race-specific associations, and selecting courses of study that emphasize separate American cultures.

William H. Gray III, president of the United Negro College Fund, defends the students' self-segregation "as a way of feeling refuge for what they perceive as hostile, non-nurturing environments." Gray feels that separate dormitories and associations can help black students feel comfortable and succeed in colleges that are mostly white and are set up to make whites feel comfortable. He believes that this mostly white environment—and American society in general—is structurally inimical to the success of blacks. "Instead of asking why are black students separating from whites at white college campuses," Gray states, "we should be asking what is wrong with white America and its institutions that blacks don't feel welcome."

Strongly opposed to self-segregation, Donald Eastman, a vice president at the University of Georgia in Athens, says, "The contention that American blacks need separatist clubs, schools and colleges because of the continuing abuses of the white culture is racist cant." Having witnessed what he feels is significant progress in the struggle for desegregation, Eastman believes that resegregation will deny blacks opportunities for success in American society: "Those with the most to lose from the new segregation are black students, who will either learn to prosper in an integrated society or will not prosper at all." Eastman, among other educators, characterizes the trend toward self-segregation at schools and universities as detrimental to race relations in American society.

The merits of self-segregation and integration as strategies for improving race relations are debated in the following chapter.

"For both whites and blacks, the notion that we
are unalterably 'different' is poisoning our lives."

Integration in a Color-Blind Society Should Be the Goal

Tamar Jacoby

From the late 1960s to the mid-1980s, busing students from inner city neighborhoods to suburban schools (and vice versa) was seen as a way to integrate society. In the following viewpoint, Tamar Jacoby argues that government integration policies, such as busing and affirmative action, failed to improve race relations because they encouraged people to emphasize their color differences rather than their commonalities. In her opinion, it is time to abandon such policies in favor of color-blind approaches. Jacoby is the author of a forthcoming book on the history of race relations.

As you read, consider the following questions:

1. How are stereotypes of blacks disguised, according to Jacoby?
2. What was the real lesson of the busing battle, according to the author?
3. What could public policies do to increase integration, according to Jacoby?

It was near the end of the dinner party when the conversation turned to race. We were talking about what we thought was wrong, and I found myself describing my nostalgia for the ideals of the 1960s. "What ever happened to integration," I asked, "to the idea that we are one community?" No one answered the rhetorical question, but I noticed the black woman at the other end of the table staring intently. "What happened," I went on, "to the idea that underneath the skin we are all the same?" The woman, whom I'd never met before that evening, jumped up from the table. "We woke up," she answered icily and walked out of the room.

The evening ended soon after, but I could not shake my astonishment. Did the woman's racial resentment really loom that large—so large that she had to leave the room when I mentioned our common humanity?

What ever happened to integration? A Rip Van Winkle who went to sleep in 1964, when the mainstream more or less accepted Martin Luther King's vision, would not recognize the way the racial landscape has evolved in just thirty years. "Community" now suggests not one integrated nation—as Dr. King meant it—but a minority enclave, as in "the black community." "Brother" evokes not the brotherhood of man but the solidarity of skin color. "It's a black thing, you wouldn't understand," the T-shirts say—and few of us question the underlying assumption.

Sentimental Luxury

When did this happen? How and why? Have we really agreed to give up on a common humanity? I don't think we have. I believe that most people, at heart, still feel they share something beneath their surface differences. But if most Americans still believe in inclusion, they don't know how to reconcile it with diversity—and meanwhile we are sliding willy-nilly toward a future that leaves little room for commonality.

Even many who still talk about integration think of it as a sentimental luxury, hardly relevant to today's real racial problems. In fact, for both whites and blacks, the notion that we are unalterably "different" is poisoning our lives. Underclass youths decline to make an effort in "the white man's school"; others refuse to obey the "white" law. Middle-class black students struggle, often in vain, to reconcile their anger and their mainstream ambitions. Whites—even whites who feel they are free of prejudice—still nurse half-conscious notions of racial inferiority. Cut off from all but superficial contact with blacks, their stereotypes only grow worse, often disguised as well-intentioned double standards.

Can the integration ideal be revived and reshaped to make more sense in the racially jaded 1990s? I don't see any alternative.

Integration's critics base their argument on history: We tried it, they say, and it failed. Remember busing? Remember those white faces filled with hate—in Little Rock and Boston? Other skeptics, just as disappointed, think it was black not white anger that ruined things. Black Power, the Black Panthers, Louis Farrakhan: Blacks don't seem to want integration, these people say, so why are we forcing it on them?

The Age of Integration?

We are now in the third great period in the American history of white-black relations. The first was the age of slavery, which lasted from the seventeenth century to the 1860s. Next came the era of racial segregation, which lasted from just after the Civil War until the 1960s. Since the late '60s we have been living in an era which, as yet, has no definitive name.

When it first began, we thought this third age would be called "the age of integration." But we now see, after thirty years of bitter and disappointing experience, that it can hardly be called that.

David R. Carlin Jr., *Commonweal*, January 27, 1995.

To a degree, the skeptics are right. Much of what we've tried in the past thirty years hasn't worked. Most blacks still live in largely black neighborhoods. School desegregation, though successful in some towns, has proved a failure in the big cities where most blacks live. Many workplaces are now racially mixed, but the mingling ends abruptly at the end of the work day. More often than not, what desegregation there is feels forced and mechanical, a mockery of the color-blind harmony that Dr. King and others once envisioned.

Just why past efforts failed is a long story, with enough blame for whites and blacks to share. Bigotry played a part, but so, on both sides, did misunderstanding. Well-intentioned efforts to force the races together, often in already tense circumstances, led instead to heightened mistrust and nastier stereotypes than before.

Busing was the classic example of what could go wrong. It sounded great on paper. Neighborhood patterns and old stereotypes were working together to block voluntary mingling. Contact, it was reasoned, would bring understanding—and understanding learned in childhood would last a lifetime. What policy makers didn't reckon on was the size of the gaps they were trying to bridge: gaps in educational achievement and in standards of behavior, not to mention inflammable reservoirs of fear on both sides of the color line. Instead of teaching black and white to get along, busing only confirmed black fears of white bigotry even as it encouraged whites to equate "black" with poor and uneducated.

A Renewed Pursuit of Integration

The history of the busing battle teaches an important lesson, but not the lesson most people think. It says nothing about the desirability of color-blind understanding, nor does it prove that America is "too racist" to achieve integration. All it teaches is that forced mingling bears little fruit, particularly when those being forced are not social equals. The road back to Martin Luther King's vision will have to run along different lines.

There are many possibilities, including the one that prevailed into the 1960s: At home, on the weekend, in the family and the neighborhood, Jews were Jews and Italians Italians; under the law and in their careers, they operated as individual Americans. Ethnicity, race and religion were important parts of identity, but so was citizenship, and most people had no trouble reconciling these different claims. Today's fascination with multiculturalism makes it a little harder to find that balance between clan and commonweal, but not, I suspect, as hard as some demagogues of identity politics would have us believe.

A renewed pursuit of integration need not mean a return to '60s-style social engineering. Washington can provide some opportunities for black and white to get to know each other: a conscripted national service corps, for example. And government can create incentives for voluntary, color-blind racial mingling, as in public-school choice programs. But the best path toward inclusion is still the old-fashioned one: up the escalator of schooling, employment and a stake in the system.

Integration is already taking hold on the job, especially in jobs where the same rules apply to everyone and merit makes color irrelevant. And it is most likely to stick where blacks and whites share basic values and concerns—a commitment, say, in a mixed neighborhood, to safe streets, property values and good schools.

For many blacks, plainly, some additional boosts are needed to make up for generations of exclusion—scholarships, aggressive recruitment and the like. Even these measures are unlikely to bring the poorest blacks onto the escalator. But the first steps toward Dr. King's vision need not—cannot—wait for the elimination of the underclass. There is plenty to be done in the meantime, and any inclusion of middle-class and working-poor blacks will surely help open the way to others. For government and the rest of us the challenge is to let this mingling happen.

Why doesn't it happen? The real obstacle, even for blacks already on the escalator, is one of attitudes—on both sides of the color line. No real integration will be possible without renewed faith in one community, and rekindling that faith will require nothing less than a radical shift in racial mores.

It will take many small steps to make the revolution. Locally and nationally, public policy could start by de-emphasizing the difference that color makes, whether in the voting booth or on an application for a government contract. Mainstream institutions, too, could replace race-conscious remedies with color-blind ones: affirmative-action programs, say, that target any and all disadvantaged candidates.

Preaching Trust

Whites have plenty of work to do, re-examining old stereotypes and natural clannishness. But black leadership has at least as far to go—not just denouncing separatism but actually encouraging racial mingling. *Newsweek* columnist Joe Klein has suggested "interracial Martin Luther King tables [and] Frederick Douglass houses" on campus. The role of racial caucuses and "community liaison offices" might be reconsidered: Are they really helping their constituents by emphasizing only how they are different? Politicians, entertainers, sports heroes and others—black and white—could use their bully pulpits to preach not "solidarity" and suspicion but an open trust in the other race.

The shift that's needed looks unlikely today. To the degree it happens, it will build slowly and will suffer many zigzagging reversals. Still, if we do not eventually change course, it's hard to see how the nation will hold together in the long run—how the law will stick, or the social contract.

In every case, change will begin with someone who says "no" to the tribalist nonsense that most of us now accept on faith as the first law of race relations. "It's a black thing, you wouldn't understand," a white thing, a gay thing or a Jewish thing. Whatever "it" is, isn't it about time we started trying to explain it to each other?

"The permanence of racism thesis criticizes the idea that most White people in America will grant Black people equal rights."

Integration in a Color-Blind Society Is Not Possible

John C. Brittain

The civil rights movement of the 1950s and 1960s sought the integration of blacks into American society. In the following viewpoint, John C. Brittain argues that integration failed to achieve equality for blacks because of the entrenched racism of white people. He contends that a permanent struggle against racism is necessary to ensure equality for blacks. Brittain is a professor of law at the University of Connecticut in Storrs.

As you read, consider the following questions:

1. What was the traditional civil rights ideology founded on, according to Brittain?
2. What is the argument of antiessentialists, as defined by the author?
3. According to the woman in the author's anecdote, how had black people won?

John C. Brittain's contribution to "Is Racism Permanent? A Symposium," in *Poverty & Race*, November/December 1993. Reprinted with permission.

In his 1992 book *Faces at the Bottom of the Well*, Derrick Bell posited a provocative thesis:

> Black people will never gain full equality in this country. Even those herculean efforts we hail as successful will produce no more than temporary "peaks of progress," short-lived victories that slide into irrelevance as racial patterns adapt in ways that maintain white dominance. This is a hard-to-accept fact that all history verifies. We must acknowledge it, not as a sign of submission, but as an act of ultimate defiance.

Other civil rights advocates have expressed similar views. Robert Carter, a veteran civil rights lawyer and later federal district court judge, once said that the pioneer civil rights leaders thought that racial segregation was the disease. Once the civil rights movement eliminated the segregation, the society would achieve racial equality for the African American people. Instead, the leaders discovered that the segregation was only the symptom, and White racism was the disease. Still further, Kenneth B. Clark, a brilliant psychologist who conducted the studies concerning the adverse impact of segregated education on the learning abilities of Black children, recently lamented (see his contribution in *Race In America: The Struggle for Equality*, Herbert Hill and James E. Jones, Jr., eds.):

> Reluctantly, I am forced to face the likely possibility that the United States will never rid itself of racism and reach true integration. I look back and shudder at how naive we all were in our belief in the steady progress racial minorities would make through programs of litigation and education, and while I very much hope for the emergence of a revived civil rights movement with innovative programs and educated leaders, I am forced to recognize that my life has, in fact, been a series of glorious defeats.

The Permanence of Racism

I agree with the thoughts of these civil rights activists about the "permanence of racism" in America. The conditions of White racism remain the same, but some of the underlying assumptions may have changed.

The traditional civil rights ideology was founded on the unstated assumption that human beings are equal in the eyes of God—the same; and that human nature unites us all in a common *essence*. Together we will, in the words of Dr. Martin Luther King, reach the "promised land" of racial equality. The permanence of racism thesis attacks that "sameness" theory. Black feminists have stood up to say, "I am not the same as you and do not speak for me." This movement, dubbed anti-essentialism, suggests that no essence unites us as human beings. Rather, we are all individuals leading the attack with unique experiences that can neither be classified nor categorized. (For example, the Black lesbian faces a dilemma about which civil rights organizations to join. Should she join the National Organization for Women [NOW], led by White women, or the National Association for the Advancement of Colored People [NAACP], led by Black men, or the AIDS Coalition to Unleash Power [ACT-UP], led by gay and lesbian White people?) Anti-essentialists argue that unity must be built more by realistic connections, instead of relying on abstract and unreal notions of a common essence.

Black Americans Believed in Integration

The civil-rights movement asked precious little. A deeply Christian man [Martin Luther King Jr.] and the crusade he symbolized were warmly embraced by a large portion of white America for all the wrong reasons: namely, that the movement preached the perfectibility of the majority and of the society over which they hold sway. . . .

The government offered to make amends, and we (black Americans) believed in the constitutional connection between a government and its people. . . . We believed that the government actions represented the will of its people. We believed in the goodwill of our countrymen based upon the displays of their "representative" government.

We believed so much that we made the naturally illogical progression to looking to the government to sway its people, looking to political change to stimulate cultural change, asking the cart to pull the horse under the best circumstances—in the forms of, for instance, busing and affirmative action.

Leonce E. Gaiter, *Los Angeles Times*, February 5, 1995.

Similarly, the permanence of racism thesis criticizes the idea that most White people in America will grant Black people equal rights. In fact, according to Bell, African Americans advanced socially, politically and economically when the particular principle appealed to White Americans' self-interest. This means that people of color cannot rely on the majority of White people for a shared commonality of all human beings for equal treatment.

The Failure of the Civil Rights Movement

The permanence of racism thesis exposes the idealist aspects that racial integration will lead to equality. Today, many commentators cite the failure of the civil rights movement in the past forty years to fully reach the promises and hopes of *Brown v. Board of Education* of Topeka, Kansas (1959), for racial integration and quality. While the goal that racial integration will lead to greater equality remains paramount, the reality of not achieving significant progress anytime soon more accurately reflects the nature of the struggle. To match racism's resolve of perpetuation, the anti-racist forces must unite with equal strength of resistance. In her book *Possessing the Secret of Joy*, Alice Walker says that for African American people, "Resistance is the secret of joy." The battle against the permanence of racism will never end. Therefore society must continue to study racism and devise new strategies to combat it.

I recall a personal experience when I was a civil rights lawyer in Mississippi involving an old Black woman in Sunflower County with a fighting spirit like [civil rights activist] Fannie Lou Hamer. We came out of the federal court house one day after the judge praised the Black people for challenging some obvious vestige of racial segregation, but he denied their request for relief on some seemingly unpersuasive legal technicality. I sought to comfort her with condolences about the case that the people had lost. She taught me a lesson based on the knowledge that she acquired in life rather than by formal schooling. I never forgot. When she insisted that they had won, I tried to correct her on the legality of the decision, but she interrupted. She said they won because the Black people had the White people in town very scared about the potential impact of a favorable decision for them. True, everyone knew the White people were extremely concerned about a major change in the political relations with Black people. I thought to myself, how could this Black lady think that they had won? Then she said, "Lawyer Brittain, I just lives to upset these White folks and today we upset them."

Hence, the permanence of racism theory means that this work will never end, only the battle fronts and tactics change.

VIEWPOINT

---

*"The politics of difference is overtaking
education. Those with grievance identities . . .
all want to be segregated universities within
the universities."*

Self-Segregation
Should Be Condemned

Shelby Steele

Conservative black scholars and others charge that the establishment of separate study programs for minorities and women
worsens race relations on college and university campuses. In
the following viewpoint, Shelby Steele argues that demands for
such programs encourage self-segregation and a permanent status of victimhood among minorities and women. He contends
that self-segregation movements have turned away from the goal
of a color-blind society and caused a deterioration in race relations. Steele is a professor of English at San Jose State University
in California and author of *The Content of Our Character: A New
Vision of Race in America*.

As you read, consider the following questions:

1. According to Steele, why did the civil rights movement
   produce rage in blacks?
2. What are grievance identities, according to the author?
3. What are the three reactions of whites to accusations of
   racism, in the author's opinion?

Shelby Steele, "Rise of 'The New Segregation.'" Reprinted, with permission, from *USA Today*
magazine, March 1993. Copyright 1993 by the Society for the Advancement of Education.

The civil rights movement of the 1950s and 1960s culminated in the 1964 Civil Rights and 1965 Voting Rights Acts—two monumental pieces of legislation that dramatically have altered the fabric of American life. During the struggle for their passage, a new source of power came into full force. Black Americans and their supporters tapped into the moral power inspired by a 300-year history of victimization and oppression and used it to help transform society, humanize it, and make it more tolerant and open. They realized, moreover, that the victimization and oppression blacks had endured came from a marriage of race and power. They had to stop those who maintained that, merely because they are white, they have the power to dominate, enslave, segregate, and discriminate.

Race should not be a source of power or advantage or disadvantage for anyone in a free society. This was one of the most important lessons of the original civil rights movement. The legislation it championed during the 1960s constituted a "new emancipation proclamation." For the first time, segregation and discrimination were made illegal. Blacks began to enjoy a degree of freedom they never had experienced before.

Black Rage in the 1960s

This did not mean that things changed overnight for blacks. Nor did it ensure that their memory of past injustice was obliterated. I hesitate to borrow analogies from the psychological community, but I think this one does apply: Abused children usually do not feel anger until many years after the abuse has ended—that is, after they have experienced a degree of freedom and normalcy. Only once civil rights legislation had been enacted did blacks at long last begin to feel the rage they had suppressed. I can remember that period vividly. I had a tremendous sense of delayed anger at having been forced to attend segregated schools. (My grade school was the first to be involved in a desegregation suit in the North.) My rage, like that of other blacks, threatened for a time to become all consuming.

Anger was both inevitable and necessary. When suppressed, it eats a person alive; it must come out, and certainly did during the 1960s. One form was the black power movement in all its many manifestations, some of which were violent. There is no question that we should condemn violence, but we also should understand why it occurs. You cannot oppress people for more than three centuries and then say it is all over and expect them to put on suits and ties and become decent attache-carrying citizens and go to work on Wall Street.

Once my own anger was released, my reaction was that I no longer had to apologize for being black. That was a tremendous benefit and helped me come to terms with my own personal development. The problem is that many blacks never progressed beyond their anger.

A Permanent State of Rage and Victimhood

The black power movement encouraged a permanent state of rage and victimhood. An even greater failing was that it rejoined race and power—the very "marriage" that civil rights legislation had been designed to break up. The leaders of the original movement said, "*Anytime* you make race a source of power you are going to guarantee suffering, misery, and inequity." Black power leaders declared: "We're going to have power because we're *black*."

Is there any conceivable difference between black and white power? When you demand power based on the color of your skin, aren't you saying that equality and justice are impossible? Somebody is going to be in, someone else out. Somebody is going to win or lose, and race again is a source of advantage for some and disadvantage for others. Ultimately, black power was not about equality or justice, but, as its name suggests, about power.

When blacks began to demand entitlements based on their race, feminists soon responded with enthusiasm, "We've been oppressed, too!" Hispanics maintained, "We're not going to let this bus pass us by," and Asians stated, "We're not going to be left out either." Eskimos and Native Americans quickly hopped on the bandwagon, as did gays, lesbians, the disabled, and other self-defined minorities.

By the 1970s, the marriage of race and power was firmly established again. Equality was out; the "politics of difference" was in. From then on, people would rally around the single quality that makes them different and pursue power based on that characteristic. It is a very simple formula. All you have to do is identify that quality, whatever it may be, with victimization, which is itself, after all, a tremendous source of moral power.

The Politics of Grievance Identities

The politics of difference demanded shifting the entire basis of entitlement in America. Historically, it was based on the rights of citizenship elaborated in the Declaration of Independence and the U.S. Constitution. This was the kind of entitlement the original civil rights movement leaders claimed for blacks—recognition of their rights as American citizens to equal treatment under the law. They did not insist, "We deserve rights and entitlements because we are black," but "We deserve them because we are citizens of the United States and like all other citizens are due these rights." The politics of difference changed all that. Blacks and other minorities began demanding entitlement solely based on their history of oppression, their race, sex, ethnicity, or whatever quality that allegedly made them victims.

By the 1980s, the politics of difference, in turn, had led to the establishment of "grievance identities." These are not about such things as the great contributions of women throughout history or the rich culture of black Americans. To have a strong identity as a female, for example, means that you are against the "oppressive male patriarchy"—period. To have a strong identity as a black means you are against racist white America—period. You have no choice but to fulfill a carefully defined politically correct role. You must document the grievance of your group, testify to its abiding and ongoing alienation, and support its sovereignty. As a black who fails any of these three requirements, you not only are politically incorrect, you are a traitor, an "Uncle Tom." You are blaming the victim, letting whites off the hook, and betraying your people.

In establishing your grievance identity, you must turn your back on the enormous and varied fabric of life. There is no legacy of universal ideas or common human experience. There is only one dimension to your identity—anger against oppression. Grievance identities are thus "sovereignties" that compete with those of the nation itself. Blacks, women, Hispanics, and other minorities are not even American citizens anymore. They are citizens of sovereignties with their own right to autonomy.

The New Segregation on Campus

The marriage of race and power, politics of difference, and grievance identities is nurtured by the American educational establishment. They also have acted on that establishment and affected it in significant ways. After a talk I gave at a well-known university, a woman introduced herself as the chairperson of the women's studies department. She was very proud of the fact that the university had a separate degree-granting program in women's studies. I stressed that I always had been very much in favor of teaching students about the contributions of women, but asked her what it was they gained from segregated women's studies that could not be learned within the traditional liberal arts disciplines. Her background was in English, as was mine, so I added, "What is a female English professor in the English department doing that is different from what a female English professor in the women's studies department is doing? Is she going to bring a different methodology to bear? What is it that academically justifies a segregated program for women, or for blacks, or any other group? Why not incorporate such studies into the English department, the history department, the biology department, or into any of the other regular departments?"

As soon as I began to ask such questions, I noticed a shift in her eyes and a tension in her attitude. She began to see me as an enemy and quickly made an excuse to end the conversation. This wasn't about a rational academic discussion of women's studies. It was about the sovereignty of the feminist identity and, unless I tipped my hat to that identity by saying, "Yes, you have the right to a separate department," no further discussion or debate was possible.

Self-Segregation at Universities

While predominantly white colleges and universities now enroll a majority of the more than 1.3 million black college students, the fact is that on many of those campuses, segregation remains alive and well. All too often, black and white students live apart, eat apart and eventually grow apart. A variety of organizations representing blacks, Hispanics, Asian-Americans and others seek the very kind of "separate-but-equal" privileges and facilities which the civil rights movement and men and women of good-will of all races sought to eliminate.

"We have a campus of 25,000 students and there is no mixing across cultural and racial lines," reports Christine Romans, the editor of the student newspaper at Iowa State University. Even during a campus rally for unity after a racial incident, she reported, "all the blacks clustered together and all the whites clustered together."

J.A. Parker, *Lincoln Review*, Spring/Summer 1994.

Meanwhile, the politics of difference is overtaking education. Those with grievance identities demand separate buildings, classrooms, offices, clerical staff—even Xerox machines. They all want to be segregated universities within the universities. They insist on their own space, their sovereign territory. Metaphorically, and sometimes literally, they insist that not only the university, but society at large, must pay tribute to their sovereignty.

Today, there are some 500 women's studies departments. There are black, Hispanic, Jewish, and Asian studies departments. They all have to have space, staff, and budgets. What are they studying that can't be done in other departments? They don't have to answer this question, of course, but when political entitlement shifted away from citizenship to race, class, and gender, a shift in cultural entitlement became inevitable.

Those with grievance identities also demand *extra* entitlements far beyond what should come to us citizens. As a black, I am said to "deserve" this or that special entitlement. No longer is it enough just to have the right to attend a college or university on an equal basis with others or to be treated like anyone else. Schools must set aside special money and academic departments just for me, based on my grievance. Some campuses now have segregated dorms for black students who demand to live together with people of their "own kind." They have lobbied for separate black student unions, yearbooks, Homecoming dances, and graduation ceremonies—again, all so that they can be comfortable with their own kind.

One representative study at the University of Michigan indicated that 70 percent of the school's black undergraduates never have had a white acquaintance. Yet, across the nation, colleges and universities like Michigan readily and even eagerly continue to encourage more segregation by granting the demands of every vocal grievance identity.

White Guilt

A great contributing factor is white guilt—specifically a knowledge of ill-gotten advantage. Ignorance is innocence and knowledge is guilt. Whites in America generally know that there is at least a slight advantage in being white. If a white person walks into a department store, chances are he or she is not going to be followed by the security guard as I am. This kind of knowledge makes whites vulnerable. (Incidentally, I do not mean to deride all forms of guilt. It can be a wonderful thing, a truly civilized emotion. Prisons are full of people incapable of feeling guilt.)

A member of a grievance identity points a finger and says, "Hey, whitey, you've oppressed my people! You have had generations to build up wealth and opportunity while I've had nothing." Almost automatically, the white person's first reaction is: "Am I guilty? Am I a racist?"

The second reaction is escapism: "All right, what do you want? What is it going to take to prove to you that I am not racist?" White college and university administrators say, "You want a black student lounge? You got it. We have a little extra money, so we can pay for a black yearbook. We can hold a separate graduation just for you. What else do you want?"

The third reaction is blindness. Obviously, when you are preoccupied with escaping your own feelings of guilt, you are utterly blind to the people causing it. So, college and university administrators blindly grant black students extra entitlements, from dorms to yearbooks, and build an entire machinery of segregation on campus while ignoring the fact that 72 percent of black American college students are dropping out.

Blacks Don't Need Separation

Blacks have the lowest grade point average of any student group. If whites were not so preoccupied with escaping their own guilt, they would see that the real problem is not racism—it

214

is that black undergraduates are failing in tragic numbers. They don't need separate dorms and yearbooks. They need basic academic skills. Instead, they are taught that extra entitlements are their due and that the greatest power of all is the power that comes to them as victims. If they want to get anywhere in American life, they had better wear their victimization on their sleeve and tap into white guilt, making whites want to escape by offering money, status, racial preferences—something, anything—in return. Is this the way for a race that has been oppressed to come into its own? Is this the way to achieve independence?

Colleges and universities not only are segregating their campuses, they are segregating learning. If only for the sake of historical accuracy, we should teach all students—black, white, female, male—about many broad and diverse cultures. Yet, those with grievance identities use the multicultural approach as an all-out assault on the liberal arts curriculum, American heritage, and Western culture. They have made our differences, rather than our common bonds, sacred. Often, they do so in the name of building the "self-esteem" of minorities. However, they are not going to build anyone's self-esteem by condemning American culture as the product of "dead white males."

We *do* share a common history and a common culture, and that must be the central premise of education. If we are to end the new segregation on campus, and everywhere else it exists, we need to recall the spirit of the original civil rights movement, which was dedicated to the "self-evident truth" that all men are created equal.

Even the most humble experiences unite us. We all have grown up on the same sitcoms, eaten the same fast food, and laughed at the same jokes. We have practiced the same religions, lived under the same political system, read the same books, and worked in the same marketplace. We have the same dreams and aspirations as well as fears and doubts for ourselves and for our children. How, then, can our differences be so overwhelming?

"When blacks are 'being ethnic,' whites see them as 'being racial.' Thus they view the identity politics of students who want to celebrate their blackness . . . as racially offensive."

Self-Segregation Should Be Accepted

Bob Blauner

Many colleges and universities have experienced a deterioration in race relations on campus and a trend toward ethnic self-segregation among student groups. In the following viewpoint, Bob Blauner argues that this deterioration results from differences in the way blacks and whites define racism. Whites associate racism with discrimination, according to Blauner, while blacks view it as the result of a society that is set up to benefit whites. He contends that it is not racist for blacks to emphasize their ethnicity and self-segregate in their own organizations. Blauner is a professor of sociology at the University of California, Berkeley, and author of *Black Lives, White Lives*.

As you read, consider the following questions:

1. According to Blauner, where do whites locate racism?
2. According to the author, why does the idea of institutional racism not make sense to most whites?
3. How is an ethnic group different from a racial group, according to the author?

Excerpted from "Talking Past Each Other: Black and White Languages of Race" by Bob Blauner. Reprinted with permission from *The American Prospect*, Summer 1992, ©1992 New Prospect Inc.

I want to advance the proposition that there are two languages of race in America. I am not talking about black English and standard English, which refer to different structures of grammar and dialect. "Language" here signifies a system of implicit understandings about social reality, and a racial language encompasses a worldview.

Different Languages of Race

Blacks and whites differ on their interpretations of social change from the 1960s through the 1990s because their racial languages define the central terms, especially "racism," differently. Their racial languages incorporate different views of American society itself, especially the question of how central race and racism are to America's very existence, past and present. Blacks believe in this centrality, while most whites, except for the more race-conscious extremists, see race as a peripheral reality. Even successful, middle-class black professionals experience slights and humiliations—incidents when they are stopped by police, regarded suspiciously by clerks while shopping, or mistaken for messengers, drivers, or aides at work—that remind them they have not escaped racism's reach. For whites, race becomes central on exceptional occasions: collective, public moments such as the recent events [e.g., the 1991 beating of Rodney King by Los Angeles police officers and the Spring 1992 riot that ensued after the officers were acquitted], when the veil is lifted, and private ones, such as a family's decision to escape urban problems with a move to the suburbs. But most of the time European-Americans are able to view racial issues as aberrations in American life. . . .

Because of these differences in language and worldview, blacks and whites often talk past one another, just as men and women sometimes do. . . . Whites locate racism in color consciousness and its absence in color-blindness. They regard it as a kind of racism when students of color insistently underscore their sense of difference, their affirmation of ethnic and racial membership, which minority students have increasingly asserted. Many black, and increasingly also Latino and Asian, students cannot understand this reaction. It seems to them misinformed, even ignorant. They in turn sense a kind of racism in the whites' assumption that minorities must assimilate to mainstream values and styles. Then African-Americans will posit an idea that many whites find preposterous: Black people, they argue, cannot be racist, because racism is a system of power, and black people as a group do not have power.

In this and many other arenas, a contest rages over the meaning of racism. Racism has become the central term in the language of race. From the 1940s through the 1980s new and multiple meanings of racism have been added to the social science lexicon and public discourse. The 1960s were especially critical for what the English sociologist Robert Miles has called the "inflation" of the term "racism." Blacks tended to embrace the enlarged definitions, whites to resist them. This conflict, in my view, has been at the very center of the racial struggle since the 1980s.

The Widening Conception of Racism

The term "racism" was not commonly used in social science or American public life until the 1960s. "Racism" does not appear, for example, in the Swedish economist Gunnar Myrdal's classic 1944 study of American race relations, *An American Dilemma*. But even when the term was not directly used, it is still possible to determine the prevailing understandings of racial oppression.

In the 1940s racism referred to an ideology, an explicit system of beliefs postulating the superiority of whites based on the inherent, biological inferiority of the colored races. Ideological racism was particularly associated with the belief systems of the Deep South and was originally devised as a rationale for slavery. Theories of white supremacy, particularly in their biological versions, lost much of their legitimacy after the Second World War due to their association with Nazism. In recent years cultural explanations of "inferiority" are heard more commonly than biological ones, which today are associated with such extremist "hate groups" as the Ku Klux Klan and the White Aryan Brotherhood.

By the 1950s and early 1960s, with ideological racism discredited, the focus shifted to a more discrete approach to racially invidious attitudes and behavior, expressed in the model of prejudice and discrimination. "Prejudice" referred (and still does) to hostile feelings and beliefs about racial minorities and the web of stereotypes justifying such negative attitudes. "Discrimination" referred to actions meant to harm the members of a racial minority group. The logic of this model was that racism implied a double standard, that is, treating a person of color differently—in mind or action—than one would a member of the majority group.

By the mid-1960s the terms "prejudice" and "discrimination" and the implicit model of racial causation implied by them were seen as too weak to explain the sweep of racial conflict and change, too limited in their analytical power, and for some critics too individualistic in their assumptions. Their original meanings tended to be absorbed by a new, more encompassing idea of racism. During the 1960s the referents of racial oppression moved from individual actions and beliefs to group and institutional processes, from subjective ideas to "objective" structures or results. Instead of intent, there was now an emphasis on process: those more objective social processes of exclusion, exploitation, and discrimination that led to a racially stratified society.

The most notable of these new definitions was "institutional racism." In their 1967 book *Black Power*, Stokely Carmichael and Charles Hamilton stressed how institutional racism was different and more fundamental than individual racism. Racism, in this view, was built into society and scarcely required prejudicial attitudes to maintain racial oppression.

Reprinted by permission of Kirk Anderson.

This understanding of racism as pervasive and institutionalized spread from relatively narrow "movement" and academic circles to the larger public with the appearance in 1968 of the report of the commission on the urban riots appointed by President Lyndon Johnson and chaired by Illinois Governor Otto Kerner. The Kerner Commission identified "white racism" as a prime reality of American society and the major underlying cause of ghetto unrest. America, in this view, was moving toward two societies, one white and one black (it is not clear where other racial minorities fit in). Although its recommendations were never acted upon politically, the report legitimated the term "white racism" among politicians and opinion leaders as a key to analyzing racial inequality in America.

Another definition of racism, which I would call "racism as atmosphere," also emerged in the 1960s and 1970s. This is the

219

idea that an organization or an environment might be racist because its implicit, unconscious structures were devised for the use and comfort of white people, with the result that people of other races will not feel at home in such settings. Acting on this understanding of racism, many schools and universities, corporations, and other institutions have changed their teaching practices or work environments to encourage a greater diversity in their clientele, students, or work force.

Perhaps the most radical definition of all was the concept of "racism as result." In this sense, an institution or an occupation is racist simply because racial minorities are underrepresented in numbers or in positions of prestige and authority.

Racism Is Not a Thing of the Past

Seizing on different conceptions of racism, the blacks and whites I talked to in the late 1970s had come to different conclusions about how far America had moved toward racial justice. Whites tended to adhere to earlier, more limited notions of racism. Blacks for the most part saw the newer meanings as more basic. Thus African-Americans did not think racism had been put to rest by civil rights laws, even by the dramatic changes in the South. They felt that it still pervaded American life, indeed, had become more insidious because the subtle forms were harder to combat than old-fashioned exclusion and persecution.

Whites saw racism largely as a thing of the past. They defined it in terms of segregation and lynching, explicit white supremacist beliefs, or double standards in hiring, promotion, and admissions to colleges or other institutions. Except for affirmative action, which seemed the most blatant expression of such double standards, they were positively impressed by racial change. Many saw the relaxed and comfortable relations between whites and blacks as the heart of the matter. More crucial to blacks, on the other hand, were the underlying structures of power and position that continued to provide them with unequal portions of economic opportunity and other possibilities for the good life.

The newer, expanded definitions of racism just do not make much sense to most whites. I have experienced their frustrations directly when I try to explain the concept of institutional racism to white students and popular audiences. The idea of racism as an "impersonal force" loses all but the most theoretically inclined. Whites are more likely than blacks to view racism as a personal issue. Both sensitive to their own possible culpability (if only unconsciously) and angry at the use of the concept of racism by angry minorities, they do not differentiate well between the racism of social structures and the accusation that they as participants in that structure are personally racist. . . .

220

The question then becomes what to do about these multiple and confusing meanings of racism and their extraordinary personal and political charge. I would begin by honoring both the black and white readings of the term. Such an attitude might help facilitate the interracial dialogue so badly needed and yet so rare today.

Communication can only start from the understandings that people have. While the black understanding of racism is, in some sense, the deeper one, the white views of racism (ideology, double standard) refer to more specific and recognizable beliefs and practices. Since there is also a cross-racial consensus on the immorality of racist ideology and racial discrimination, it makes sense whenever possible to use such a concrete referent as discrimination, rather than the more global concept of racism. And reemphasizing discrimination may help remind the public that racial discrimination is not just a legacy of the past.

The intellectual power of the African-American understanding lies in its more critical and encompassing perspective. In the Rodney King events, we have an unparalleled opportunity to bridge the racial gap by pointing out that racism and racial division remain essential features of American life and that incidents such as police beatings of minority people and stacked juries are not aberrations but part of a larger pattern of racial abuse and harassment. Without resorting to the overheated rhetoric that proved counterproductive in the 1960s, it now may be possible to persuade white Americans that the most important patterns of discrimination and disadvantage are not to be found in the "reverse racism" of affirmative action but sadly still in the white racism of the dominant social system. And, when feasible, we need to try to bridge the gap by shifting from the language of race to that of ethnicity and class.

Race or Ethnicity?

In the American consciousness the imagery of race—especially along the black-white dimension—tends to be more powerful than that of class or ethnicity. As a result, legitimate ethnic affiliations are often misunderstood to be racial and illegitimate.

Race itself is a confusing concept because of the variance between scientific and commonsense definitions of the term. Physical anthropologists who study the distribution of those characteristics we use to classify "races" teach us that race is a fiction because all peoples are mixed to various degrees. Sociologists counter that this biological fiction unfortunately remains a sociological reality. People define one another racially, and thus divide society into racial groups. The "fiction" of race affects every aspect of peoples' lives, from living standards to landing in jail.

221

The consciousness of color differences, and the invidious distinctions based on them, have existed since antiquity and are not limited to any one corner of the world. And yet the peculiarly modern division of the world into a discrete number of hierarchically ranked races is a historic product of Western colonialism. In precolonial Africa the relevant group identities were national, tribal, or linguistic. There was no concept of an African or black people until this category was created by the combined effects of slavery, imperialism, and the anticolonial and Pan-African movements. The legal definitions of blackness and whiteness, which varied from one society to another in the Western hemisphere, were also crucial for the construction of modern-day races. Thus race is an essentially political construct, one that translates our tendency to see people in terms of their color or other physical attributes into structures that make it likely that people will act for or against them on such a basis.

The dynamic of ethnicity is different, even though the results at times may be similar. An ethnic group is a group that shares a belief in its common past. Members of an ethnic group hold a set of common memories that make them feel that their customs, culture, and outlook are distinctive. In short, they have a sense of peoplehood. Sharing critical experiences and sometimes a belief in their common fate, they feel an affinity for one another, a "comfort zone" that leads to congregating together, even when this is not forced by exclusionary barriers. Thus if race is associated with biology and nature, ethnicity is associated with culture. Like races, ethnic groups arise historically, transform themselves, and sometimes die out.

Whites Do Not Appreciate Ethnic Differences

Much of the popular discourse about race in America today goes awry because ethnic realities get lost under the racial umbrella. The positive meanings and potential of ethnicity are overlooked, even overrun, by the more inflammatory meanings of race. Thus white students, disturbed when blacks associate with each other, justify their objections through their commitment to *racial* integration. They do not appreciate the ethnic affinities that bring this about, or see the parallels to Jewish students meeting at the campus Hillel Foundation or Italian-Americans eating lunch at the Italian house on the Berkeley campus.

When blacks are "being ethnic," whites see them as "being racial." Thus they view the identity politics of students who want to celebrate their blackness, their *chicanoismo*, their Asian heritages, and their American Indian roots as racially offensive. Part of this reaction comes from a sincere desire, almost a yearning, of white students for a color-blind society. But because the ethnicity of darker people so often gets lost in our overracialized perceptions, the white students misread the situation. When I point out to my class that whites are talking about race and its dynamics and the students of color are talking about ethnicity and its differing meaning, they can begin to appreciate each other's agendas.

Confounding race and ethnicity is not just limited to the young. The general public, including journalists and other opinion makers, does this regularly, with serious consequences for the clarity of public dialogue and sociological analysis. A clear example comes from the Chicago mayoral election of 1983. The establishment press, including leading liberal columnists, regularly chastised the black electorate for giving virtually all its votes to Harold Washington. Such racial voting was as "racist" as whites voting for the other candidate because they did not want a black mayor. Yet African-Americans were voting for ethnic representation just as Irish-Americans, Jews, and Italians have always done. Such ethnic politics is considered the American way. What is discriminatory is the double standard that does not confer the same rights on blacks, who were not voting primarily out of fear or hatred as were many whites.

The Ambiguous Status of Blacks

Such confusions between race and ethnicity are exacerbated by the ambiguous sociological status of African-Americans. Black Americans are *both* a race and an ethnic group. Unfortunately, part of our heritage of racism has been to deny the ethnicity, the cultural heritage of black Americans. Liberal-minded whites have wanted to see blacks as essentially white people with black skins. Until the 1960s few believed that black culture was a real ethnic culture.

Because our racial language is so deep-seated, the terminology of black and white just seems more "natural" and commonsensical than more ethnic labels like African-American or European-American. But the shift to the term African-American has been a conscious attempt to move the discourse from a language of race to a language of ethnicity. "African-American," as Jesse Jackson and others have pointed out, connects the group to its history and culture in a way that the racial designation, "black," does not. The new usage parallels terms for other ethnic groups. Many whites tend to dismiss this concern about language as mere sloganeering. But "African-American" fits better into the emerging multicultural view of American ethnic and racial arrangements, one more appropriate to our growing diversity. The old race relations model was essentially a view that generalized (often inappropriately) from black-white relations. It can no longer capture—if it ever could—the complexity of a multiracial and multicultural society.

223

Periodical Bibliography

The following articles have been selected to supplement the diverse views presented in this chapter.

J.C. Billings	"Racism in the '90s: Is It Hip to Hate?" *The Education Digest*, December 1992.
John H. Bunzel	"In Democracy's Shadow," *Vital Speeches of the Day*, October 1, 1993.
Stanley Crouch	"The One Out of Many Blues," *The American Enterprise*, March/April 1995.
Mel Elfin and Sarah Burke	"Race on Campus," *U.S. News & World Report*, April 19, 1993.
Henry Louis Gates Jr.	"Two Nations . . . Both Black," *Forbes*, September 14, 1992.
Bob Herbert	"Who Will Help the Black Man?" *The New York Times Magazine*, December 4, 1994.
Leslie Inniss	"School Desegregation: Too High a Price?" *Social Policy*, Winter 1993.
Tamar Jacoby	"The Bitter Legacies of Malcolm X," *Commentary*, February 1993.
Mary Jordan	"Separate by Choice," *The Washington Post National Weekly Edition*, March 21–27, 1994. Available from 1150 15th St. NW, Washington, DC 20071.
Nicholas Lemann	"Black Nationalism on Campus," *The Atlantic Monthly*, January 1993.
John Leo	"Separatism Won't Solve Anything," *U.S. News & World Report*, April 19, 1993.
The Nation	"Broken Promise: *Brown v. Board of Education* Forty Years Later," May 23, 1994.
Hugh B. Price	"Public Discourse," *Vital Speeches of the Day*, January 15, 1995.
L.B. Randolph	"Reverse Integration," *Ebony*, January 1994.
Cornel West	"Black Politics, Black Leadership," *The Christian Century*, August 11–18, 1993.
Juan Williams	"Why Segregation Seems So Seductive," *The Washington Post National Weekly Edition*, January 24–30, 1994.

For Further Discussion

Chapter 1

1. Derrick Bell argues that economic and social disparities exist between blacks and whites as a result of the racism of whites. What evidence does he present that opportunities for blacks are limited by racism among whites? Is the evidence convincing? Why or why not?

2. According to Stanley Fish, opposition to affirmative action is a racist attempt by whites to preserve economic and social privileges for themselves. How do you think Timur Kuran would respond to Fish's argument? Whose argument is more persuasive? Why?

3. Do you think that the statements of Louis Farrakhan are anti-Semitic? In your opinion, is Farrakhan's message a positive one for blacks? Explain your answer.

Chapter 2

1. Andrew Hacker argues that statistical disparities between the representation of blacks (males especially) and others in certain professions demonstrate the persistence of discrimination. How does Jared Taylor dispute Hacker's use of statistical data? Does Taylor effectively refute Hacker's argument? Defend your answer using examples from Taylor's viewpoint.

2. Ellis Cose believes that middle-class blacks are alienated from American society as a result of discrimination in the workplace and in society. What evidence of alienation does he present? How do you think Peter N. Kirsanow would respond to Cose's argument?

3. Roger Wilkins contends that whites take for granted the everyday privileges that skin color provides them and that this attitude is racist. In contrast, how does Steven Yates define racism? How do the authors' differing definitions of racism affect their conclusions about affirmative action?

4. Thomas Muller argues that immigrants, both legal and illegal, add jobs to the economy, increasing the demand for goods and services. According to Muller, how does this benefit blacks, and which class of blacks in particular does it benefit? What does Jack Miles say is the impact of immigration on black employment, and which class of blacks is affected?

Chapter 3

1. Gerald Horne argues that blacks are imprisoned more often and for longer periods than others because of racism in the justice system. What evidence does he present to support this argument? What evidence does Patrick A. Langan present to refute arguments such as Horne's? Which author's use of evidence is more convincing? Why?

2. Wanda Coleman believes that the sentence of probation given to Korean grocer Soon Ja Du in the killing of black teenager Latasha Harlins sent a message to blacks that their lives are worth less than those of others. How does Coleman's description of the shooting differ from the one recounted by William F. Jasper? What reasons does Jasper cite for the sentence of probation given to Du?

3. Tanya E. Coke argues that racial imbalance in a jury, particularly in a high-profile case, can give the impression that a verdict is unfair. According to Coke, why is a verdict by a racially balanced jury seemingly (and actually) more just? According to Andrew Kull, why is it incorrect to believe that a verdict from a racially balanced jury is more fair? Which viewpoint do you agree with, and why?

Chapter 4

1. What criticisms does Carol M. Swain offer of both race-conscious districts and proportional representation? Is it necessary for minorities to have a member of their group as their representative? Why or why not?

2. Pete Wilson opposes illegal immigration, arguing that it costs the state of California billions of dollars per year to provide services to illegal immigrants and that this hurts the state's economy. How do you think Elizabeth Kadetsky would respond to Wilson's argument? Explain, using the viewpoint as evidence.

Chapter 5

1. Tamar Jacoby maintains that integration of blacks into a color-blind society is the best strategy for peaceful race relations. Why did past integration efforts fail, in Jacoby's opinion? What would John C. Brittain say is the reason for the failure of integration programs? Which author's argument is more convincing, and why?

2. Bob Blauner argues that blacks and whites disagree on the definition of racism. How does he define institutional racism? Do you agree with this definition? Why or why not?

Organizations to Contact

The editors have compiled the following list of organizations concerned with the issues debated in this book. The descriptions are derived from materials provided by the organizations. All have publications or information available for interested readers. The list was compiled on the date of publication of the present volume; names, addresses, and phone numbers may change. Be aware that many organizations take several weeks or longer to respond to inquiries, so allow as much time as possible.

African Americans for Humanism (AAH)
Box 664
Buffalo, NY 14226
(716) 636-7571

AAH is dedicated to developing humanism in the African-American community through outreach to those who are unchurched and is especially concerned with fighting racism through humanistic education. It publishes the quarterly newsletter *AAH Examiner*.

American-Arab Anti-Discrimination Committee
4201 Connecticut Ave. NW, Suite 500
Washington, DC 20008
(202) 244-2990

This organization fights anti-Arab stereotyping in the media and discrimination and hate crimes against Arab-Americans. It publishes a series of issue papers and a number of books, including the *1991 Report on Anti-Arab Hate Crimes*.

American Civil Liberties Union (ACLU)
132 W. 43rd St.
New York, NY 10036
(212) 944-9800

The ACLU is a national organization that works to defend Americans' civil rights guaranteed by the U.S. Constitution. The ACLU publishes and distributes policy statements, pamphlets, and the semiannual newsletter *Civil Liberties Alert*.

Anglo-Saxon Christian-Patriots
c/o E.S. (Gene) Hall
1948 Fabersham Ct.
Snellville, GA 30278
(404) 972-4445

This Christian organization promotes study of and adherence to the biblical proscription against race mixing. It publishes and distributes a Bible study book on racial separatism.

Anti-Defamation League (ADL)
823 United Nations Plaza
New York, NY 10017
(212) 490-2525

The ADL works to stop the defamation of Jews and to ensure fair treatment for all U.S. citizens. It publishes the periodic *Dimensions* and the quarterly *Facts* magazines.

Center for the Applied Study of Prejudice and Ethnoviolence
Stephens Hall Annex
Towson State University
Towson, MD 21204-7097
(410) 838-2435

The center studies responses to violence and intimidation motivated by prejudice. It publishes the quarterly newsletter *Forum* as well as numerous reports.

Center for the Study of Popular Culture
9911 W. Pico Blvd., Suite 1290
Los Angeles, CA 90035
(800) 752-6562

The center has formed a Civil Rights project to study and address the effects of affirmative action laws on the nation. The project provides legal assistance to citizens challenging affirmative action and promotes color-blind, equal opportunity for individuals. It publishes and distributes a number of books, including *Liberal Racism*.

Citizens' Commission on Civil Rights (CCCR)
2000 M St. NW, Suite 400
Washington, DC 20036
(202) 659-5565

The CCCR monitors the federal government's enforcement of laws that bar discrimination and promotes equal opportunity for all. It publishes reports on affirmative action and desegregation as well as the book *One Nation Indivisible: The Civil Rights Challenge for the 1990s*.

Euro-American Alliance
PO Box 2-1776
Milwaukee, WI 53221
(414) 423-0565

This organization opposes racial mixing and advocates self-segregation for whites. It publishes a number of pamphlets, including *Who Hates Whom?* and *Who We Really Are*.

Hispanic Policy Development Project (HPDP)
1001 Connecticut Ave. NW
Washington, DC 20036
(202) 822-8414

HPDP is a nonprofit organization that encourages analysis of public policies affecting Hispanic youth in the United States, especially in education, employment, and family issues. It publishes a number of books and pamphlets, including *Together Is Better: Building Strong Partnerships Between Schools and Hispanic Parents*.

Lincoln Institute for Research and Education
2027 Massachusetts Ave. NE
Washington, DC 20036
(202) 223-5110

The institute is a think tank that studies public policy issues affecting the lives of black Americans. It publishes the quarterly *Lincoln Review*.

Multicultural Association of Northwestern Ontario
711 Victoria Ave. E
Thunder Bay, ON P7C 5X9
CANADA
(807) 622-4666

This association sponsors multicultural educational events for young people in Ontario and among its regional affiliates. It publishes the quarterly *Regional Youth Council Newsletter* and the annual *NW Ontario Multicultural Calendar of Events*.

Multicultural Council of Saskatchewan
369 Park St.
Regina, SK S4N 5B2
CANADA
(306) 721-2767

The council sponsors multicultural educational events for young people in Saskatchewan and among its regional affiliates. It publishes the monthly *Cultural Crossings*, the quarterly *Faces—Canada's Multicultural Magazine*, and the quarterly *Check-up on Multicultural Health*.

National Association for the Advancement of Colored People (NAACP)
4805 Mt. Hope Dr.
Baltimore, MD 21215-3297
(410) 358-8900

The NAACP is the oldest and largest civil rights organization in the United States. Its principal objective is to ensure the political, educational, social, and economic equality of minority group citizens. It publishes a variety of newsletters, books, and pamphlets as well as the monthly magazine *Crisis*.

National Center for Neighborhood Enterprise
1367 Connecticut Ave. NW
Washington, DC 20036
(202) 331-1103

This organization promotes self-sufficiency in low-income communities and the revitalization or urban neighborhoods. It publishes the periodic newsletter *In the News* and *On the Road to Economic Freedom: An Agenda for Black Progress*.

National Urban League
1111 14th St. NW, 6th Fl.
Washington, DC 20005
(202) 898-1604

A community service agency, the Urban League aims to eliminate institutional racism in the United States. It also provides services for minorities who experience discrimination in employment, housing, welfare, and other areas. It publishes the report *The Price: A Study of the Costs of Racism in America* and the annual *State of Black America*.

Poverty and Race Research Action Council (PRRAC)
1711 Connecticut Ave. NW, Suite 207
Washington, DC 20077-0009
(202) 387-9887

The PRRAC is a national organization that promotes research and advocacy on behalf of poor minorities on the issues of race and poverty. It publishes the bimonthly newsletter *Poverty & Race*.

Sojourners
2401 15th St. NW
Washington, DC 20009
(202) 328-8842

Sojourners is an ecumenical Christian organization committed to racial justice and reconciliation between races. It publishes *America's Original Sin: A Study Guide on White Racism* as well as the monthly *Sojourners* magazine.

United States Commission on Civil Rights
1121 Vermont Ave. NW
Washington, DC 20425
(202) 376-8177

A fact-finding body, the commission reports directly to Congress and the president on the effectiveness of equal opportunity programs and laws. A catalog of its numerous publications can be obtained from its Publication Management Division.

Bibliography of Books

Nancy Abelmann and John Lie — *Blue Dreams: Korean Americans and the Los Angeles Riots.* Cambridge, MA: Harvard University Press, 1995.

Harry S. Ashmore — *Civil Rights and Wrongs: A Memoir of Race and Politics 1944–1994.* New York: Pantheon Books, 1994.

Derrick Bell — *Confronting Authority: Reflections of an Ardent Protester.* Boston: Beacon Press, 1994.

Mary Frances Berry — *Black Resistance, White Law: A History of Constitutional Racism in America.* New York: A. Lane, Penguin Press, 1994.

Bob Blauner — *Black Lives, White Lives: Three Decades of Race Relations in America.* Berkeley and Los Angeles: University of California Press, 1989.

Bebe Moore Campbell — *Brothers and Sisters.* New York: Putnam's, 1994.

Stephen L. Carter — *Reflections of an Affirmative Action Baby.* New York: BasicBooks, 1991.

Wanda Coleman — *Hand Dance.* Santa Rosa, CA: Black Sparrow Press, 1993.

Joseph G. Conti and Brad Stetson — *Challenging the Civil Rights Establishment: Profiles of a New Black Vanguard.* Westport, CT: Praeger, 1993.

Ellis Cose — *A Nation of Strangers: Prejudice, Politics, and the Populating of America.* New York: William Morrow, 1992.

Audrey Edwards and Craig K. Polite — *Children of the Dream: The Psychology of Black Success.* New York: Doubleday, 1992.

Richard Allen Epstein — *Forbidden Grounds: The Case Against Employment Discrimination Laws.* Cambridge, MA: Harvard University Press, 1992.

Gertrude Ezorsky — *Racism and Justice: The Case for Affirmative Action.* Ithaca, NY: Cornell University Press, 1991.

Louis Farrakhan — *Independent Black Leadership in America.* New York: Castillo International Publications, 1990.

Joe R. Feagin — *Living with Racism: The Black Middle-Class Experience.* Boston: Beacon Press, 1994.

John Hope Franklin — *The Color Line: Legacy for the Twenty-first Century.* Columbia: University of Missouri Press, 1993.

Henry Louis Gates Jr. *Colored People: A Memoir.* New York: Knopf, 1994.

William W. Goldsmith *Separate Societies: Poverty and Inequality in U.S.*
and Edward J. Blakely *Cities.* Philadelphia: Temple University Press, 1992.

Lani Guinier *The Tyranny of the Majority: Fundamental Fairness in Representative Democracy.* New York: Free Press, 1994.

Herbert Hill and *Race in America: The Struggle for Equality.* Madi-
James E. Jones Jr. son: University of Wisconsin Press, 1993.

bell hooks *Outlaw Culture: Resisting Representations.* New York: Routledge, 1994.

Gerald Horne *Reversing Discrimination: The Case for Affirmative Action.* New York: International Publishers, 1992.

Alan L. Keyes *Masters of the Dream: The Strength and Betrayal of Black America.* New York: William Morrow, 1995.

Andrew Kull *The Color-Blind Constitution.* Cambridge, MA: Harvard University Press, 1992.

Coramae Richey Mann *Unequal Justice: A Question of Color.* Bloomington: Indiana University Press, 1993.

Manning Marable *The Crisis of Color and Democracy: Essays on Race, Class, and Power.* Monroe, ME: Common Courage Press, 1992.

Douglas S. Massey *American Apartheid: Segregation and the Making of the Underclass.* Cambridge, MA: Harvard University Press, 1993.

Nathan McCall *Makes Me Wanna Holler: A Young Black Man in America.* New York: Random House, 1994.

John J. Miller *Strangers at Our Gate: Immigration in the 1990s.* Washington: Center for the New American Community, 1994.

Nicolaus Mills, ed. *Debating Affirmative Action: Race, Gender, Ethnicity, and the Politics of Inclusion.* New York: Delta Trade Paperbacks, 1994.

Toni Morrison, ed. *Race-ing Justice, En-gendering Power: Essays on Anita Hill, Clarence Thomas, and the Construction of Social Reality.* New York: Pantheon Books, 1992.

Thomas Muller *Immigrants and the American City.* New York: New York University Press, 1993.

Charles Ogletree et al. *Beyond the Rodney King Story: An Investigation of Police Conduct in Minority Communities.* Boston: Northeastern University Press, 1995.

Gary Y. Okihiro *Margins and Mainstreams: Asians in American History and Culture.* Seattle: University of Washington Press, 1994.

Gary Orfield *The Closing Door: Conservative Policy and Black Opportunity.* Chicago: University of Chicago Press, 1991.

William E. Pannell *The Coming Race Wars? A Cry for Reconciliation.* Grand Rapids, MI: Zondervan, 1993.

Phillip Perlmutter *Divided We Fall: A History of Ethnic, Religious, and Racial Prejudice in America.* Ames: Iowa State University Press, 1992.

David R. Roediger *Towards the Abolition of Whiteness: Essays on Race, Politics, and Working Class History.* London: Verso, 1994.

Peter Skerry *Mexican Americans: The Ambivalent Minority.* New York: Free Press, 1993.

Paul M. Sniderman and Thomas Piazza *The Scar of Race.* Cambridge, MA: Belknap Press of Harvard University Press, 1993.

Thomas Sowell *Race and Culture: A World View.* New York: BasicBooks, 1994.

Shelby Steele *The Content of Our Character: A New Vision of Race in America.* New York: St. Martin's Press, 1990.

Carol M. Swain *Black Faces, Black Interests: The Representation of African Americans in Congress.* Cambridge, MA: Harvard University Press, 1993.

Ronald T. Takaki *A Different Mirror: A History of Multicultural America.* Boston: Little, Brown, 1993.

Studs Terkel *Race: How Blacks and Whites Think and Feel About the American Obsession.* New York: New Press, 1992.

Cornel West *Race Matters.* Boston: Beacon Press, 1993.

Ralph Wiley *What Black People Should Do Now: Dispatches from Near the Vanguard.* New York: Ballantine Books, 1993.

Steven Yates *Civil Wrongs: What Went Wrong with Affirmative Action.* San Francisco: ICS Press, 1994.

Index

Hennepin County, Minn., 169, 170
Hernandez, Lisa, 60
Hicks, Joe, 120, 121
Hispanic Americans
  and activism, 56, 58, 62
  in California, 117, 188-90
  and Chicano *movimiento*, 65, 69
  compete with blacks, 55-63
    should form alliance, 64-70
  and L.A. riots, 68, 117-19
  and low-paid work, 121, 122
  media/white indifference to, 68, 70,
    121
  particular problems of, 61, 121
  and tension with blacks, 57-60, 190
  in Texas, 55-63
  see also immigration; politics
Hitler, Adolf, 45, 52, 53
Hochschild, Jennifer, 22
Hofstadter, Richard, 83
Hopwood v. Texas, 93
Horne, Gerald, 135
Houston, Tex., 57-58, 59-61, 62
Houston Post, 56, 60

immigrants
  illegal
    California hosts many, 187, 193
    crisis of, 194
      is federal responsibility, 195-96
    large cost of, 193-94
    measures against
      are racist, 186-91
        con, 192-96
      and citizenship rights, 188
      have widespread support, 197-88,
        190
      restrict access to welfare/schools,
        187, 189
      and Save Our State (S.O.S.) ballot,
        187
    magnet cities for, 129
    take jobs from blacks, 116-23
      con, 124-31
      because Latinos are trusted, 121
      only when jobs are low-paid, 122,
        130-31
immigration
  benefits of, 17, 27-28, 129
  growth of, 117, 125
  and growth of labor force, 123
  opposition to, 125-26
    is mostly white, 190
    by labor leaders, 121-22
    among Latinos, 119
    and S.O.S. ballot, 197-90
Immigration Act of 1990, 126
Immigration and Naturalization

Service (INS), 59, 187, 189
Immigration Reform and Control Act
  of 1986, 191, 121-22

Jackson, Jesse, 52, 89, 223
Jackson, Michael, 53
Jacob, John, 52
Jacoby, Tamar, 200
Jasper, William F., 151
Jefferson, Thomas, 69
Jewish protests, 163
Jim Crow signs
  residual effects of, 92
  and segregation, 35, 114
Jones, Franklin, 61
juries
  all-white, 158
  participation of women in, 168
  should be racially balanced, 157-64
  should not have racial quotas, 165-
    71

Kadetsky, Elizabeth, 186
Kamasaki, Charles, 61, 63
Karlin, Joyce, 150
Kean College incident, 43-49
Kennedy, Anthony, 171
Kerner Commission, 103, 219
Kiley, Barbara, 188
King, Coretta Scott, 52, 121
King, Martin Luther, Jr., 89, 206
  birthday made national holiday, 182
  dream fulfilled by middle class, 94
  inspiration missing now, 35
  wanted color-blind integration, 201,
    202, 203, 205
King, Rodney, case of, 101, 149
  defendants in, 148
  jury in, 162
  linked to L.A. riots, 117-118
  media portrayal of, 150, 153, 166
  verdict in, 34, 158
    was shocking, 101, 150
    white/black condemnation of, 34
Kirsanow, Peter N., 88
Korean Americans, 125, 128
  attacked in L.A. riots, 116, 119, 152
  in conflict with blacks, 145-46, 148-
    49
  small population of, 119
  as victims of crime, 54, 152
  as victims of media bias, 153-56
Korea Times, 152
Ku Klux Klan, 98, 218
Kull, Andrew, 165
Kuran, Timur, 29

Lacayo, Richard, 163